RICH DESSERTS
& CAPTAIN'S THIN

In 1831 Jonathan Dodgson Carr, son of a Quaker grocer, set off to walk from his home in Kendal to Carlisle, determined to launch a great enterprise. Within fifteen years, Carr's of Carlisle had become one of the largest baking businesses in Britain – and is a by-word for biscuits to this day. Following his trail to Carlisle (where she herself was born and grew up), Margaret Forster brings 19th-century daily life into vivid focus and charts the rise and rise of a new class of family – manufacturing middle-class, ambitious, newly rich yet sternly religious. This is history as it was lived by the men and women whose worlds were bound up by the enterprise – from the shop floor to the comfortable homes of the paternalistic Carrs. We see the conflict between religion and profit, the family feuds and the changing face of a city through this compelling historical narrative, told with Margaret Forster's characteristic blend of scholarship, readability and marvellous attention to the texture of everyday life.

MARGARET FORSTER

Born in Carlisle in 1938, and educated at the Carlisle and County High School for Girls, Margaret Forster read history at Oxford before making her name as a novelist and biographer. She is the author of sixteen novels and five works of non-fiction. Her recent bestselling works include the biography of Daphne du Maurier, a memoir of her own family, *Hidden Lives*, and the novel *Shadow Baby*. She lives in London and the Lake District, and is married to writer and journalist Hunter Davies.

Margaret Forster

RICH DESSERTS & CAPTAIN'S THIN

A Family and Their Times
1831–1931

VINTAGE

Published by Vintage 1998

2 4 6 8 10 9 7 5 3 1

First published in Great Britain by
Chatto & Windus 1997

Vintage
Random House, 20 Vauxhall Bridge Road,
London SW1V 2SA

Random House Australia (Pty) Limited
20 Alfred Street, Milsons Point, Sydney
New South Wales 2061, Australia

Random House New Zealand Limited
18 Poland Road, Glenfield,
Auckland 10, New Zealand

Random House South Africa (Pty) Limited
Endulini, 5A Jubilee Road, Parktown 2193,
South Africa

Random House UK Limited Reg. No. 954009

A CIP catalogue record for this book
is available from the British Library

ISBN 0 09 974891 6

Papers used by Random House UK Ltd are natural,
recyclable products made from wood grown in sustain-
able forests. The manufacturing processes conform to the
environmental regulations of the country of origin

Printed and bound in Great Britain by
Mackays of Chatham PLC, Chatham, Kent

Contents

List of Illustrations

———————— • ————————

———————— • ————————

M Y SCHOOL IN Carlisle, a mixed Infants and Junior state primary, stood on a slight hill above Holy Trinity Church. The biscuit factory was to the left, as you looked towards the city from the school, built below the level of the church, at the junction of the road to the west-coast ports and the road to the empty marshes of the Solway Firth. The playgrounds of the school, two of them, were squares of concrete surrounded by high brick walls, but these grim barriers, dirty with smoke, could not keep out the glorious aroma of chocolate. It floated over us children, invisible but definite, and made us rush even more wildly round the ugly confines of the barren playing area. It seemed to madden us, intoxicate us, we could hardly bear not to storm the factory and seize the chocolate-coated biscuits that we knew were being made in their thousands. Visions of these biscuits floated so enticingly before us that we thought of the factory as a kind of heaven. We never imagined a place of noise and weariness, never contemplated the monotony and the physical labour for little return that went into making the biscuits. Instead we envied those lucky enough to work there.

Carr's of Carlisle was a name of which we were in awe. Carr's could give us what we craved.

*

During the 1950s, once examinations were over for the sixteen-year-olds, the Carlisle and County High School for Girls organised tours of the city's various factories. It was thought salutary to encourage clever and not-so-clever girls alike to go round at least one factory, so that they could witness what they might come to if they turned out to have disgraced the school and failed to pass their O-Levels. Besides, there were a few weeks of term still to go and the practice of simply turning fifth-formers out of school to please themselves had not yet taken hold. So a tour of a factory it was.

The list of options went up quite early. There was a choice, among others, of the Metal Box, Ferguson's or Carr's. Nobody wanted to go to the Metal Box (I certainly didn't – my father worked there) and though Ferguson's (which made textiles) had a few takers, Carr's was by far the most popular choice. We might be sixteen, but the lure of those chocolate biscuits was as strong as it had been at six. Everyone knew that at the end of a tour of Carr's each girl would be given a packet of biscuits (and there was no need to mention the thieving from the conveyor belts that would go on along the way).

We met outside the factory, accompanied by a teacher, and though I had passed the gates of Carr's every day of my life, once I was through them I was amazed at how little I had been able to envisage the scale of what lay inside. It was like going into another town, which had its own roads, crossings and traffic rules, a town where, without a guide, we would have needed a detailed map to make our way from storehouses to doughing rooms, from the building where empties were kept to the foundries and sawyards, from the icing and decorating departments to the chocolate and toffee rooms.

But we did have a guide, a man in a khaki-coloured coat, who was extremely brisk and bossy and called us 'young ladies' in every sentence. He was used to taking parties round the factory – Carr's prided itself on always being open to inspection – and probably did not even listen to himself any longer. We listened, and sniggered (but then, in groups, we sniggered at everything). He gave us white overalls and caps to put on. The caps had hair-nets inside them, which caused a crisis of vanity – what, tuck *all* our hair inside, every strand? But we would look *awful*. The white overalls, though, were another matter. We liked those. They were pristine and starched, and it was easy to pretend we were doctors. And there were two roomy pockets, which seemed promising . . .

Once we were all uniformed, off we went, nudging each other as we followed our strutting guide, mimicking his walk as he led us through the corridors to the wash-basins situated outside the doors that opened into the first factory floor. Lots of splashing, lots of unnecessary shrieking, lots of 'Now, now, young ladies' and then, severely reprimanded by our teacher, we quietened down and stood in line. Suddenly there was a curious sense of expectancy, a sense of theatre, of a curtain going up as we waited to go through the big, heavy doors. The moment we were inside, we no longer wanted to make fun of our tour leader, but instead scurried obediently after him, scared that we would really get lost among all the thundering machines churning and grinding around us. He led us at such a rapid pace, pointing and shouting and explaining, that we hardly caught a word, though we clustered anxiously around him whenever he paused.

We were stunned by the power of it all. It was incomprehensible how everything worked, how any kind of order could come out of what seemed to us frightening chaos, in which the machines had a life of their own. Yet everywhere there were people, mostly women, who appeared perfectly at ease. They fed and tended the monstrous machines and conveyor belts, deftly lifting and setting down, apparently oblivious to the constant, appalling noise. But they had more than noise to cope with. The smells and the heat bothered us just as much. No glorious odour of chocolate when we got to the chocolate room: now it was an overwhelmingly rich, sickly smell, more like a stench, and it made us instantly nauseous. So did the sight of the melted chocolate running into a machine in thick, dark globules, and the vats of disgusting-looking yellow stuff, the cream waiting to be put into the sandwiching machine.

We got our free biscuits. Somehow, we had no appetite for them, not immediately anyway. We were all very quiet on the way back to school, our heads full of nightmare visions of failing O-Levels and having to become cracker-packers at Carr's. It was not a joke any longer.

*

Forty years on and I was eager to go round Carr's again, ready to see it with new, well-informed eyes. I wanted to match its history with present-day reality. But those regular tours, the welcome to all-comers, have stopped. And Carr's is not Carr's any more. Since 1972 the factory has belonged to McVities, part of the United Biscuits empire. A nonsense as far as everyone in Carlisle is concerned, of course – how can Carr's be anything but Carr's, even if the McVities name is writ large, in gaudy blue and yellow, above the old, plain white Carr's name on the front of the factory? *It* persuades nobody. This factory has a soul and its name is always going to be Carr's.

But the place seems like a fortress now. Across the

wide road leading into the main forecourt there is a barrier where all cars must stop and drivers and passengers report to reception. It is only the first of the obstacles to entering, whether by car or on foot. Once in reception, a plastic card has to be issued, which operates a turnstile (what are they making here, guns or biscuits?). Then we were through: myself, a member of the Carr family and our guide.

We went first along a wood-panelled corridor and up some wide stairs, relic of a more gracious era indeed (and not glimpsed by us as schoolgirls), into the boardroom. There they all were, the past bosses and owners, the Carrs, with not a McVitie in sight. Jonathan Dodgson, the founder, his sons Henry, James and Thomas, his grandsons, Theodore, Bertram and Harold, with only Ronald missing. None of the great-grandsons, though they too played their part. Paintings of the factory as it used to be adorn the walls (inaccurate in some details, but attractive). It could be the boardroom of any family business: there is no sense of frenzied manufacturing activity here. The adjoining offices are busy but equally removed from the product they manage. In one of them we are given the white coats and hats that I remembered so well, with the addition of special shoes, black for feet under size six, white for those over. I wished I had bigger feet – white shoes look so much more in keeping with the coats. We were also given cute little earplugs this time, dangling on a string, whereas before our young ears were left unprotected (or was the noise less deafening then?).

Certainly it is ferocious now, even worse than I recalled. So is the feeling of claustrophobia. The rooms – sheds? caverns? halls? – are vast and high-ceilinged, but the atmosphere is still one of being trapped and crushed. The machines and conveyor belts seem so tightly packed together, so dominant and huge, that it is an effort to look upwards and beyond them to see that in fact there is plenty of space, plenty of light and air. When we walk up the narrow iron staircases and on to the narrow galleries there is a different perspective.

Peering down at the biscuits going past, quite slowly for the most part, armies of biscuits, all perfectly regimented, it is easier to adjust. This is much less intimidating than actually standing beside the belts, where the feeling is one of being hemmed in by some motorway, the traffic heavily congested but curiously obedient, and absolutely relentless – on and on it flows, enough to cause dizziness or to hypnotise. The spell is broken when the biscuits suddenly flip, turn over on their tummies ready for coating with cream or chocolate. The jumps are synchronised, immensely satisfying to watch in their precision. Otherwise, it is like watching a river full of tiny logs sweeping towards the sea. There are so many intricate patterns to note, not only those made by the arrangement of the biscuits themselves but by the belts carrying them. These twist and wind throughout the factory like tangled string but without the knots, heading miraculously to some smoothly planned but unseen destination. As choreography it is remarkable.

Back on the factory floor, we have the new technology pointed out to us. There are computer screens alongside the conveyor belts, with all kinds of data to do with baking times flashing away upon them. Nobody seems to pay any attention to them, however important they may be. There are shelves in front of them with sample biscuits laid out in rows, like offerings to a god. But the computers do not seem like gods, even if they are – it is the belts that are revered. They are watched all the time, at every stage. Eyes are ever upon them, hands moving in time with their motion. We watch assorted biscuits being packed. One woman picks up a box, snaps a red Cellophane lining into it and passes it on. Reach, snap, pass. On and on, swift and smooth. The next woman has a chute in front of her delivering two kinds of biscuit, a small round one with a smile on its iced face and an oblong pink wafer. These have to be put into the correctly shaped holes. In they go. The box, now with two biscuits in place, travels to the third woman in the line. She adds a square biscuit to the vacant square hole and three chocolate fingers to the narrow gap left for them in the centre. All done by hand. So much still done by hand, that is the surprise. So much work that is entirely mechanical and yet it needs the human hand to do it. Easy? Only on one level.

But the measuring and mixing of ingredients are now fully automated. Vague memories of watching women stirring things vanish. Now, the flour is not even seen. It comes directly from the silos, by chute, into the mixers, where it joins all the other ingredients. A giant set of blades rotates the resulting mass, pummelling it violently, before it drops into a bin from which, in another operation, the dough will be sent on its way. A man stands by the machine setting a timer on the computer: 180 seconds and then thud, thud, and the beating begins, the mixture hurled about like clods of pale mud. 'That is my job,' he says, deadpan, 'in all its splendour.' Later, we see the dough that this machine has made travelling along a conveyor belt in one broad, flat mass, ready to be cut into shapes. It looks like a blanket in need of a wash, a dirty yellow, and when there are two layers, and currants are slipped between, these look like bits of grit caught in fibres of wool. Beside the belts stand enormous bins, some with currants, like stones now, waiting to be spread on tarmac, others with nuts, which look more like bullets. There is nothing enticing about these foodstuffs, not even about the chocolate, an ocean of slime oozing its way along.

We use our earplugs in some areas but not in others. When the noise is so awful that we are obliged to pop them in, we see that, incredibly, the workers' mouths are moving – they are somehow managing to communicate with each other. It is hard not to stare. Nobody seems to mind being stared at. There are bland smiles and nods, or complete blankness, but no visible resentment or hostility. This is the factory, after all, saved from closure, because of its excellent labour relations, when United Biscuits closed so many other factories down. This is Carr's, the family firm, where that family, true or false, believed its workers to be well looked after and happy. Some working families clocked up hundreds of years between them, down the generations – the Reids, the Pattinsons, the Stubbs, the MacGregors, the Taylors, the Robsons, the McBrides – hundreds of years, father to son, father to daughter, granddaughter and great-granddaughter, before it all came to an end and Carr's was no more. It is all hard to credit.

Leaving the factory floor, it is the silence that blesses us first. No quiet anywhere inside. In the areas where the noise of production does not deafen, music plays over the Tannoy. Silence is impossible. Literally. So, on exiting, the silence is a huge relief, but so is the escape from the heat. This is oppressive almost everywhere, not because the temperature is actually high, but because of the nature of the heat. It is cloying, stifling, the sweet, rich smell of baking, lovely in a domestic kitchen, but suffocating on this grand scale. I often felt near to fainting on the tour. I know I could not stand this, hour after hour, poor tender thing that I am. It was such a pleasure in the cooling room – oh, the bliss of those cold draughts setting the chocolate or the icing on the biscuits. There was less noise there too, more of a rhythmic clanging than a shattering grinding, and fewer workers about. There was an altogether more scientific atmosphere – an illusion, but there it was.

Of the actual laboratories we see nothing. They are not part of the tour, nor are the many offices and administrative departments. Two hours, and we have seen only a fraction of the works. But what we have seen is the real work of production, the actual manufacturing of the goods. All over the country, all over the world, there are factories like this. Most of us are so familiar with the shops where the goods end up, but ignorant of the factories where they are made. The origins of these factories are buried in the history of the industrial revolution, and their humble, but hugely significant, beginnings have long since been forgotten. What went into the creation of these strange and powerful places is a little-known story. The history of Carr's of Carlisle is only one small strand in a complex web – a tale of one man, with a good idea and great entrepreneurial flair and energy, from whom a successful, worldwide business sprang, based on one factory in a small northern city. J. D. Carr, manufacturer of biscuits, had his battles, his campaigns, his victories, just as the soldiers and politicians of his day did, and, being a Quaker, he had his moral dilemmas too.

When the entrepreneurial spirit clashed with religious conviction in Victorian England, something very interesting happened, with repercussions right down to our own times.

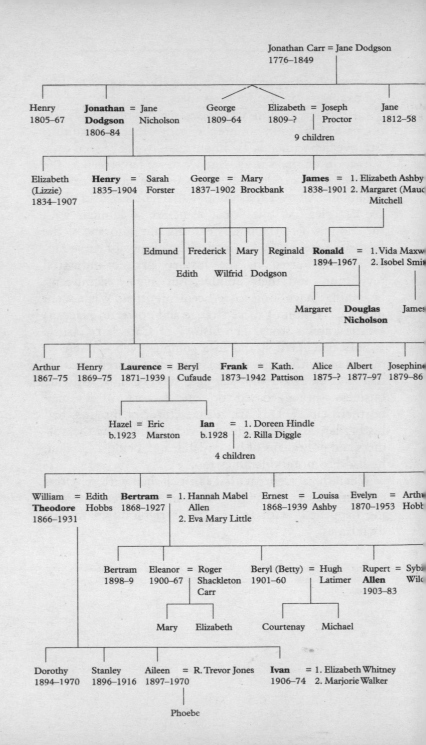

Jonathan Carr = Jane Dodgson
1776–1849

Henry
1805–67

Jonathan Dodgson = Jane Nicholson
1806–84

George
1809–64

Elizabeth = Joseph Proctor
1809–?
9 children

Jane
1812–58

Elizabeth (Lizzie)
1834–1907

Henry = Sarah Forster
1835–1904

George = Mary Brockbank
1837–1902

James = 1. Elizabeth Ashby
1838–1901   2. Margaret (Maud) Mitchell

Edmund   Frederick   Mary   Reginald   **Ronald** = 1. Vida Maxwell
          Edith   Wilfrid   Dodgson   1894–1967   2. Isobel Smith

Margaret   **Douglas Nicholson**   James

Arthur
1867–75

Henry
1869–75

Laurence = Beryl Cufaude
1871–1939

Frank = Kath. Pattison
1873–1942

Alice
1875–?

Albert
1877–97

Josephine
1879–86

Hazel = Eric Marston
b.1923

Ian = 1. Doreen Hindle
b.1928   2. Rilla Diggle
4 children

William **Theodore** = Edith Hobbs
1866–1931

Bertram = 1. Hannah Mabel Allen
1868–1927   2. Eva Mary Little

Ernest = Louisa Ashby
1868–1939

Evelyn = Arthur Hobbs
1870–1953

Bertram
1898–9

Eleanor = Roger Shackleton Carr
1900–67

Beryl (Betty) = Hugh Latimer
1901–60

Rupert **Allen** = Sybil Wild
1903–83

Mary   Elizabeth

Courtenay   Michael

Dorothy
1894–1970

Stanley
1896–1916

Aileen = R. Trevor Jones
1897–1970

Ivan = 1. Elizabeth Whitney
1906–74   2. Marjorie Walker

Phoebe

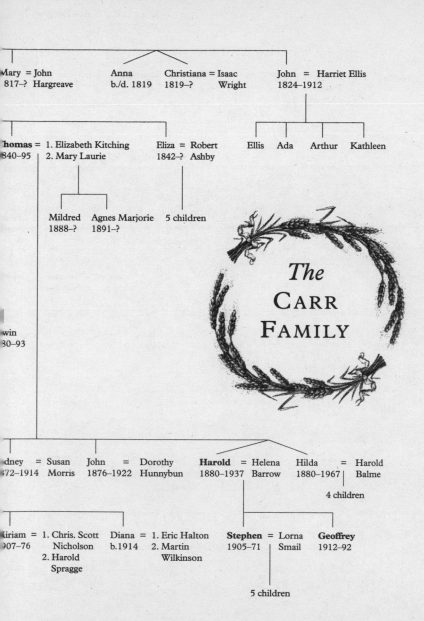

Mary = John
1817–? Hargreave

Anna
b./d. 1819

Christiana = Isaac
1819–? Wright

John = Harriet Ellis
1824–1912

Ellis   Ada   Arthur   Kathleen

Thomas = 1. Elizabeth Kitching
1840–95   2. Mary Laurie

Eliza = Robert
1842–? Ashby

Mildred
1888–?

Agnes Marjorie
1891–?

5 children

The CARR FAMILY

...win
...30–93

...dney = Susan
...72–1914 Morris

John = Dorothy
1876–1922 Hunnybun

Harold = Helena
1880–1937 Barrow

Hilda = Harold
1880–1967 Balme

4 children

...iriam = 1. Chris. Scott
...07–76   Nicholson
              2. Harold
                 Spragge

Diana = 1. Eric Halton
b.1914   2. Martin
             Wilkinson

Stephen = Lorna
1905–71   Smail

Geoffrey
1912–92

5 children

Note: the names in **bold type** are those who worked in the family business

Chapter One

A QUAKER CHILDHOOD
IN KENDAL

NOISE WAS something to which Jonathan Dodgson Carr was accustomed long before he ever experienced factory noise. It was ironic, really, since silence was so essential to the well-being of his people, the Quakers. They needed complete silence so that they could sense the spirit, which they believed to be in every one of them, and hear it speak. But it was only in the meeting-house that the young Jonathan Dodgson found peace. At home, above his father's wholesale grocery business in Highgate, Kendal, every minute of every day was noisy, and so were most hours of the night.

Highgate was the principal street in this small Westmorland town at the turn of the nineteenth century and it was always busy. It was paved with particularly large, rough cobbles of local stone, so that the wagons and carts making their way up the long, narrow, hilly stretch of road from south to north had the grinding of their metal rimmed wheels magnified many times over. The hooves of the dray horses pulling the wagons, four to each vehicle, slipped and slithered on these same wickedly uneven cobbles and the drivers, dressed in blue linen, had to stand, legs wide apart, feet braced, to keep their balance. They yelled at the horses and pulled at the reins and were forever looking down anxiously at the three broad iron bands, twelve to fifteen inches in width, round each wheel, always apprehensive that small stones might spring from between the cobbles, stick into the joins and split the iron tyre.

The building in which Jonathan Dodgson was born on 9 December 1806 was impossible to insulate from this constant racket. It stood squeezed between the premises of a milliner, which had a doctor's surgery behind it, and a larger house owned by another Quaker family, the influential Braithwaites. The street was lined with shops mixed with inns and the occasional private house, all straggling up the hill in untidy architectural lines. There were butchers' stalls, known as shambles, on both sides and cattle were still sold in the street itself. The actual shops – every variety of them, from clothes shops to pawnbrokers and confectioners – were often sited partly below ground level. They had no windows but were protected by heavy wooden shutters which, when let down in a horizontal position, acted as tables from which goods could be sold. It was enough to make shoppers feel quite disorientated when they found that to reach articles on the top shelf they had to bend down to do so. Altogether, main street or not, Highgate was very odd-looking, not at all grand or imposing, but then no street or area of Kendal was thought any smarter than another.

At night, too, the Carr family house was unfortunately placed. There were a great many public houses in Highgate and all night long drunkards swarmed out of them, making their unsteady way over the lethal cobbles, difficult enough to negotiate when sober, but impossible when intoxicated. There were no policemen to caution them against rowdy behaviour. There was only the solitary night watchman, standing in his sentry box in the middle of the street, calling out the time and the state of the weather. At least during the night the noise of the town bells stopped, ceasing at 6 p.m. in the winter and 7 p.m. in the summer, and there were no clocks striking. The most constant sound, when it could be heard above all the other louder ones, was that of the heavy rain on the roof. It was no myth that it seemed to rain all the time in Kendal. Records show that, on average, the rain during this period was steady and unremitting on half the days of every year. It could douse the oil lamps, by which the town was lit, if the wicks were not most carefully protected. The town clerk, putting the maintenance of the 140 lamps out to contract, was stern about the quality of thread used in the wicks. If the lamps were to burn from sunset to daybreak through the habitual, torrential rain and lighten the thick gloom, then the thread had to be strong.

But in spite of the noise and the rain, Kendal was not a bad place in which to be born and brought up in the first part of the nineteenth century. According to a Dr Ainslie, writing to a local newspaper a few years before Jonathan Dodgson's birth, it was a sociable and cheerful place. The countryside around it might previously have been described by Daniel Defoe in his *Tour of the Whole Island of Great Britain* (1726) as 'barren and frightful', but the town itself was stable and peaceful. The very isolation of Kendal, cut off as it was by the surrounding mountains and a river that regularly flooded, sweeping away the bridges, had kept it safe from disturbances. The last time Kendal had suffered from a marauding army was in 1745, when Bonnie Prince Charlie's retreating troops had swept through it. Since then there had been nothing to fear and people had grown quite complacent and self-satisfied. There was not even a local militia ready in case of any threat to the peace, though, three years before Jonathan Dodgson's birth, a volunteer force had been hastily formed in response to the belief that Napoleon would invade. The panic over, it was disbanded.

So, to be born in 1806 in Kendal was thought, by the inhabitants at least, to be fortunate, though it was not the healthiest of towns. Typhoid was prevalent and the weavers – Kendal was first and foremost a weaving town, producing cloth too coarse for export but highly popular at home – were prone to suffer most in the regular epidemics. Their sedentary, indoor occupation in overcrowded conditions gave them little resistance, though they did not suffer anything like the mortality rate of weaving communities in the larger manufacturing towns. Jonathan Dodgson's grandfather, Henry Carr, had been a weaver, but neither he nor any of his family died of typhoid. In his day the Carrs had lived on the outskirts of Kendal, at Far Cross Bank, which offered some protection from infection; and Jonathan Carr, even when his family moved to Highgate, also escaped the disease. According to Dr Ainslie, 'the natives' preserved themselves from illness 'by a plaster taken inwardly called thick poddish'. The Quakers had something else, though. They placed great faith in a concoction called Black Drop. It was sold by various Quakeresses in Kendal and consisted of a four-ounce phial, priced at ten shillings, of opium mixed with the juice of quinces. This mixture had been gently heated before having added to it saffron, cloves, nutmeg and cinnamon. Left to stand for a week, the 'Black Drop' was strained and the resulting liquid evaporated to a syrup. It was hardly surprising that the women who did the work wore masks. The claims made for this medicine were extravagant – it was said 'to stimulate energy' and yet 'to reduce excessive activity'.

Jonathan Dodgson, if ever his Quaker mother Jane dosed him with Black Drop, was more in need of the latter benefit. He was a big, strong boy, taller and heavier than his older brother Henry, and from the first was noted as being full of energy. But it was an energy at odds with the child's remarkable gentleness – strong, energetic little boys are more likely to be wild, even destructive, than gentle, hardly capable when young of knowing their own power. Jonathan Dodgson – his middle name was his mother's maiden name – seemed able to control his strength. He was mentally as well as physically strong, very determined, intent on doing his best. It was an odd combination in a child, his size concealing an unexpected thoughtfulness and calm.

He was the leader of the children – Henry (a year older), the twins George and Elizabeth (three years younger), Jane (six years younger), Mary (ten years younger), Christiana (thirteen years younger, the survivor of twin girls), and finally John, who was born when Jonathan Dodgson was eighteen, bringing to an end his mother's twenty years of childbearing. It was a big family, though average-sized for the times. The grocery business supported them all comfortably, but then Quakers lived plainly. The wealth of this Quaker family was certainly not great, and caused no clash, as yet, between their ideals and the temptations of affluence. Jonathan Dodgson was brought up to believe that his duty was to see that his own needs were modest, and to help others less fortunate than himself.

But the Carrs were not well known in Kendal for doing good works. No outstanding acts of benevolence are recorded under their name. The leading Quaker families of the day were the Wakefields, the Crewdsons, the Braithwaites and the Wilsons. These were the ranks from whom came the founders of the local banks, the Schools of Industry. These were the Quakers who had connections with the famous Gurneys and Barclays. The Carrs took no lead in charity work, nor does their name appear in any list of rank-and-file workers. They are not noted as having attended public meetings or as contributing money to good causes. If they did these things they did them anonymously, unlike the prominent Quakers in Kendal. And yet they were devout and earnest, diligently attending Quaker meetings, and pleased to perform the various duties asked of them.

Jane, in spite of her large family, served regularly on committees, given the unenviable job of visiting members who were reported to have transgressed. Alcohol was regarded by Quakers as utterly evil, so if one of the Friends had been seen drunk, a deputation was sent to point out the error of his ways and to help him, through prayer, redeem himself. Even more gravely in breach of the society's code was immoral conduct, especially in a woman. Jane Carr was often called upon to visit such women, which indicates a certain feeling for the task, but she was also active in serving as a representative to the monthly meetings and to the much bigger and more important quarterly meetings. Her local worshipping group in Kendal, known as a 'particular meeting', clearly trusted her to go on their behalf to those monthly meetings, where representatives from several particular meetings met together. And those meetings in turn thought Jane well able to go on to the quarterly meetings for the whole county. Jane's name does not appear on surviving minutes for the big yearly meeting, when Quakers from the whole country met in London, but then it was the men who were chosen to represent their group in the capital (though the women eventually had their own representatives). Even if, in the town itself, the Carr parents had no connection with the other eminent Quaker families, within the walls of the meeting-house they were on a par with them and contributed as much.

As a child, the meeting-house was Jonathan Dodgson's second home. It lay just round the corner from the family house, in Stramongate, the street that led off Highgate down to the River Kent. In 1816, when Jonathan Dodgson was ten, a new meeting-house was built at a cost of £3,637 (the highest cost being for the limestone and the timber). It was a very attractive building, though simple and modest, in keeping with Quaker principles, with a large, oblong main hall, which had a minister's stand on one side and a stepped loft round the other. There was a screen across the middle, with four arched openings, and most unusually the hall was heated (the 'warming apparatus' cost £35 18s). The place held 850 people – the Quakers were strong in Kendal – but, in spite of its size, it was not intimidating for a child. The Quaker religion was friendly towards children, who were encouraged to consider themselves important members. They were welcomed and there was nothing to overawe them, as there was in 'steeple-houses' (the Quaker name for traditional churches) – no darkness, no stained glass, no tombs, no music, no pomp and ceremony. Of all the seventy-four meeting-houses in the north-west of England, the Kendal house was one of the most substantial and yet most appealing. It even had a garden front and back, and its situation near the river made it especially pleasant.

Jonathan Dodgson was an intelligent, thoughtful boy who took in everything happening around him, using his eyes and ears to good effect. The sober clothes of his people told him that the Quakers disliked show of any kind. They were all dressed in dark-coloured garments made of serviceable materials and without any adornment, whereas outside the meeting-house what did he see? Women at that time were wearing romantically inspired dresses, with even the less well-off trying to ape the high waistline of the fashionable dresses, which emphasised the bust, and managing to find from somewhere woven gauze and handmade lace to lavish on trimmings. Colour was everywhere, especially luscious pinks and blues, and hairstyles and hats were very elaborate. Even some of the men had a certain dash, with the woollen dress-coat being in vogue, thickly padded on the front to accentuate the chest and shoulders, while the more daring young men sported 'Cossack' trousers. Kendal was not London, but it had its share of dandies and any child could see the vanity involved. It was strange to go from the streets into the meeting-house with its stone floor and whitewashed walls. Once inside, the shouts, oaths and jeers of the streets faded. Nobody ever shouted, nobody swore, nobody traded insults. All was silence and calm, the loudest noise a cough, or a heavy footstep on the floor. All was courtesy, making the loud dealings between traders outside seem rough and unpleasant.

To some children, this withdrawal from what was so vibrant and active became boring – it was dull in the meeting-house, with everything so quiet and all the procedures agonisingly slow. Yawns could set in very quickly. But Jonathan Dodgson was, from the first, temperamentally suited to belonging to the Society of Friends. The few remarks surviving in family memoirs all speak of his exemplary devotion and his quick grasp of what being a Quaker meant. He appeared to like the idea, central to his religion, of having to listen for God within himself. This scared some children – it was frightening to strain to listen, then hear nothing – but he responded to it. He liked the notion of being responsible for himself and all his actions: it fitted in with his sense of independence. Nor did he have any problem with the instruction to be truthful at all costs: it seemed to him obvious that if a person said yes, they should mean it. Lies, fibs and half-truths only led to confusion. Children lied because they were afraid, but in the meeting-house fear was not the spur. No one threatened or coerced young Jonathan Dodgson. He learned by example, and that example was of lives lived in a dignified and peaceful way.

A little harder to cope with, for a child, were the rules governing pleasure. Pleasure was a problem for the Quakers. They were not Puritans, but on the other hand they were against pleasures that produced an over-excitement likely to deflect the faithful from listening for, and to, God. Jonathan Dodgson and his siblings could play, but in playing they could not dance or sing, not even nursery rhymes. At home there were no pianos or violins and on the walls there were no pictures. The natural ebullience of most children could find no outlet in organised games, either – kicking or knocking balls about in contests was a waste of time. But, remarkable though it may be, these rules seem to have appealed to Jonathan Dodgson. He hated to waste time, always liked to see some result for any effort he made. He willingly ran errands for his father, and there were plenty to run, and he enjoyed using his precocious strength to lift and carry for his mother. Since he liked to be so physically active and was not of a bookish disposition, it did not grieve him that there were few books in the house – no poetry, no novels, no plays.

School might have come as something of a shock, given that he disliked being confined, but Jonathan Dodgson took to it well. He and Henry went to Stramongate, the school their parents had attended, next to the Kendal meeting-house. Jonathan and Jane Carr had enjoyed their schooldays and saw no reason to send their eldest two children elsewhere (though they later sent two others to Ackworth in Yorkshire, founded in 1779, which became one of the most famous Quaker boarding schools). In their day, most classical texts had been banned and so had foreign languages. They had had a very plain education indeed, with a heavy emphasis on the useful – reading, writing and arithmetic.

They therefore knew no Latin, Greek or French and their knowledge of literature was extremely limited, though their familiarity with the Bible was hardly to be rivalled. Jonathan Carr was a grocer, a merchant, and what he had learned at Stramongate he considered perfectly adequate for his sons. The teaching there had in fact changed since his own day, as indeed it had been forced to do throughout all Quaker schools. By the first quarter of the nineteenth century the facts had been faced and those facts were that a Quaker education was often of a low standard. Good teachers were hard to attract. The best teachers came from the universities, and Quakers could not attend university (they were banned, by the Test Acts of 1673 and 1678, which demanded an oath of loyalty to the established Church). In order to procure better-educated teachers, Latin, Greek and French had all been allowed into the curriculum, in the hope that in future some of the pupils would become teachers themselves and so raise the general standard. It had also been decided that not all poetry and dramatic texts should be prohibited, and a very carefully chosen selection had become available. So Henry and Jonathan Dodgson Carr received a wider education than their parents, but in many other ways their experience of school was the same. They, too, dug the school garden – easy for both of them – enjoying the manual labour as an alternative to sport, and, just as their parents had done, they studied nature, highly important in a Quaker education.

But Stramongate was a tougher place by 1813. The classes were larger, and more unruly as a result; the tranquillity of the meeting-house did not quite extend to the school. During the years that the Carr brothers attended there were several vicious schoolmasters who were expert at the use of the tawse (a whip with short leather thongs). Sometimes the tawse was used so enthusiastically that the services of a surgeon were required to staunch the blood. No protest was registered, but then it is a mistake to think that because Quakers were peaceful people, their schools were run on peaceful lines. It was alarming for Jonathan Dodgson to discover this, although because he towered over his contemporaries and was heavily built, he was less likely to be the victim of any brutality. At least at Stramongate there were no punishment cells, eight feet square with heavy shutters, as there were at Ackworth, where offenders, for sins as trivial as stealing an onion from the garden, were shut in for anything up to three days. But the discipline was equally strict. Rigid silence was enforced during lessons and absolute obedience demanded. In this atmosphere learning was hardly pleasurable, but Jonathan Dodgson recorded no complaints. He could look after himself, in the playground as well as the schoolroom. If a fight broke out, and even in Quaker schools fights did of course occur, he acquitted himself well. He was reputed to be a sensible, pleasant boy, not at all aggressive in spite of his muscular appearance, but, if called upon to defend himself, he could not resist the temptation. He could box, though he had never been taught, and sometimes did so, even if he knew he should turn the other cheek.

When Jonathan Dodgson was not at school or in the meeting-house, he was helping his father in the Highgate premises of his wholesale grocery business. He and Henry, since they were both strong boys, were well able from a young age to help with carrying goods from carts to shop, with stacking boxes as they arrived, with splitting open the big wooden crates in which so many goods were packed and with helping to keep the place clean at all times, which involved punishing daily rituals of sweeping up dust and straw, and spilled substances that had leaked out of sacks. Jonathan Carr dealt mainly in dry goods – tea, coffee, sugar, flour – all arriving and departing in large quantities. Every day deliveries were made and the unloading of goods was a perilous business, with so little room in the narrow streets, back and front, for the drivers to negotiate. Everything had to be inspected, counted and paid for, and then checked again, with no room for mistakes in the accounting. Nothing was bought on credit, nor was credit given. The despatch of goods was handled with the same scrupulous attention to fairness – no short measures, no slipping in of anything even slightly damaged. All day long suppliers and customers were pouring through the shop, which was more like a warehouse, making it a permanently busy place in which two boys were hardly noticed. But from their point of view, they were ideally placed to absorb effortlessly whatever business was about and to see how it was organised. They were involved in the proceedings and nothing about their father's trade was strange to them. Family life revolved round it.

There was little time in this regime – school, meeting-house, helping in the business – for the boys to enjoy any of the pleasures that Kendal had to offer, but then for Quakers most of these were banned. They were not allowed to go to the theatre, nor to frequent the new racecourse, nor to watch cock-fighting. In that respect they were not part of the community, though since their own particular community, of Quakers, was so large at the time, they felt no sense of loss. Occasionally, of course, an event would occur that they experienced with everyone else in Kendal – such as when Jonathan Dodgson was ten and the tremors of an earthquake were felt; or the magnificent aquatic procession as it set off from the new canal basin, when he was twelve, on its way to Lancaster, which was considered harmless enough as an entertainment and significant enough to be educational. (Canals, after all, were going to affect the Carrs' business.) But mostly Jonathan Dodgson's growing up was not influenced by anything that the town itself had to offer. The influences were Quaker ones and were not dependent on place.

There was no indication that this promising youth would do anything but follow his older brother Henry into the family business and then, as Henry quickly did, branch out into an allied field on his own, perhaps becoming a retailer instead of a wholesaler, perhaps specialising in tea or coffee. Henry, thoroughly grounded in the handling of a business, chose to be a retail grocer, operating in the same street as his father and helped by him. Jonathan Dodgson was expected to follow the same kind of path. Nothing rebellious, or even enterprising, had been noted about him to indicate otherwise. What appears to have struck his family most was not any lurking desire to be different but his very conformity. He was obedient. He was helpful. He showed concern for others. He was kind. He got on well with everyone. In short, he was a paragon of all the Quaker virtues, or so he was remembered. And, of course, his size – he was remembered most vividly for that. In an age when a man of five foot nine inches was reckoned tall, Jonathan Dodgson was being referred to as 'a giant' by the age of sixteen, when he had already reached that height and was still growing fast. The width of his shoulders, the breadth of his back, the muscles in his arms and legs – all were remarked on and admired. People were fascinated by what they thought of as a contradiction between his appearance and his temperament. His square, open face with its calm blue eyes and pleasant smile was somehow at odds with his body, the body surely of a pugilist, a bruiser.

But not, after all, so very much at odds because, although he was not aggressive or belligerent in the physical sense, the bland countenance hid another kind of fighting spirit. Jonathan Dodgson was tougher than his face and expression made him appear and every bit as determined and strong as his body suggested. He was not going to go into his father's business, though he had an absolute respect for it, nor was he going to follow Henry. To everyone's surprise, he chose to be apprenticed to a baker the moment he left school. This might look like a harmless, even unadventurous, variation – baking, after all, was not exactly a startling departure from the trade of grocer of one sort or another – but in 1820 it was a very strange choice indeed. It seemed almost wilful, given that bakers then were less respected than other tradesmen and the work they did both hard and poorly paid. And there were too many bakers in Kendal, as well as everywhere else, so wages were low.

As a baker's apprentice, Jonathan Dodgson had to rise at three in the morning and his day was unlikely to finish before five in the evening. The bakehouse was a stifling place, extremely hot, very unhealthy, and the only time he escaped from this atmosphere in his fourteen-hour working day was when he carried bread out to the customers. He carried the loaves on wooden boards balanced on his head. The boards were large, roughly three feet by four, and held up to thirty loaves each, which made them extremely heavy. Apprentices were often seen to stagger under their weight and if they fell, which was all too easy on Kendal's cobbles, the cost of the spoiled bread was deducted from their wage (if they received a wage at all – often they got only their keep). The contrast in winter between the hot bakehouse and the freezing outside air was not conducive to good health, and bakers' apprentices were notorious for their pallor. They suffered from all kinds of lung diseases, through absorbing the flour dust, and ruptures were common because of the heavy sacks of flour they were obliged to carry. Various enquiries into the condition of bakers and their apprentices, reported in journals such as *Chambers Edinburgh Journal*, concluded that the situation in the baking industry during the early nineteenth century was appalling.

Jonathan Dodgson stood up well to the life. His strength at last came in useful. All the lifting and carrying required of an apprentice developed his already strong muscles further and he was in danger of thinking himself an Atlas or a Samson, so easily did he perform the physical labour. And of course he went home each evening, unlike so many bakers' apprentices, who were obliged to sleep on the premises in rooms that were little better than cupboards. His home became even more comfortable towards the end of his apprenticeship, because in 1824 the Carrs moved out of Highgate to a new house on Thorney Hills. This was less than a mile away, but the area was entirely different in atmosphere. The new house was one in a terrace, Kent Terrace, in a quiet location across the river, with beautiful views over the rooftops opposite to the hills behind. The hurly-burly of Highgate was forgotten in this tranquil setting and there was suddenly space for the eight children on a scale they had never before experienced. This was as near to gracious living as anyone in Kendal could come, and the sort of house and locality to which very few bakers' apprentices returned at the end of their day. In fact, the Carrs' new house was so comfortably furnished and equipped that it calls into question just how strict they were in every respect as Quakers.

In absolutely strict Quaker homes in the first quarter of the nineteenth century there were only plain, serviceable furnishings and utensils, but the Carr parents slept in a fine four-poster mahogany bed with thick curtains around it to protect them from draughts, and in their dining-room they had a splendid mahogany sideboard, upon which rested glass decanters, wine glasses and fine china rather than plain wooden platters. Jonathan Dodgson himself slept on an iron bedstead with a proper mattress and had in his room a washstand and commode. There was not a great deal he had to do for himself, since three servants looked after everything. Were the Carrs becoming what was known as 'gay Friends' – those who liked pretty things and were rejecting the simplicity of the life imposed upon them, now that they were affluent and it was becoming too rigorous? The presence of the decanters is extremely odd – what were decanters used for, except for alcohol? – because, whatever else, the Carrs remained temperance lovers.

The move to Thorney Hills coincided with Jonathan Dodgson seeing a bit more of the world beyond Kendal. As children, the Carrs had seen little of the outside world, but once they were young adults they began to go further afield to the towns and villages of the two northern counties, Cumberland and Westmorland. The opportunities to travel afforded by attending monthly and quarterly meetings were eagerly taken by parents and children alike – it was not just the chance to see other places that appealed, but the delights of other company. Within Kendal, the Carrs moved in highly restricted circles, but once attending the bigger meetings they were able to mix with new people and benefit from being in touch with that wider Quaker family that they knew existed, but of which they normally had no experience.

These larger meetings, bringing together Quakers who lived far apart, were valuable in practical ways, too, and not just for strengthening faith. Men and women met to discuss business, as well as for worship, and to exchange information about their respective trades. They gave help and advice to each other, the equivalent of modern networking. Socially, the meetings were also important because they acted as marriage markets.

Young people taken along by their parents met in a safe Quaker atmosphere and were smiled upon indulgently. Quakers could only marry other Quakers. If they 'married out' they were disowned, so every Quaker parent was anxious to bring together prospective couples. If a son or daughter failed to find a partner within their own local meeting, then the best hope was to take them to the bigger gatherings. There was consequently often quite a party atmosphere, and there were instances of a most un-Quaker-like attention being paid to appearance.

Henry and Jonathan Dodgson Carr began to go on their own as representatives to the quarterly meetings towards the mid-1820s. By then Henry was established in his own business in Highgate, and Jonathan Dodgson, just out of his apprenticeship, was trying to set up as a baker himself. Both of them quickly learned how vital these quarterly meetings were for discovering what was going on throughout the whole of the North of England. The talk was all of canals and railways, or rather the coming of railways. Where would these railways run? How would this dramatic development in transport revolutionise business? Which towns would benefit and which effectively decline, because they were inaccessible to the railways? Would Kendal be inaccessible, situated as it was surrounded by mountains? If so, what would happen to its trade? There were twelve stagecoaches a day leaving Kendal to connect it with the various westcoast ports and the big industrial towns to the south, but would they, and all the wagons and carts laboriously and slowly travelling the roads, be enough to compete with the railways serving other centres of trade?

This was the kind of speculation that heated the air at meetings, and which was of more interest to Jonathan Dodgson than to any other member of the Carr family. He was well aware that there were already too many bakers in Kendal (twenty-six of them in 1829), all vying for custom and experiencing hard times. The imposition of the Corn Laws in 1815 had made things even worse than they already were. A baker could no longer sell whatever size of loaf he wished or charge whatever price he thought fair. The weight of a loaf was now regulated and anyone selling short weight was promptly fined, as well as often having the offending loaf hung around his neck.

Bread as the most basic of foodstuffs was always needed, which made producing it especially attractive to the Quakers, since they saw the prime function of trade as providing essentials, but the life of a baker was hedged about with all kinds of rules and restrictions. Jonathan Dodgson had had plenty of time to observe them and had come to object to them. Quakers, though not supposed to be motivated by thoughts of profit, nevertheless had a duty to do good business. Material gain rightfully acquired was fully justified, and indeed *failure* in business was punished. But he was never going to do very well in Kendal as the twenty-seventh baker, and he knew it. He was, though no one in his family had suspected it, ambitious and there was no room for him in his home town. He listened attentively at the bigger Quaker gatherings to the talk of the railways planned and it was obvious to him that Kendal was no place to be. Carlisle was the coming place, Carlisle because it would soon be connected by railway to Newcastle. His sister Elizabeth was going to marry Joseph Proctor of Newcastle and acquaintance with the Proctors, who ran a flour mill on the Tyne, left Jonathan Dodgson in no doubt as to what the smart move would be. He had not yet married and still lived at home, so he had managed to save some money, but he was not finally ready to make the jump until the summer of 1831, when he was twenty-four years old. By then, the first stretch of the all-important Carlisle–Newcastle railway was in the process of being built.

But what precisely precipitated Jonathan Dodgson's departure for Carlisle in June 1831 is not known. Something as trivial as the weather could have been a deciding factor. The summer of 1830 had been wretchedly cold, wet and miserable. Kendal, often referred to as 'the auld grey town' because of the limestone of which it was built, had rarely looked so bleak. All summer the rain dripped from the grey-green roofs, and the hills round about could hardly be seen for mist. The winter that followed was even worse. In February, the River Kent flooded, as it very often did, but this was a spectacular flood, which swept over the whole of the lower part of Stramongate as far as the Nag's Head Yard. The meeting-house and the school were both surrounded by dirty brown floodwater and the damage was considerable. The arches of the bridge that Jonathan Dodgson crossed daily on his way to work were filled with river water to within a few inches of the keystones. There seemed no respite from the misery inflicted by the weather, and Kendal had never seemed less attractive. Anyone planning to leave was surely encouraged to do so.

But leaving was not that simple. The Carrs, originally from Yorkshire, had been settled in Kendal for the last hundred years. None of them had left for 'foreign parts'. Visits, on Quaker business, to other towns hardly counted – they were quickly home. They were a tightly knit family, as most Quaker families were, so for a cherished son to leave his parents and siblings and remove himself to a city where he had no family was quite a drastic thing to do. Whether his family backed him, whether indeed they did more by actually encouraging him, or even *sent* him on behalf of them all, is not known, but certainly they did nothing to stop him. If they had, Jonathan Dodgson would never have gone against their wishes. It was not the Quaker way, especially not in a happy and supportive family. Agreement, conciliation, these were the watchwords. There may have been some rivalry with Henry, but that was unlikely. Henry was not a baker and future events were to indicate that he was more of a follower than a leader, more prone to listen to his younger brother than to challenge him.

If the reason for Jonathan Dodgson's departure from Kendal in 1831 is not precisely known, the manner in which he left was to become the stuff of family legend and, like all such legends, is highly romantic and suspect. He was said to have set off to walk the long, rough road to Carlisle, forty-three miles away, a veritable Dick Whittington. This was later amended, and he was said to have been given a lift when he was only a few miles out of the town by one Thomas Brockbank, a tea merchant. Even then, he was portrayed as arriving in Carlisle with nothing but the shirt on his back, and with nowhere to stay. This charming story made his instant success all the more remarkable of course, but there are many puzzling and impossible-to-prove details. Why, for a start, would Jonathan Dodgson choose to walk? Long walks were common, but not for young men actually moving house and business, and not for those well able to afford the coach fare. Stagecoaches travelled regularly from Kendal to Carlisle, three days a week. The most favoured left at 5 a.m. (no problem for a baker used to rising before dawn) from the White Hart Inn, at a cost of ten shillings outside, twelve inside. Not cheap, but not out of the reach of a Carr. Then, unless Jonathan Dodgson proposed to arrive in Carlisle, take a look and then walk back, all in one day, he would need at least some modest luggage, which would have made walking impractical.

What is certain is that Thomas Brockbank gave him

a lift, though, once again, the story that he picked up young Jonathan Dodgson along the way is questionable. Brockbank was no stranger to the Carr family. He was a Quaker and supplied both Jonathan senior and Henry with tea, making regular calls on them. His daughter Mary described in her memoir how well her father was doing at this time as a tea dealer, living in Stanwix, Carlisle's only well-to-do district. He had business all over Cumberland and Westmorland, and his visits were expected. What more natural than that he should take Jonathan Dodgson with him, by agreement rather than by accident? At any rate, take the young man he did, saving him from a gruelling tramp over Shap Fell and down on to the Eden plain, as far as Carlisle, where Jonathan Dodgson hoped to start his own business and prosper.

Chapter Two

'CHEAP BREAD'

THOSE FORTY-THREE miles Jonathan Dodgson travelled with Thomas Brockbank, who was neat and gentlemanly in his suit of light grey and his black satin cravat, were slow ones. It was uphill all the way to Penrith and, though two turnpike trusts had been set up, the road was still rough, hard work for the horse pulling the two men and a trap laden with tea chests. The countryside through which they passed was beautiful but wild, mile after mile of moorland with few trees and no flowers. In the distance, to the west, were the mountains of the Lake District, dark blue and grey in a jagged line along the horizon, and to the east the swollen flanks of the Pennines. There was a pleasant smell of tea leaves – however closely sealed the wooden crates were, the scent of the different teas seeped through them – and the wind, mercifully gentle at this time of year (it was June), jangled the horse's harness. Thomas Brockbank did not drive his horse hard. In all ways he was a true Quaker, calm and kind, content to take all day over the journey and show consideration for animals as well as people.

Once through Penrith, the pace quickened. The road was not only downhill now, but in a much better state thanks to the efforts of John McAdam, who only recently had supervised improvements. He had seen the need to reduce gradients and to make sure that the road surface was well drained. Jonathan Dodgson and Thomas Brockbank fairly rattled down from the hills and on to the Eden plain towards Carlisle. This was a cathedral city, built mostly of red sandstone, quite different in appearance from Kendal. Here, the castle was not a ruin, as it was in Kendal. It stood squat and strong, just beyond the beautiful cathedral with its magnificent east window, giving to the city an air of solidity and permanence. Castle Street, running past the cathedral, was broad and open, site of the better-class shops, though not too grand a thoroughfare to have potato stalls along it once a week. It ended in the market square where, in front of the Town Hall, Thomas Brockbank had his stall. Here George Fox himself, founder of the Society of Friends, had preached against 'the deceitful ways of merchants' and had urged them to let their 'yea be yea' and 'do unto others as they would have others do unto them'. He had wanted honesty in trade relations, and the foundation had to be fixed, fair prices – exactly Jonathan Dodgson's own philosophy. But he hoped to escape, in his own kinder times, the fate of George Fox, who had been imprisoned in Carlisle jail by two huge jailers, who had looked like 'two great bear wards' and had beat with a cudgel anyone who came to visit him in that 'nasty, filthy place'.

English Street, the main street, led the other way from the market square and was nothing like Highgate in Kendal. It was wide and the buildings, many with attractive gardens, were better built and spaced. The whole atmosphere, for a young man arriving from Kendal, was much less claustrophobic. He felt there was room to move in this city, in a way there was not in his home town. But though, to Jonathan Dodgson, Carlisle seemed superior and rather grand, a newspaper report of the time on the 'Condition of the People of England' had not found the city impressive. On the contrary, Carlisle was condemned in Douglas Jerrold's weekly Newcastle paper for showing few features of modern improvement. Its market was 'rude', its pavements cluttered with sacks, many of them showing the heads of geese protruding through the holes, and the clothes of the vast majority of the inhabitants were seen to be in tatters. In addition the bread was 'awful', a promising opinion for a newly arrived baker with a mission to bake good bread. But first Jonathan Dodgson had to find somewhere to stay.

Quakers were extremely hospitable and it is almost certain that at first he lodged with Thomas Brockbank. Not for long, though. Within a month he was resident in Castle Street, renting a shop there next to a bonnet shop and living above the premises. For a young man supposedly arriving in Carlisle on his own, with just what he stood up in, it was a remarkable achievement. No young man without means could possibly have managed it. So what were his means?

Here we come to the whole mystery of stories such as Jonathan Dodgson Carr's and those like him. He was first of all a baker, a tradesman, and then a manufacturer, a businessman, and in both cases he had little interest in recording personal details of his life. What he did record, carefully and minutely, were his accounts – what things had cost, what he had paid, what his profits and losses were. As a child he had attended, as all Quaker children did, those business meetings that were held after, but as part of, meetings for worship, and he had been taught the importance of recording all dealings involving money. A Quaker businessman's reputation was for fair dealing and honesty, and without it he was nothing. So from the beginning Jonathan Dodgson wrote down and filed all business transactions, which as far as he was concerned told all that needed to be said about his life.

These have mostly survived, but what have not survived, because they barely existed in the first place, are those intimate personal records – what he did each day apart from work, what he thought, his personal likes and dislikes. These have to be pieced together from sources other than his own hand (which, fortunately, exist). Even letters home to his family, such as they are, turn out to be about business and nothing else. They are informative, sticking strictly to the point, which was the establishing of himself in a bakery. But even here, records of his launch as a baker in Carlisle do not include the most important information: where did he get his original capital from?

It is possible that he used his own earnings, saved during his previous three years as a journeyman baker after his apprenticeship ended, but these could hardly have financed the renting of a Castle Street shop with accommodation, the equipping of the bakehouse behind it and the payment of wages to staff. Did he have help from his father, either as a loan or a gift? Did he borrow from a Quaker bank? Impossible to tell, but wherever the money came from, he capitalised on it very rapidly. There were not as many bakers and flour dealers in Carlisle as there had been in Kendal (twelve compared with twenty-six), and only one operated in Castle Street, but even so there was little room for manoeuvre. Jonathan Dodgson (who from his arrival in Carlisle became known as J.D.) worked harder than he had ever done to establish his shop, and this was not simply to make it pay but to finance his ambitious ideas. He had not come to Carlisle just to succeed as a baker. It seemed to J.D. that it was ridiculously obvious what was wrong with the baking industry: it depended on too many stages of production. Surely it made more sense for a baker to mill the flour, from which he made the bread, himself and for him to organise and control its distribution far beyond the confines of his shop's counter. Throughout the country there were at that time thousands of small mills grinding corn into flour and then despatching it by horse transport, very slowly and in modest quantities, to the bakers, who were therefore always hostage to the varying fortunes of their suppliers. Nobody had yet thought of building a factory in which everything could be done. The baker who owned his own mill and produced his own flour on the premises would be independent and could increase his profits. This was exactly what J. D. Carr set out to do.

It took him six years to achieve it. The problem was not only financing his ambitious venture, but finding a site for the factory. His choice fell on a piece of land near the canal basin in Caldewgate, one of Carlisle's poorest areas but one which within the previous twenty-five years had become its industrial heart. This was thanks to the River Caldew, which flowed through the flat, low-lying district. Its water turned out to be excellent for various processes used in the textile industry and Caldewgate had boomed as the centre of the weaving trade. Joseph Ferguson, a cloth manufacturer, had sited two of his mills here in 1824 and another manufacturer, Peter Dixon, was planning to follow suit and build Shaddon Mill there for his textile business. From a manufacturing point of view, Caldewgate was the place to be, particularly because of the canal basin, which was beautifully situated for the easy transport of goods. J.D. was thinking way ahead of merely producing perishable bread. His intention was to make biscuits, which would have a far longer life and could be sent nationwide. The canal, about which everyone in the North had heard so much, had opened in 1823 with a tremendous show. Practically the whole of Carlisle had gathered to watch the first ship, the *Robert Burns*, sail up it and their cheers were matched by the boom of

cannon and the frenzied playing of the bandsmen following in their own boat. The canal was vital to J.D.'s
plans, even though he knew that the coming railway
might supersede it.

But in other ways Caldewgate was a dangerous
choice. J.D. knew this perfectly well. He had eyes and
ears and he was a man who walked everywhere, dis-
daining carriages and traps except for long distances. He
walked through Caldewgate every day, inspecting the
canal basin and negotiating to buy land, and what he
saw told a sorry tale. The buildings were crowded
together, full of weavers plying their trade and becoming
more desperate by the year. The moment J.D. left his
Castle Street shop and rounded the corner to cross the
west wall of the city over the River Caldew he was
confronted by visible evidence of abject poverty, such
as he had never witnessed in Kendal. The first sanitary
inspection of Carlisle, in 1831, the year that J.D. arrived
there, revealed proof, if it were needed, of the appalling
living conditions, an obstacle to any hope of good
health. This was where cholera epidemics easily took
hold (there were three in the next twenty years) and
where typhoid and scarlet fever erupted regularly. One
William Farish, a man born above a weaver's shop in
Caldewgate in 1818, recorded what had happened after
the Corn Laws were passed in 1815. A period of such
poverty began that 'the wail of famished women and
helpless children could be heard in every street'. What
made the plight of these families even worse was that
the little money earned by the weavers so often went
on drink. There were twelve public houses in the half-
mile between the Caldew Bridge and Port Road and,
according to Farish, these were heavily patronised,
leading to 'pandemoniums' on Sunday mornings. Fights
went on till dawn and 'rowdyism and blasphemy reigned
supreme'. There were sights degrading enough to turn

hardened stomachs, never mind those of teetotal Quakers – scenes where crowds gathered to watch a man, challenged to crawl through a sewer for a drink, do just that.

It was not the place, then, for a quiet, peace-loving man like young J. D. Carr to choose to work, but his factory had to be near the canal. Caldewgate had another disadvantage and one that might affect business rather more significantly than the living conditions and drunkenness of its inhabitants. It was a place of extreme political tension. There had been constant trouble in Caldewgate for the last thirty years: it was the reason why, just before J.D. arrived, the Armoury in the nearby castle had been converted into a barracks. Here, in 1819, the Radical Reformers had taken to the streets, 400 of them, marching three abreast through Church Street, the Lady Radicals among them wearing red shawls and green veils, and black bonnets and dresses. Robert Johnson, a famous northern agitator arriving from Preston to encourage them to arm, had found a ready audience, and in the riots of 1826 Sir Philip Musgrave, the Tory candidate for the election that year, was roughly manhandled. J.D. was all in favour of parliamentary reform but not of rioting. He worked for the Reform Act together with the other manufacturing families, the Dixons and Fergusons, regularly attending meetings and lending his support to all peaceful measures necessary to achieve the passing of such an act. He celebrated with all the reformers when, in 1832, the bill got through. Nowhere was this more celebrated than in Carlisle, according to William Farish, who was pleased that 'the gentlemen of the town subscribed liberally' to the celebrations. J. D. Carr was among them, though he was not yet prosperous (but he gave every prisoner in the jail a loaf). There was a great procession through Carlisle, the weavers joining in wearing white aprons with REFORM printed on the sashes across them, and the Dixons and Fergusons marched alongside the working men (though J. D. Carr was not recorded as doing so).

But anyone who thought the passing of the Reform Act would make Caldewgate peaceful was a fool. There was still a long way to go before the Radical Reformers would be satisfied, and their headquarters were in Caldewgate. Voting rights in Carlisle had hardly changed at all: 330 freemen and 587 £10 householders were now allowed to vote, but that totalled only 917 new voters out of a population of over 20,000. It was no wonder the Chartists found support. J.D. watched the marches and knew Caldewgate would see further trouble. Nevertheless, he bought the land for his factory bang in the middle of this disturbed area, opposite the new church, Holy Trinity, which had just been completed, and right beside the canal, as he had intended. It cost him £800 and this time there was no mystery about its financing, for the money came from a bank loan. Then he put out to tender the building work, 'To Masons and Builders, to be let, the Building of a Corn Mill, Warehouse, Bakehouse and other Buildings in Caldewgate. Plans and specifications to be seen at J. D. Carr, Castle St.' This advertisement ran in the *Carlisle Journal* over several months in the mid-1830s, while J.D. schemed and worked to bring his great enterprise to fruition. He had a vision of a wholly self-contained biscuit works and bakery, from which boats bearing his goods would sail down the eleven miles from the canal basin to Port Carlisle. There they would be transferred to ships going on to Liverpool and from there, in time, all over the world.

This grandiose dream was kept alive through the six difficult years it took to build the factory, not by any greedy expectation of eventual immense wealth but by the notion of service. J.D. had a deep and genuine sense of mission, one that at first was simple: he wanted to make good, cheap bread to feed the poor. It angered him to see bread out of the reach of those who needed it most, simply because of the iniquitous Corn Laws. These laws, which had been in operation throughout his entire working life, first as an apprentice, then as a journeyman and now as a master baker, had been meant to protect home agrarian interests. The monopoly of the English farmers' market had been preserved in 1815 by prohibiting the import of foreign wheat until the price of English wheat had reached 80 shillings a quarter. Only when it had reached this high price was cheaper, foreign wheat allowed in. In this way, the price of bread was kept artificially high.

In his time as a baker J.D. had seen bread go from being the staple diet of the poor to become in some instances a luxury item, especially in areas like Caldewgate. No one in Caldewgate could afford to come to J. D. Carr's smart Castle Street shop to buy bread. William Farish, years later, still remembered that 'it was no uncommon thing in our house to be without bread for weeks together'. One of the first things J.D. did when he came to live in Carlisle was to seek out others intent on finding a way round the brutal operation of the Corn Laws. Objections to them had been so violent that a sliding scale had been fixed in 1828, but the principle was still the same: protect the home market and keep foreign wheat out for as long as possible.

J.D. found such like-minded souls at the meeting-house. He went there, with Thomas Brockbank, his very first week in the city and involved himself enthusiastically in Quaker business. The Carlisle meeting-house was different from the Kendal building he had known so well. It was in Fisher Street, just round the corner from where he lived and worked in Castle Street, a long, narrow but deep building with a lobby running from the street frontage right to the back. It could hold only 400 people, to Kendal's 850, and its membership was not as strong, though it was growing. By October 1831 J.D. had been selected as representative to the monthly meeting and from then on filled that role for three months of every year for the next decade, as well as acting as clerk and treasurer.

But it was the friends that J.D. made there who were more important than any position he held. Of these, Hudson Scott was the most significant. Like J.D. he was young and ambitious, full of ideas and eager to experiment. He was the nephew of a well-known Carlisle figure, Benjamin Scott, who had begun to trade as a bookseller and printer the previous century. Hudson Scott took over this business the year that J.D. came to Carlisle and was using a steam engine to power his presses, something that interested his new friend very much indeed. The two of them were put on the library committee and, while concentrating on re-cataloguing the books (commenting loftily that they found them 'in a state of extreme incorrectness'), they discussed the whole application of steam engines and the potential uses for them in their respective trades. Hudson Scott took J.D. to see his printing works, where he was also now making metal boxes, and there the idea was born: why not apply the same process to biscuit dough? If a steam-powered machine could, as J.D. had seen, cut metal, then how much more easily it could cut dough and thereby mechanise a slow, labour-intensive job.

But first J.D. needed to get his factory built and this proved a long, drawn-out business fraught with difficulty. He did not know Carlisle, or its masons and builders, and his project was an unusual one, never tackled before. He had to keep a close eye on everything happening down near the canal basin and at the same time keep up trade in his shop. It was his energy, his powers of organisation and his expertise upon which everything depended. It needed a prodigious imagination to envisage any building at all rising from the wasteland of mud that J.D. had bought. It might be on the very lip of the canal, but otherwise it had nothing to recommend it and he had no one to help and guide him as to the best way of setting about getting a factory constructed. Advice could have come from the Ferguson and Dixon families, both of whom had already built their own factories in which to carry out their textile industries (and the Dixons were in the process of building yet another factory), but J.D. did not know these other manufacturers properly yet. They were not Quakers, so they did not go to the Fisher Street meeting-house where he enjoyed the only sort of social life he had. He had seen Joseph Ferguson and the brothers Peter and John Dixon at political reform meetings, and he knew them to share his concern for the welfare of Carlisle's poor, but he was not their friend. J.D. was on his own, still a stranger to Carlisle and, as such, at a distinct disadvantage.

Even though he had only come from Kendal in the next county, a mere forty-odd miles away, his accent (never mind his appearance) marked him out as a stranger. The Kendal accent was much closer to the Lancashire than the Cumbrian accent, and Carlisle people had an accent different again from those who lived outside the city in the rest of Cumberland. J.D. had to negotiate with builders who found him difficult to understand and whom he very often found incomprehensible, not just because of accent difficulties but because of the very language they used. His own speech was formal, full of 'thees' and 'thous', and lacked not only any exaggeration but any cursing. He knew none of the local figures of speech and euphemisms or slang. But he was determined to supervise everything himself and so each day, at some time or another, he appeared on the site, a strange-looking figure in his Quaker clothes to the navvies working there.

The local builders hired Irish and Scottish navvies to do the hard digging and shifting of stones and soil, and a desperate-looking and -sounding lot they were. J.D. had no control over them, of course, and could do nothing about their occasional drunkenness, their frequent brawling or the constant oaths they exchanged. They were the responsibility of the builders, who paid them little and wanted to be rid of them as soon as possible. Once the ground had been prepared, other manual labour was brought in, of a more reliable and settled kind. So many trades were involved in the building of the factory – masons, bricklayers, carpenters, plasterers, plumbers – all of them working in an industry virtually untouched by any technological change since the Middle Ages. No builder in Carlisle employed more than ten men (not counting temporary labourers) and on a big job like this one the builder had to become a kind of entrepreneur himself, contracting out much of the work. J.D. was well aware of this and knew that he had to trust his builder, but he could not give that trust without an element of personal supervision. The local newspapers, reporting this exciting development in Caldewgate from time to time as the factory went up, never failed to comment that the owner was 'ever present'.

J.D. had decided that he wanted his factory built of bricks, not stone which was more widely used locally, so bricks were hauled in carts by the labourers from Botcherby and Kingmoor, two miles respectively to the south and north of the city, where there were brickworks. The people of Carlisle grew used to the noise of these heavily laden carts pulled by strong dray-horses trundling through the city, swaying alarmingly under the weight and damaging the roads as they went. Not all the roads they had to follow were well tarmacked and there were complaints about the terrible mess left by the deep ruts of the brick carts, which filled with water and then, in cold weather, froze over. Sometimes, the carts collapsed and the bricks thundered down, blocking the way and causing chaos. So they were not popular, and unfortunately a great many had to pass through Carlisle over a three-year period, with the factory needing so many bricks.

Everything in the construction of the factory was of necessity done by hand, but the lack of machinery did not make the building work any less noisy. On the contrary, the noise was shattering, since there were so many men using tools and yelling orders from one end of the vast site to the other. Often J.D. was seen to stand observing from a bit of ground that was slightly raised, looking towards the road side where the factory would be. Before his eyes was the timber scaffolding, erected with much difficulty and after the discarding of many lengths of wood, and all round it piles of bricks, which men collected in barrows and wheeled on demand to the teams of bricklayers who had at their service apprentices mixing mortar. There *was* order in it all, but it was difficult to find, and doubtless J.D. was trying to see it. If anything, the apparent confusion was worse once the outer shell was up, because then the interior crawled with even more workmen doing even more jobs.

But J.D. went on visiting, even though he was working hard in his Castle Street shop doing the baking. He was not a man who could, or would want to, delegate, but there were many times when it would have been more than useful to have someone he could absolutely trust at his side. His brother Henry was a possibility, but the rest of the family he had left behind in Kendal had, most unexpectedly, moved to Manchester. So J.D. had to manage on his own, but not quite alone, because in 1833, when the first tenders had gone out to build the factory, he got married.

He met his wife, Jane Nicholson, daughter of the widowed Elizabeth Nicholson of the coastal town of Whitehaven, at a quarterly meeting that she attended with her mother who, like J.D., was a representative to it. Jane was three years younger than he was, a bright-eyed, gentle young woman who appeared very small and frail beside the strapping J.D. He made his mind up quickly and the necessary clearing for marriage went ahead. A committee of three was appointed to investigate the circumstances of each of them, to make sure there was no impediment to their marrying. Then, on 20 November 1833, the marriage duly took place in the rather grand Whitehaven meeting-house.

The meeting-house was in Sandhills Lane, right in front of the newly laid-out town, and, though outside it was unremarkable, inside its grandeur was revealed. There were vast stone pillars holding up the centre valley of the double roof, making the place look more like the interior of a despised 'steeple-house' than felt quite comfortable for a Quaker. Nor was it physically comfortable for the wedding guests, half of whom could not see what was going on because of the pillars. An excessive number of witnesses signed the marriage certificate, but then Quakers were still nervous about their ceremonies being recognised as valid, so they took every precaution. There were fifty-four witnesses altogether, thirty-three women and twenty-one men, of whom ten were relations. J.D.'s brother Henry came to the wedding, as did his sister Jane, but, though they approved of the marriage, his parents did not make the long journey. J.D.'s new friend Hudson Scott came, however, together with hordes of Nicholsons and a contingent of local families. No rings were exchanged and, as was the Quaker custom, most of the ceremony took place in silence, except for the exchange of vows.

Life changed at once for J.D. No longer did he live above the shop in Castle Street, but took his new wife back to a house in Lowther Street. At least this lay a healthy distance from Caldewgate, although it was a modest house with fields opposite it, a mere few yards to the east of Rickergate, another of Carlisle's poor areas. By cutting through the old medieval lanes that joined Lowther Street to Scotch Street and so to the market place, J.D. could be at his shop in five minutes. He left the house early, often before dawn, still keeping the hours of the working baker he was, and returned late, leaving Jane to adjust on her own to life in a strange city.

This was not as difficult as it was for many women, because the fact that Jane was a Quaker gave her a ready-made family wherever she went. The meeting-house in Fisher Street was the centre of her social life, just as the Sandhills Lane house had been for her own family in Whitehaven. But the difference between the towns was marked. Whitehaven was a port, with the arrival and departure of ships its most important activity. It was a small town and, since it was so newly created – built to the specifications of the Lowther family, who owned it (and had enough interest and taste to make the town architecturally attractive, with streets elegantly laid out) – it was far cleaner and less crowded than Carlisle. Jane was used to the sea air and the open streets and freshness of Whitehaven, and Carlisle was at first overwhelming. But her life was spent almost entirely in the house or the meeting-house, so she was not obliged to cope with the contrast in the way that her husband had had to (though he thrived on it).

A year after they were married the Carrs had their first child, a girl named Elizabeth, followed fifteen months later by a son, Henry, and a second son, George Thompson, sixteen months after that. All very satisfactory: a man building up a new business needed sons to give it the future he planned. The year Jonathan Dodgson's second son was born, 1837, was the year that the new factory finally opened.

For the previous two years the wretched inhabitants of Caldewgate had watched the great brick building go up, until it towered over the canal basin, a mighty edifice with an impressive gateway fit for a palace. The main building had five floors and the adjoining ones three, and behind these were the yards and sheds. There was a mill, a bakehouse, a warehouse, storage rooms, stables and a shop – it was like a small town on its own. Even before these works were operational, everyone in Carlisle knew about them, not just because they had seen the building work but because J.D. had taken a front-page advertisement in the *Carlisle Journal*. He might be a Quaker, a believer in modesty, and he might seem to all who observed him quiet and reticent in manner, but his instinct was always to advertise his own progress and aims. The heading to the advertisement could not have been bolder or, to the authorities administering the Corn Laws, more challenging.

CHEAP BREAD

J. D. Carr, Corn & Flour Merchant, Miller, Bread & Biscuit Baker, having in addition to the one in Castle Street opened his new shop in Caldewgate and nearly completed the extensive premises . . . has pleasure in announcing to the public that, from the combined advantages of grinding his own materials and working both bread and biscuits by steampower, he is able to sell at the lowest possible rate, there being great economy as regards time and labour . . . In the manufacture of biscuits by a newly invented patent machine, he has made considerable improvements, the quality being superior, owing to the astonishing rapidity of the process.

What made the opening of the factory even more exciting was that it coincided with the opening, only six weeks before, of a railway line from a station in the south-east of Carlisle to the canal basin, right beside it. This was a distance of only one and a half miles, but every yard was significant, linking the canal, as it did (and therefore the new factory), with the western end of the long-promised Carlisle to Newcastle railway. It represented the meeting of rail with water, and Carr's were at the very point of contact, with their own length of line joining the railway just above the canal basin. At the railway opening there was a great dinner for 300 of the city's worthies, but J. D. Carr did not attend the sumptuous banquet. He did not approve of this kind of conspicuous consumption and self-indulgence. But he was as thrilled as everyone else to see the transport revolution become reality, just as he had envisaged.

Nobody else in Carlisle, no other manufacturer, was as well placed as J.D. now was to benefit from it. But to do so, he could no longer stretch himself so thin. The time had come to delegate, and there was no one he would rather trust than his own family. Henry, impressed during a visit by what he saw his younger brother had already achieved, sold his own business in Kendal and joined J.D. in Carlisle. He was followed soon afterwards by John, the youngest brother, only fourteen but already an apprentice baker as J.D. had been. Then, in 1840, all of the rest of the family, except George, arrived in Carlisle. The clan had finally gathered, clustered round their one outstanding entrepreneurial figure.

J.D. and Jane still lived in Lowther Street, though with the birth of two more sons, James Nicholson in 1838 and Thomas William in 1840, the house was becoming crowded. The rest of the Carrs rented a house in George Street, just five minutes away, and now Jane had plenty of company, with three sisters-in-law (Jane was twenty-eight, Mary twenty-three and Christiana twenty one) all unmarried at that time, ready and willing to help look after their nephews and nieces. All their fortunes and their futures depended on J.D., but he showed no signs of finding this a strain. As far as he was concerned he had hardly begun, even though he already appeared to be so successful. He knew precisely how perilous that success really was. Quickly built up, his business could just as quickly collapse, since it lacked the solid basis of the securely, almost limitlessly, wealthy families in and around Carlisle.

The landed gentry were the powerful people of Carlisle, the ones who controlled the city even if, since the 1832 Reform Act, the manufacturers and industrialists had begun to challenge their position. The new men became mayors and councillors, town clerks and eventually MPs. J.D. had no such political ambitions, local or otherwise, unlike his manufacturing neighbours, the Dixons and the Fergusons, and could not in any case, as a strict Quaker, hold any office that required the swearing of an oath or even an affirmation (a solemn declaration permitted on grounds of conscience instead of an actual oath). But he was interested in how the local grandees used their power and, since he was passionate about all kinds of reform, he was aware that nothing could be done without their co-operation. Quaker contacts, very useful when he started off, were no longer enough. He needed to have some connection with Sir James Graham of Netherby Castle and Philip Henry Howard of Corby Castle, men with whom in the ordinary course of events he would have no dealings, nor would he have wanted them.

This was just as well, because, should J.D. have wanted to break into Cumberland society, he would have found it impossible. It would have required the purchase of land in the order of something like 10,000 acres to be on a par with the county's élite (the city of Carlisle itself had no such élite) and even then he would not have been accepted. Adam Smith had noted in 1776 that 'Merchants are commonly ambitious to become country gentlemen' but that, though they might manage to be received by some of the local gentry, they were unable to break into the upper echelons of county society. Richard Cobden despaired of them even trying to do so – 'Manufacturers and merchants . . . seem only to desire riches that they may be able to prostrate themselves at the feet of feudalism. See how every successful trader buys an estate . . .' *Land* was power, not money, and the possession of substantial amounts of it kept society everywhere small and exclusive.

In Cumberland (and therefore Carlisle) the three most important landed families around whom society revolved were the Lowthers (Earls of Lonsdale), the Howards (Earls of Carlisle) and the Grahams of Netherby. None of them lived in Carlisle, though they all at some time or another owned town houses there. They had grand estates within a ten-mile radius of the city and consorted with each other, which, in the days of horse traffic and poor roads, and because of the distance between estates, meant that mutual visiting was fairly limited. By far the most important and influential magnate at this time from Carlisle's point of view was Sir James Graham, who lived in some splendour at Netherby Castle. He had begun his political life as Whig MP for the city, but when he lost his seat in 1820 he had spent his temporary retirement from Parliament developing his estate, converting thousands of acres of wet soil into arable land. J.D. was interested in him because, once back in Parliament, Sir James had made a speech exposing corruption in the Civil List, and because he had been one of a committee of four who had prepared the first electoral reform bill. But what J.D. admired most about Sir James was that he had changed his mind on the Corn Laws and was now against them, saying 'the object of political economy is not the greater accumulation but the better distributing of wealth and the happiness and well-being of the greatest number'. Exactly so. But though his sentiments sounded Liberal, Sir James styled himself a Liberal-Conservative and was not well liked, even by those who shared his views. He was aloof, very much the lord in his haughty bearing, and not a good mixer. J.D. would never have received an invitation to his table.

More approachable, and regarded far less warily by Carlisle people, were Philip Henry Howard, who was one of the junior Howards and lived in Corby Castle, and later on George James Howard, another 'junior', who lived at Naworth. Philip Henry was a Liberal, as was George James, who became the eccentric father of eleven children. The Howards – there was yet another branch, living at Greystoke, near Penrith – thought themselves intellectually superior to the rest of the county magnates, referring to them scathingly as 'Tally-ho mugs' who thought of nothing but hunting, shooting and fishing. Philip Henry became a Liberal MP for Carlisle in 1835 (and held on to his seat in the elections of 1837 and 1841). J.D. encountered him at political and public meetings in Carlisle, but in no sense were they friends.

The situation was no different for other manufacturers. The Dixons and Fergusons did not socialise with these powerful people either. On the other hand, they themselves were busy creating a new social class, doing their best to ape their supposed betters by building impressive houses, if not purchasing the elusive estates. Peter Dixon had a house built for himself in 1837 at Holme Eden, and Richard Ferguson had actually had his own small stately home built at Harker Lodge as early as 1807. They did not move far out into the country to do this, but stayed near to the city, which made them a far more important part of it than the landed magnates had ever been. They were physically *in* Carlisle all the time – working there, going to its theatre, joining its societies, supporting its library, museum and infirmary. Now this was the type of society that J.D. could have joined and been a part of, but because he was a strict Quaker when he arrived in Carlisle he sought no entry to it. Again, it was a matter of meeting his contemporaries in public gatherings to do with reform and the welfare of the poor, but never dining in their homes or inviting them into his own. It was the same with the lawyers and architects, the accountants and the clerks: he lived among them but did not socialise. He was marked out by his beliefs and as such was far more isolated than he had been in Kendal, where there were many more Friends and he was not so remarkable. Only the influential Scott family and other Carlisle Quaker families socialised with the Carrs.

But J.D. was quite content with this situation. There was no question of him desiring to be upwardly mobile socially – that was never of any interest to him – although public meetings afforded ample opportunity in the next decade for some kind of recognition and growing respect, which in turn brought him even more to the notice of those local magnates who were also Members of Parliament. J.D. continued to attend a great many of these meetings and spoke frequently at them, on any number of causes close to his heart. First and foremost was the Anti-Corn Law movement, then anti-slavery and anti-militia, plus support for the temperance movement. His name appears again and again in the two Carlisle newspapers, with his comments and questions from the floor reported in detail. The reputation that he was acquiring through the growth and success of his biscuit works, soon to be referred to as the biggest in England, was matched by his name for being a reformer, if a curious one without a political platform. J.D. was an oddity in every way and no one in Carlisle quite understood him. It was rare to find a man who appeared to have no desire for personal advancement in the accepted sense, and who stood up at meeting after meeting to speak on behalf of others without wishing to represent them. He was rarely on the platform, though invited on to it, and even more rarely accepted any kind of office, whether as treasurer or secretary or any similar modest function. He seemed to want to be in the thick of the fray and yet always slightly apart.

But what was unmistakable was J. D. Carr's obvious sense of purpose. There was a point to everything he said at these public meetings; he was not becoming prominent simply as a 'good' man, one inspired only by Christian duty. What emerged was his practical nature, his desire that systems should work well, whether the factory system, the political system or the social system. He hated waste and exploitation of all kinds. None of his speeches ever comprised high-flown rhetoric, but concerned themselves with how things could be made more effective, so that everyone would benefit. It was clear to him that common sense should be the basis for every kind of reform: it was not *sensible* to have in operation laws that prohibited cheap bread for the poor. But however strongly J.D. felt, and he felt very strongly indeed on any number of issues, he never called anyone who disagreed with him a fool, or treated him with contempt. That was what evidently struck journalists – his politeness, his even temper, his courtesy, even to those who sneered at him. All ideal Quaker attributes, but still surprising to witness. He was gaining a reputation of an unusual kind, one for compassion and concern running side by side with an aggressive business sense, and it confused people. How could J. D. Carr be, at one and the same time, so caring and yet so ruthless? How did his Quaker beliefs allow him to be so?

Within his own family, J.D. was seen only as kind and gentle. As a father to his six children (another daughter, the last child, Eliza, was born in 1842) he ruled by example and had no need of the rod. None of his young children feared him, and all of them later had happy memories of his benevolence. His household was run on strictly Quaker lines, but it was not a gloomy place: he had a sense of fun and approved of simple games. And when he was at home, which was not a great deal, his influence was felt not only in the attention to prayers but in his love of the outdoors. He took all his children out into the countryside, making them aware of the beauty of nature and the value of fresh air and exercise. Since he was such a tall, strong man, who wore the sombre clothes of the conventional Quaker, he looked striking surrounded by his small children as he walked them through Carlisle on their way to the River Eden or to the meeting-house. It was hard to equate this benign, fatherly figure with a man who was running a factory, employing some eighty people and expanding all the time.

But those within the factory recorded a similar dichotomy.

Maps of Carlisle

Carlisle, late 19th century

Caldewgate in 1865

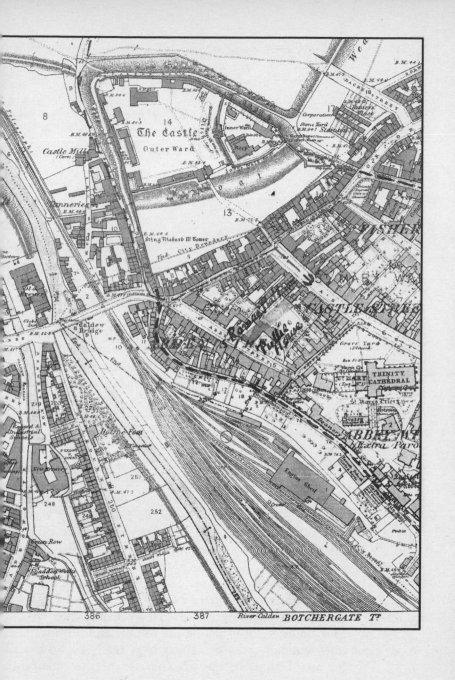

Chapter Three

•

A GIANT OF A MAN

J.D. NEVER INTENDED to remain a mere baker of bread. That held no challenge, beyond making bread as wholesome and cheap as possible, and no real worthwhile profit, which would give him the means to put into practice the many ideas he had in his head. To bake only bread in his bakehouse was wasteful. It left the factory under-used, because bread had to be baked at night, so there was no work done for most of the day. The future lay in biscuits, sweet biscuits, and he was quick to realise this. When J.D. was a boy, the word 'biscuit' commonly meant ship's biscuit, a kind of solid, dry, unleavened dough shaped into rounds and baked very hard several times. This was carried on long sea voyages because it lasted so much longer than bread, since it contained no ingredients that would go bad quickly. Not that this longer life made ship's biscuits palatable – the first thing a sailor was said to do with his biscuit was tap it on a hard surface to dislodge the maggots.

Ship's biscuits were made at the ports before the ships set off. The navy's bakers would set up in the victualling yards, mix up the crude dough by hand, then bake it four times, before shaping the rounds and putting them into wooden casks or canvas bags ready to be loaded on board ship. In the first quarter of the nineteenth century some basic machinery had been invented to speed up this process, but it was only a matter of a mixer, a roller and a cutter operating one after the other, and the operation still relied on human hands in the interim stages. The machinery, such as it was, was in any case used only in the preparation of this particular type of biscuit. Sweet biscuits, known as 'fancy' biscuits, were made elsewhere, entirely by hand and in small quantities. They were concoctions of very fine flour and sugar mixed with a selection of other ingredients – almonds, currants, preserved fruits – and often flavoured with orange or rose water, and they had been in existence since the Middle Ages. Housewives and cooks made fancy biscuits from their own invented recipes, largely for consumption by their own households, although sometimes they might make more than they needed and then sell them from trays in the streets. But no baker manufactured fancy biscuits on a large scale at the time J.D. began to do so in Carlisle. Down in the South, George Palmer was baking fancy biscuits and selling them in his Reading shop, as were several other bakers around the country, but these were all made by hand in small quantities and were not widely distributed.

Yet it was obvious – to J.D., to George Palmer – that these fancy biscuits were in growing demand. For one thing, they kept well. Packed carefully into airtight tin boxes, which were then sealed, they could be preserved, quite crisp and fresh, for months, even years, and so they could be transported. But of course, however carefully packed, biscuits were fragile. They could not survive intact if carried on carts and wagons along bad roads. Times, however, were changing, just as J.D. began his business: water transport (in other words, the canals) gave biscuits a much better chance of survival. With a factory right next to a canal basin, J.D. was perfectly situated to send his biscuits far and wide. The export of

Carr's biscuits began in the early 1840s, managed through the shipping connection with Maryport. Ships sailed regularly then from Maryport all over the world and it was easy to persuade captains to take boxes of biscuits to deliver with the other goods they were carrying. The biscuits went by canal to Port Carlisle and from there by small ships to Maryport, ready for transfer to larger ones.

Once the railways came, their significance for the biscuit trade, along with so many other trades, was immense. It was not just that transport was safer for the product, but that this new method of travel actually fuelled the need for biscuits. All over the country, from the late 1830s onwards, railways were being completed and more and more travellers were using them instead of the roads. Once they did, they needed provisions and, unlike the stagecoaches, which stopped at inns, the train stations had no dining facilities as yet, and neither did the trains. Biscuits were the perfect form of snack, and snacks instead of proper meals were becoming more and more usual as working hours changed. There was also a feeling of luxury about fancy biscuits – they were treats, a refined form of food, and middle-class women especially liked to offer them with tea (as they do in Mrs Gaskell's *Cranford* and other novels of the period). Whereas bought cakes were a sign of household failure, bought biscuits were not. They had a strange allure, because they were so attractive to look at. They appealed to the eye and often had a delicious smell: in short, they were ladylike.

So J.D. turned his attention from concentrating almost entirely on bread in his first Castle Street shop to turning out fancy biscuits in his new factory in Caldewgate in larger and larger quantities. He had his premises ready, equipped with thirteen new ovens formed of stones of great thickness, and he had his mill, capable of producing

8,000 bags of flour a year. Next he had to find the all-important work force. Choosing the workers was difficult. There was no shortage of applicants, in 1837, to work in his impressive new factory. It was, as the *Carlisle Journal* remarked, 'a time of panic'. The very month that the factory opened there was a march past it, and through Caldewgate, of textile workers going to Ferguson's factory to ask for more money (they were refused), and the area swarmed with men desperate for work of any kind in any trade. J.D. did not want the desperate. The desperate, in his experience, drank and he was determined to employ only teetotallers, or at least those who could convincingly claim to be so. Nor did he want mature men set in their ways and with their health and strength perhaps already in jeopardy, if not actually ruined by their work. He knew all about that. He knew, from personal observation, that hernias were common among those who had worked for a long time in the baking industry and that lung diseases were easily contracted in the hot, badly ventilated bakehouses. His aim was to take on younger men and train them himself, but he needed some experienced hands to start with, apart from his own and his brother John's (though John was still an apprentice), so he recruited from Scottish bakeries, finding accommodation for the men himself.

Care of his workers was to be paramount. J.D. had shown it already, in the design of his factory. The windows were large, the ceilings high, the whole effect airy and spacious. He had fixed the starting time at 5.15 a.m. and the finishing time at 6 p.m., with money wages paid to everyone (three to five shillings a week for the boys, seventeen shillings for the men), and with a daily allowance of biscuits to all. Anyone doing overtime would be paid extra. A room was set aside as a schoolroom, because he knew it was unlikely that all his men, never mind his boys, would be able to read and write, and another room as a library. He had even shown consideration not only for cleanliness but for fun and exercise – there was a swimming-bath provided, fourteen feet square, which was filled with warm water, and here the boys swam three days a week. Sometimes the water, which came off the steam engine mechanising the production of the biscuits, was far too hot, in which case the boys had the additional fun of being hosed down with cold water as they came out. Dr Henry Lonsdale, when he inspected Carr's for a paper he was writing for the *Journal of Public Health* on conditions in bakeries, could not get over 'the airiness of the apartments, the arrangements for ensuring cleanliness, the temperate habits of all concerned . . .' But he was sharp enough to notice that none of the above was as significant as the example set by J. D. Carr himself, which he concluded 'kindled a kindred spirit among the men'.

It came as a shock not only for Dr Lonsdale but for a journalist from *Chambers Edinburgh Journal* (and several others who visited Carr's to report on it) to see J.D. himself actually working alongside the men. He started at the same time as they did, donned his white apron as they did (all the workers were issued with aprons) and sat beside them doing exactly the same work, moving from one part of the factory to another regularly, so that he was beside every man at some point. His was a calm, authoritative presence with no hint of threat about it. He did not ask anyone to do what he had not demonstrated he was willing and able to do himself, and this included the most menial of tasks. He lifted and humped about great sacks of flour. He could lift a twenty-stone sack with ease and carry it the length of the warehouse floor. Then he would dust the flour off his hands, smile and ask if anyone else would like to try. His visible strength was a very important part of his influence: men respected a boss who was stronger than the strongest among them. They were always surprised, though, that such strength went with such mildness of manner. J.D. unfailingly used the Quaker form of address – it was 'thee' and 'thou' to everyone and a refusal to use any form of title, even 'Mr' or 'Mistress' – and this made him seem quaint. It was altogether confusing to have a man in charge of everything who never shouted or bawled anyone out, one who used politeness almost as a weapon, and whose slow, even walk was the very opposite of the strutting posture of a characteristic all-powerful owner.

And yet they were in no doubt that J.D. was the owner (or the Founder as he was known). His constant presence in the factory was not the only indication that he was passionately involved in his trade, though it was the most obvious one. He was strict and did not hesitate to act on his extremely well-known principles. Take temperance: no allowances were made for drunkenness. Every apprentice, as part of his sworn indenture, had to promise not to go to the taverns (as well as not to gamble or visit the playhouse) and every journeyman had to take a pledge not to touch alcohol. Any man who thought J.D. could not be serious, and that this was pure idealism which would not be expected to last, quickly discovered his mistake. Sobriety was the watchword and it was rigorously enforced. To that extent, his workers went in fear of J.D., even if there was nothing about him otherwise to arouse that emotion.

J.D.'s genial air, which made him look like a benign gentleman farmer, was misleading. He was tough in the cause of righteousness and ambitious not just for the success of his business but for improvement in the lives of his work force. This had its disadvantages for them, as well as its advantages. Certainly, the workers at Carr's felt cared for within the factory environment, but they also felt unnerved. It was unsettling for many of them to sit or stand next to the owner – too much room for comparisons (were you doing the job as well as he was and had he noticed?), too uncomfortable a feeling of being tested and in due course perhaps found wanting. How could you work all day next to the man who employed you and paid you, and not occasionally exceed the permissible level of conversation? One wrong or hasty word, one bout of swearing, and you were done for. The necessary respect for the man who had such power over you, and whose own conduct seemed so irreproachable, could be forgotten and you, not he, would be the loser. It took a particular type of man to adapt to Carr's, but then it was just such a man for whom J.D. was searching. He knew what kind of places his workers had come from, how they had been ruled by those impervious to their needs, and he knew the risk of treating them with kindness. It might be misinterpreted. Nobody had taught J.D. how to manage a large unit of industrial employment – such a thing was, in fact, in its infancy everywhere – and he made his own rules, inspired by his Quaker beliefs.

One of these was that the workers should have some say in their own welfare. This was not to give them any actual decision-making power but to endeavour to settle any possible grievances, which might in time affect the smooth running of the factory. It might look like a liberal approach, but it was not: it was a purely practical one. As in so much else that he did, J.D. was motivated by common sense. It was not that he thought his workers had the *right* to be consulted, but that by allowing some measure of consultation he would isolate and deal with any trouble before it took hold. So, from the beginning, he held a foremen's meeting twice a week at which he himself or Henry, and later George and finally John (the only brother to work alongside the men with J.D., once he was qualified), was also present.

The foremen from every department were invited to report any cause of dissatisfaction and then it was earnestly discussed before action, if any, was taken. It was this, more than the hygienic conditions in the factory, which astounded visitors in the 1840s. To them, this consultation, however admirable, was potentially dangerous. Who knew what ideas it would put into the workers' heads? But J.D. had absolute confidence that to consult was to placate. He did not see that he surrendered one iota of control.

Yet, however successful he was within his own factory, he knew that the real battle for better conditions, which would in turn be conducive to better business, lay outside it. He never entertained any illusions. Each day as he walked to work, passing over Caldew Bridge into Caldewgate, he witnessed the utter wretchedness in which his workers lived once they left his clean, light factory. He had to cross Dow Beck, the stream that ran down the main street, to get there and this was little better than an open sewer. Refuse was thrown into it by everyone and was swept along into the river when the water was high, but lay rotting and stinking in summer when the water was low. The fastidious J.D. stepped over it but, even with the beck negotiated, walking the rest of the way down Bridge Street was treacherous. There was little proper paving and the walkways were rarely swept clean.

Here was the greatest degradation of all – 200 people used ten filthy privies and inhabited damp, miserable cellars. The lanes going off Bridge Street were full of dunghills and stagnant pools, while between the canal basin and Bread Street, opposite his factory, there was a vast overflowing cesspool. Of the ten places listed in Carlisle as most at risk from cholera, eight were in Caldewgate in the immediate vicinity of Carr's. Walking to work was a daily reminder for J.D. that his workers were more at risk from disease at home than from anywhere in his factory, more liable to infection of every kind. Home pulled them down and made them miserable, and misery led them into temptation. In his factory, they would don their pristine white aprons, they would swim in the bath from which they emerged fresh and clean, but they went home to appalling conditions.

J.D. made it his business to know as much as possible about the living circumstances of his employees, dutifully attending every meeting to do with the condition of the poor in Carlisle, and in the 1830s and 1840s there were a great many of these. It was well known, due to various reports, that as many as *half* the population of the city were living in dire poverty and another quarter surviving only with a struggle. J.D.'s workers were obviously not among the destitute, but nevertheless most of them had big families and lived in houses that were grossly overcrowded and without even the most basic amenities. He had done his best, when he brought down the experienced bakers he needed from Scotland to start off his business, to see that they were as well housed as possible, but the choice of accommodation had been limited and he was far from satisfied.

James MacGregor, one of J.D.'s best workers, was living in just two rooms in John Street with his wife, three daughters and two sons. The rooms were dark, low-ceilinged and either roasting hot when the fire (used for all cooking) was lit, or freezing cold when it was not. There was no running water of course – this came from a shallow well and was of extremely dubious purity, though it could also be bought from a cart for one penny a gallon – and the privy was shared with several other families. The MacGregor family were good people and not in the least feckless – James had signed the pledge, so did not drink his wage away – and their rooms were clean, but James was glad to leave them for the factory.

Before he set off for work (just across the road) James had porridge with milk for his breakfast, making him well fed compared with so many others, who had only a thin oatmeal gruel. For dinner he ate potatoes with perhaps a little bacon, and once a week meat in a stew. Meat was so expensive then that few workers could afford it and it hardly featured in their diet. But James's wife bought scrag end and stewed it well, and the stew lasted three days. The family drank tea, without sugar. It was not a very varied diet but it was sufficient and the family never went hungry. Clothes were more of a problem. J.D. had noted how thin and worn the clothes of his employees tended to be. Men came to work even in the coldest weather without any kind of top coat, and James MacGregor was no exception. With a wife and five children to clothe, he could not afford to buy good thick garments for himself and wore the same patched woollen trousers and jacket, winter and summer, adding a muffler and thick, long stockings underneath his trousers in the coldest weather. He never took his cap off, but then few of the men did.

What most concerned J.D. was not just the poor conditions in which this respectable Scottish workman lived, together with many others like him, but the strain they were under living so closely together with people unlike themselves – people, in other words, who drank and lived without regard for morals. They deserved better. Provided with decent houses, his sober hardworking employees would benefit enormously.

He intended to try to see that they got them, but at first, in the late 1830s and the early 1840s, he directed his energies to the running of the biscuit works, which left little time for attempts at social reform. The fancy biscuits he turned out initially were of only two kinds (the popular alphabet variety and a finger shortbread), but what was significant was *how* they were manufactured. J.D. was using a steam machine in the process, one that could make a ton of flour into biscuits in an hour. According to the *Carlisle Journal*, in its issue of 7 May 1837, J. D. Carr had read about a machine invented in America that could do this and, 'being a practical man, determined to inquire into the facts of the case. He soon found that the statement was true in all its parts and, like a sensible man, determined to profit by his knowledge. A machine was ordered...' It was installed in Carr's by 1838 and was considered a wonder to behold. Even George Palmer, who joined forces with Joseph Huntley to form a biscuit-manufacturing firm much bigger than Carr's, was forced to admit, if through gritted teeth, that J.D. had introduced machinery into the trade before he did, although he asserted that it was so crude it did not really count.

What did count and what nobody could dispute, not even the envious George Palmer, was that J.D. pulled off the most amazing *coup* in May 1841, when he became the first biscuit manufacturer to gain a Royal Warrant. Queen Victoria started issuing warrants almost immediately after her accession and in 1841 issued a total of 356, of which only one was to a biscuit manufacturer. A Royal Warrant of appointment was, of course, a mark of recognition to an individual supplier. The warrants were dated and signed by the Lord Chamberlain and made out to Her Majesty's Gentleman Usher in Daily Waiting, who had to administer a fairly elaborate oath to the grantee. The oath was taken on the Bible, but Quakers used the special Form of Affirmation.

How an obscure biscuit manufacturer up in a small northern city managed to get such a prestigious warrant, which he immediately exploited for all it was worth, remains a mystery. J.D. had no connections at Court

J.D. Carr with his family in the late 1850s (from left, George, James, Eliza, Henry, J.D., Lizzie, Jane, Thomas).

J.D. Carr, late 1860s – note the shabbiness of his 'quaintly Quaker' clothes and the top hat he raised to no one.

Jane Carr – the fur on her coat shows she had left strictly Quaker habits behind.

The market place in Carlisle, painted by W.H. Nutter in 1835, soon after J.D. opened his first shop.

Carr's Biscuit Factory and Caldewgate, the industrial heart of the Victorian city.

Girls and young women working in the packing room, all neatly dressed in regulation white aprons, and with hair tied back.

The biscuit machine room, where the women collected the heavy trays from the men who minded the machines.

The original biscuit cutting machine of the 1840s.

An example of the pristine white uniform every woman had to wear.

Henry Carr, his wife Sarah, and six children, three of whom died of scarlet fever soon afterwards.

Thomas William Carr with his children, a year after the death of his wife who died giving birth to the twins.

The brothers Carr, c. 1900 (from left, doctors Sydney and John, Ernest the rebel, Theodore the managing director, Bertram, Harold).

A typical late-Victorian family picnic: James Carr in the deckchair, Theodore centre (with moustache), Henry standing beside the invalid carriage.

*The centre of Carlisle towards the end of the 19th century,
with horse-drawn city omnibuses.*

Workers leaving Carr's factory to catch the tram home in the early 1900s.

and no influential friends. He may have asked Carlisle's MP at that date, Philip Henry Howard of Corby Castle, to help him, but, if so, he committed nothing to paper. He knew Howard of course, having met him at meetings to discuss the establishing of an infirmary and the proposed setting-up of a building society to enable working men to buy their own homes, but there is no available written record of this local grandee interceding for him. The approach to the Palace must have come from J.D., putting himself and his biscuits forward (he would have had to send samples), and that has one very odd aspect to it. J.D. knew that an oath had to be sworn and that, should he be granted the coveted Royal Warrant, he would have to use the Form of Affirmation, as other Quakers had been prepared to do. But even affirming was to him a form of compromise and he had vowed never to do it. He said so, frequently. He stated this in writing, both before and long after 1841. Once, in a long and serious letter to the *Carlisle Journal*, in which he was explaining why he could never hold municipal office, he said that it was because, though other Quakers had found ways to compromise, 'I can agree no compromise.' He dissented, he wrote, from the established Church and objected to the control of the state in religious matters, and that was that.

Yet there were other Quakers, of the very highest calibre, upholding the strictest views of their religion, who by this time were having no problems with affirming. After Parliament had been opened to dissenters in 1832, Joseph Pease of Darlington sought election and made history as the first MP to affirm rather than take an oath. Nobody appears to have thought any the less of him for doing so. But as yet none of the other Quaker food families had been put to the test in this particular way – a fairly trivial test, after all. J.D. was the first to get a Royal Warrant and for business reasons made the necessary compromise, which he was not prepared to do in any other area of his life. Perhaps he managed to obtain a wording that seemed to him *not* to be a compromise. The oath, for those who took it, was elaborate, but the Form of Affirmation could vary. J.D. undoubtedly persuaded himself that whatever he said to Her Majesty's Gentleman Usher in Daily Waiting did not compromise him.

Once he had his Royal Warrant, he let everyone know. The *Carlisle Journal*, in a state of great excitement, reported, 'We understand Mr J. D. Carr has by special licence been appointed Biscuit Maker to Her Majesty and has received orders for the supply of the Royal Household with his delicious biscuits. We hear he is now engaged in preparing a supply for the Princess Royal.' 'By Royal Appointment' was stuck on every communication from Carr's and went into every advertisement. For a Quaker, with an obligation to tell the literal truth at all times, J.D. strayed suspiciously close to exaggeration in the wording of some advertisements. One read, 'The Queen's biscuits, manufactured by J. D. Carr of Carlisle, are in general use at the Royal Household . . .' How could he be sure of that? The mere fact of having a Royal Warrant did not guarantee that his biscuits were 'in general use'. Hair-splitting, but then Quakers did split hairs.

At the age of thirty-five J.D. was entering upon the most successful decade of his life, but he was also on the brink of experiencing conflict between his very sincerely held Quaker principles and his entrepreneurial style of business. He was beginning to make money, big money for a Carlisle manufacturer. Three years after he received the Royal Warrant, he was turning out not two but twenty-one varieties of fancy biscuit (of which the Rich Desserts were the most popular), as well as the ship's biscuits, which still made up two-thirds of production. He had enough money to make him feel rich and he had to decide how to adapt to his new wealth.

The most obvious answer was to build himself a house that would satisfy his needs and inevitably reflect his new status. Before the birth of Eliza in 1842, J.D. moved his family out of the Lowther Street house and back into Castle Street, but this was only a temporary measure while he was building a new house across the River Eden in Stanwix, Carlisle's most desirable area. He had bought some land there, more land than he needed for his own house, because he advertised 'Freehold Building Ground for Sale' in the *Journal*: '24 valuable freehold building sites . . . greatly elevated above the river . . . pure air and salubrity unrivalled'.

The house he went on to have built for himself was a two-storey building with sash windows and a stone balcony between the two floors at the front. Only the best materials were used – local green slates for the roof, sandstone dressings, wrought-iron balusters and, inside, panelled doors, moulded ceiling cornices, scrolled cast-iron balusters and moulded mahogany hand-rails. The site was high above the river, set back from the road that led to Brampton, but screened by trees. J.D. called it, perhaps slightly ironically, The Villa, and he and his family intended to move there as soon as it was completed. There would be room, at last, for his six children to run around and it represented a very big jump from living above the shop in Castle Street. This looked like a plan for gracious living, or as near to it as anyone in Carlisle could come, infinitely superior to anything within the city, though not on a par with the true grandeur of Corby, or Netherby, or Scaleby, or Rose Castle, those houses of the aristocracy and the bishop situated at various points around Carlisle.

J.D. now had a position to keep up, but the only public position he accepted was within the Quaker movement. He was happy to serve, as he had been doing all his adult life, as representative to monthly and quarterly meetings, and even in 1842 and 1845 (and again in 1853, 1859 and 1861) to the yearly meeting in London. Going to London, in May, was a big event. The meeting lasted ten days and required a fairly extensive wardrobe, even for the plainest dressed of Quakers: ten white shirts, six neck cloths, eight stocks, two night caps, four pairs of stockings, six handkerchiefs, two coats and two pairs of breeches. A total of 154 representatives from the twenty-three quarterly meetings gathered in a most sedate assembly to debate matters troubling Quakers all over the country and to worship together in separate meetings held at different venues in the capital. J.D. was one of four representatives for the whole of Cumberland and Northumberland, and he was appointed as an auditor of the accounts.

The main topics discussed in the 1842 meeting were education (William Forster, who later, in 1870, was to introduce an important Education Act, was there), marriages (should Quakers be allowed to marry out?) and slavery in the colonies. J.D. did not speak but he listened very attentively, especially to what was said about slavery, and he made good use of the opportunity for contacts afforded by being gathered together with influential men from so many different places. He met James Cadbury (representative for Berkshire) and his rival Joseph Huntley, as well as members of the Clark, Palmer and Fry families. When he was not fully occupied within the yearly meeting he attended others in London connected with his other interests, such as the Anti-Corn Law protests, and he also found time to remember his employees. John Irving, his foreman in the sugar biscuit department, was extremely pleased to receive on J.D.'s return a pair of spectacles, priced eighteen shillings. John could not read but J.D. hoped that the spectacles would help him, since he was making slow progress with the phonetic method taught in the factory.

Once back in Carlisle, J.D. felt more than ever that, as a man of some standing now as well as a Quaker, he ought to contribute something more positive to society than a well-run factory. In fact, he had been putting his head above the parapet for the last four years, ever since he had felt securely established in his new premises. He had joined the Carlisle branch of the Anti-Corn Law League as soon as it was formed in 1838 and quickly became its most fervent member, bombarding the two local newspapers with letters pointing out how iniquitous the Corn Laws were. In August 1838 he had written a particularly long and serious letter setting out his position, which the *Journal* printed in full. 'I have been looking', he began modestly, 'for some weeks past to the subject being taken up by someone more conversant with the subject than myself, but as this has not been done I am anxious that the present time should not pass without a few remarks made on the subject.' These 'few remarks' turned into a detailed and damning explanation of exactly why the Corn Laws were 'evil', followed by a complicated set of tables that he had drawn up to demonstrate why they were unnecessary anyway. He attacked the supporters of the Corn Laws, asking what on earth they had to fear from foreign grain when, as he pointed out, even if all the corn on the continent were purchased instead of home grain, it would keep the country for only five weeks. He ended by urging free trade, not all at once but gradually.

But letters, though increasingly sharp, had not been J.D.'s only form of attack. In April 1841 he did something much more daring and much more likely to bring him into conflict with the authorities. He put two sets of loaves in the window of his most prominent shop, the original Castle Street one (nobody was going to notice anything in his factory shop-window, or no one of influence, because the good citizens of Carlisle tried not to walk through Caldewgate at all). One set were shilling loaves, one set sixpenny. He put a notice in front of each set saying 'taxed' on the smaller loaf and 'untaxed' on the larger loaf. Since the loaf sizes were dramatically different but the prices the same, this drew everyone's attention and soon a crowd had gathered. The *Carlisle Journal* (founded in 1798 and strongly Liberal in its views) reported the event approvingly but unfortunately got its facts wrong, muddling up the weights and prices of the loaves and making nonsense of its own conclusion that 'here was a palpable demonstration of the effect of taxation adapted to the plainest understanding'. It also declared that 'the character of Mr Carr requires no defence', which provoked a sarcastic response from an anonymous correspondent calling himself 'Fairplay', who had written in to correct the errors of fact. 'You say the character of Mr Carr requires no defence . . . [but] if he *will* take it into his head to think himself a great luminary whose rays can light the doubting traveller through the devious paths of political economy he must excuse us if we hesitate to exclaim "Behold, the sun!" And Indian-like adore him.'

The *Carlisle Patriot* (as Tory as the *Journal* was Liberal) called J.D. and all the Anti-Corn Law League members 'a little knot of mischievous busybodies', but in the *Journal* another anonymous writer, calling himself simply 'A Working Man', defended J.D. against Fairplay's accusations. He wanted to duff Fairplay up – 'many of the fellers in our village wish to have him in our hands awhile . . . he would soon find whether your printer's devil or our dung forks were heaviest . . . I can alus live better when corn is cheap.'

All this was entertaining but meanwhile everyone,

including J.D., waited to see if the authorities would act. It was illegal to sell bread untaxed and, though he had not exactly done that – anyone buying the bigger, untaxed loaves still had to pay the tax separately – a case against him could have been attempted. But nothing was done.

The *Journal* had been correct to say that J.D. was of irreproachable character. He was already famous for his honesty. This, after all, was the man who, finding that his workmen had collected two extra bags of grain for which he had not paid, had the grain milled into flour, then took it down to the police superintendent saying it was not his and he must find the owner and return the flour to him. One of the authorities, in the shape of the vicar of Stanwix, where J.D. was having his house built, had already tried to challenge him and had failed. As a Quaker, J.D. refused to pay tithes. When the vicar claimed them from him and was refused, he had a bag of flour removed forcibly from Carr's and proceeded to try to auction it in Carlisle market place. Not a single person would bid for it. The vicar then applied to the magistrates for a warrant to distrain on J.D.'s goods because of his non-payment of tithes, and when it was granted a bailiff arrived and took away some silver spoons.

But returning from London in 1842, J.D., in spite of his previous efforts, felt that something more was due from him. That year the poverty in Carlisle was terrible. The *Journal* reported that out of a population of 22,000, there were 5,561 reduced to such a state of suffering that immediate relief was needed to save them from actual famine. It took care to point out that 'the details have not been furnished by any member of the Anti-Corn Law League . . . they have been obtained by a committee composed of all parties'. Philip Henry Howard (Carlisle's MP) had been moved to beg on behalf of the poor in Carlisle in a letter to the editor of *The Times*, 'I grieve to say that the means at the disposal of the committee of the Carlisle Relief Fund are nearly exhausted . . . any donation however modest can be forwarded . . . to the Mayor or the writer.' He helpfully pointed out that 'Postal Orders facilitate the transport of small sums.' The money did not flood in and the position became desperate.

It was all, J.D. was convinced, the fault of the Corn Laws, so he redoubled his efforts to get them repealed. It was he who organised a huge meeting in December 1842 when a deputation from the Manchester branch of the Anti-Corn Law League came to the Athenaeum (a big hall in Lowther Street) and addressed 800 members, including women. The *Patriot* was shocked and even the *Journal* was uneasy – 'the presence of women at such meetings forms a new era in the history' (in Carlisle, anyway). John Bright (MP first for Durham, then for Manchester, and founder, with Richard Cobden, of the Anti-Corn Law League) attended and made a tremendous speech, and J.D. seconded the motion put to the meeting that evidence against the imposition of the Corn Laws should be put into the hands of everyone with a vote.

J.D. did everything he could to help get the Corn Laws repealed during the next four years. Some of his efforts were, for a Quaker, quite flamboyant. Since he was ever aware of the power of advertising, he had made for himself a splendid waistcoat of a rich brown velvet, bearing a design of ears of corn embroidered upon it in a lighter shade. The word 'free' was worked into the pattern and the whole effect was enough to attract close attention whenever he wore it. To those innocents who failed to appreciate the symbolism, he delivered a lecture they were unlikely to forget. His own workers were proud of him and when, in April 1845, J.D. offered to supply the great Anti-Corn Law League Bazaar, which was held in London, with a quarter-ton of biscuits free of charge, they offered their labour free. But the climax of all the agitation in Carlisle that J.D. fomented came in January 1846, when Anti-Corn Law fever reached its height throughout the country. Richard Cobden and John Bright came to Carlisle together to rally the troops for the coming final onslaught, and J.D. was in charge of the organisation. The Athenaeum, which held an official maximum of 800, was besieged for tickets and three times that number tried to squash in. Finally, 1,300 were crammed in, making the hall dangerously overcrowded. Cobden and Bright duly arrived from Newcastle and the atmosphere was thrilling. It seemed impossible, listening to the applause that greeted the speakers and the cheers that erupted at the end, to doubt that repeal was inevitable. Proposing the vote of thanks, J.D. commended the League's 'zeal, judgement and perseverance'. Victory must surely come.

It did, very soon after, and a party was held in the large packing-room of the biscuit works. It was actually the workers who held it: they and their wives were the hosts, inviting J.D. and all his family to join them. The room had been beautifully decorated with flags and evergreens, and over the chair given to J.D. was a banner reading 'Be Just and Fear Not'. He wore his waistcoat, of course, and was delighted with all the speeches and with the songs and recitations that followed, especially since the jollity was not caused by alcoholic consumption. Tea, biscuits and cakes were all that were needed to celebrate, and that pleased their employer most. The hilarity and excitement came from a sense that conditions would now be better, that a great battle had been fought and won. J.D. had a sense of true identification with his workers which made him proud and which he did not want to lose. Carr's was, above all, a *family* firm and he was the paterfamilias.

He felt that his workers were well looked after and certainly none of them would ever starve, but his concern was never entirely focused only on them. He was well aware that in other parts of Britain there was still terrible destitution, repeal of the Corn Laws notwithstanding. That very year, in November 1846, the plight of the poor in the West Highlands was widely publicised, and J.D. wrote to Mr Blamire, Chief Tithe Commissioner, offering to provide his rye and maize bread free if the Government could arrange transportation. Mr Blamire tasted the bread and pronounced it very nutritious, but said that it was too impractical a suggestion – by the time the loaves reached the West Highlands, such were the difficulties of transport to the region, it would be inedible. But he was very interested in J.D.'s version of the old ship's biscuit, a coarse, plain biscuit, much more palatable than the original and kept much fresher now that it could be sealed in tins. Lord John Russell, the Whig Prime Minister of the time, sampled the biscuit and agreed with Mr Blamire. He asked for 'a large pack' to be sent to Windsor, where a Cabinet meeting was to be held. The *Carlisle Journal*, reporting all this, delighted in the image of the entire Cabinet sitting munching Carr's biscuits while deciding matters of State. The Queen... the Prime Minister... the Cabinet – J.D.'s fame seemed never-ending. Meanwhile, biscuits (two tons were produced each hour) were conveyed to the Highlands to help prevent starvation.

Chapter Four

•

THE RICH DESSERTS

A FTER THE spring of 1846, when he and his wife, their six children and three servants had moved into The Villa, J.D. had a very different walk to work. He no longer simply crossed the road, cut through Paternoster Row to the right of the cathedral, and strode along West Walls to Caldew Bridge and so into crowded, filthy Caldewgate. The contrast in that five-minute walk was marked enough, but walking from The Villa it was even greater. Stanwix was green and leafy, situated so high above the River Eden – a much cleaner and far more beautiful, meandering river than its tributary the Caldew – that, as J.D. had said in his advertisements when trying to sell land there, the air felt fresh and pure. Coming down his drive and stepping out onto the Brampton road, he could see through the trees the open parkland on the east side of the river and then, as he came to the top of the steep hill that swooped down to cross the river, the whole of Carlisle was spread before him, with the castle and the cathedral clearly outlined on the horizon. He was above all the noise and bustle, the dirt and the crowds, when he began his walk and then, reaching the bridge, peace departed.

He cut through Rickergate now, skirting the Sands where cattle were herded to be sold and slaughtered, and it was a route full of depressing and ugly sights,

71

made all the more striking because of the contrast with the area from which he had just come. Rickergate was a slum just as Caldewgate was, but it lacked the factories, the industrial energy, which at least gave Caldewgate some feeling of purpose behind the grime of its living conditions. This area, between his factory and his home, gave J.D. a twice-daily determination to try to make things better for the poor. He had the will, he had the money and even if he would not accept responsibility in the form of municipal office, he accepted it in other ways. There was hardly an evening he was at home with his wife and six children, so busy was he with meetings and committees on social reform. For twenty years, from the early 1840s to the early 1860s, his name was never out of the newspapers, as they reported on the various schemes in the city to try to ameliorate the lot of the poor. J. D. Carr was forever speaking from the floor and proposing motions and votes of thanks, so that at one time it seemed no gathering was able to start without his presence. People, especially reporters, looked around and if they could not see his tall figure, usually standing at the back of the hall, they could not settle.

Some of the reforms that he interested himself in had begun before he came to Carlisle. Since 1828 there had been efforts to establish a proper infirmary and a committee had been formed to organise the raising of funds and the building of the place. This was well on its way before J.D. became involved, and indeed the infirmary opened, not far from his factory, in 1841. The first annual subscription list has no record of anything given by J.D., though every year after that he contributed £2 2s (but the Dixons and Fergusons gave very much more), although he never served on the committee. But health was very much his concern and he saw good health as beginning in the home. How could those who lived in such hovels in Rickergate and Caldewgate possibly be healthy? What they needed, as he had acknowledged for a long time, was proper housing. And it was not only for health reasons that housing mattered. J.D. had always considered bad living conditions to be directly connected to the violence and immorality that reigned in these districts. Nobody could behave decently when they had to live like pigs (and often *with* pigs). His solution was that working men should be assisted to buy their own homes. This was in accordance with his Quaker principles: people should be helped to be independent and should not have to depend on charity. He wanted people to have the pride of ownership, and to that end he was willing to become one of the vice-presidents of the Cumberland Co-operative Benefit Building Society. It took a long time for this to be established, but J.D. was working towards it for the rest of the 1840s, together with others inspired in the same way.

Carlisle had grown dramatically since he had first arrived in 1831 and its housing problems had grown with it. The situation had been bad enough when J.D. had gone in search of decent lodgings for his workers nearly twenty years ago, but now it was not just areas like Caldewgate, where his factory was situated, that were slums – the very centre of the city had been filled in with lanes and courts where living conditions were, if anything, even worse. It saddened him to walk through Carlisle now and see that those gardens he had enjoyed admiring – gardens once attached to the houses in the main streets – had all gone. They had been built on, and many of the houses themselves had become hotels and shops when their owners had sold up and moved to quieter areas. There had been no control over this kind of 'in-filling' building, and no restrictions. Every day, on his way to the factory, J.D. passed through an area that had once been pleasant and was now unbelievably congested. This lay between Fisher Street (where the meeting-house was), St Alban's Row (next to the Town Hall), Scotch Street and Rosemary Lane (joining Fisher Street to Castle Street, where J.D. had his first shop). So rapidly and so carelessly had this block been filled in with houses that the privies were situated below the bedrooms and next to the kitchens. There was no proper drainage, and a report made in 1850 seethed with disgust as it listed the details: 'surface channels alone have been provided, not however with any view to refuse drainage for this purpose. They ought not to be used, but merely to carry away rainfall.' The privies leaked and, when they did, the liquid refuse 'in contact with the wall ... passes through, to the great inconvenience of the occupants'. This situation was at its worst when it occurred in back-to-back dwellings with no ventilation in the rear walls.

People were crammed into these new buildings in enormous numbers. The report described, almost incredulously, how five or six people were sleeping in each bed and that most rooms had two beds in them, meaning that as many as twelve slept together, adults and children of both sexes. It came to the same conclusion as J.D. – '[this] constitutes one large forcing area for the generation of vice'. Some inhabitants did not even have access to a privy, disgusting though these were. Their human waste was taken by them to open ash-pits in the street, and barrows came to take it away at night. It was reckoned that between nine and ten thousand people were living in Carlisle in these kind of circumstances and that they had no hope, as things stood, of rehousing, even if they were in employment. People came to the city because there was work available and they could not afford to care where they had to live in order to get it. What alarmed J.D., and others concerned with this housing problem, was not only the misery and lack of decency, but the danger to health – everyone's health. Once cholera or typhus started in places like this, these fatal diseases would sweep through the whole city without respect for any person. The last typhus epidemic had been in 1840–1, with 1,223 recorded cases; the last cholera epidemic in 1834, when twenty-two of the thirty-three victims had died before it was contained. It was fear of the consequences for health that at last precipitated the formation of a building society that would try to alleviate the distressing shortage of acceptable housing.

The first meeting of the new and, for Carlisle, quite revolutionary building society did not take place until April 1850. It began at 7.30 p.m. in the Athenaeum (as most important meetings in Carlisle tended to), with the Mayor in the chair. As usual when anything exciting was happening there were far too many people crammed in, 1,000 of them, again exceeding the hall's official capacity, and most were working men, many of them J.D.'s workers. The shares in the existing building societies in the city had always been too high for working men to buy, but this new society, formed precisely with them in mind, was to charge only sixpence, or at the most one shilling a week. By the end of April, 2,894 shares had been taken up and two estates bought: Edentown, for £1,200, which would be divided into eighty-eight building plots, and Belle Vue for £630, to be divided into fifty-six. The society was an outstanding success and J.D.'s chief supporter, Dr Eliot, coroner of Carlisle and the society's treasurer, saw it as part of a larger programme of sanitary reform in which the old 'fever nests' would be swept away. By the eighth annual meeting, when J.D. for once actually took the chair, building plans were more ambitious and included extensive construction in Denton Holme, which became an industrial suburb where the respectable working class came to live. J.D. made a speech pointing out that, now there was no tax on glass, bricks or windows, and only a small duty on timber, there was no reason for houses to be expensive. Everyone agreed with him.

In fact, where this cause was concerned, there was little or no opposition. The problems were all practical ones, to do with finance and organisation. But in other campaigns J.D., to his surprise, met outright hostility and had to learn how to deal with it. As a Quaker, he was against war and therefore opposed to the raising of armies, including local militias. The Government could still, in Carlisle and elsewhere in the mid-nineteenth century, summon up the militia (an organisation of citizens with some rudimentary military training, available to be called from their normal occupation to serve as a defence force). The militia had often been called out to be used in Caldewgate when there was civil unrest there and it was extremely unpopular, so much so that in February 1846 a public meeting was called to petition against it. J.D. moved the first resolution, in which he stated firmly his own beliefs, 'that . . . the practice of war [is] equally repugnant to religion and humanity . . . that large military preparations tend to increase the probability of its occurrence . . . [we] regard with the deepest regret and disapproval . . . the contemplated enrolment of the militia and hold it to be the duty of every lover of this country to oppose the measure by all peaceful and Christian means'.

It quickly became clear that among the thousand people present at the meeting were many who had come to oppose the abolition of the militia and were all for enrolment. When J.D. got up to speak, after his resolution had been hotly debated for some considerable time, he said that he had been reading the Articles of War and contrasting them with his New Testament, but as he began quoting he was interrupted by the chairman (the Mayor), who irritably said that there was no time for 'abstract questions' and that if they started on this kind of comparison 'we could argue for a month whether war was in accordance with Christianity'.

J.D. sat down and was not, according to the newspaper reports, heard from again. He chose not to fight his corner, or protest that his point had been important enough to be considered, but appeared to give in, however offended or annoyed he may have been at the Mayor's brusque intervention. But this illustrated not that he lacked determination when challenged, so much as that he lacked vanity and false pride. He could accept being publicly reprimanded without seeing it as a loss of face. He was, in short, a man whom it was difficult to insult and this became a great asset to him in all his dealings. The sense of fair play that had been his as a child was still there; business success had not in the least gone to his head, and he did not imagine he was now so important that everyone should listen to him.

But though he cared about preventing enrolment in the militia, this cause did not arouse in J.D. the same passion as his feelings about slavery. The movement that was as close to his heart as the Anti-Corn Law League was the anti-slavery campaign. This was a cause dear to every Quaker, and one for which all Quakers worked right from the beginning. At the yearly meetings that J.D. attended, the wrongs of slavery were debated endlessly, and it was through the invaluable help of the Quakers that the emancipation of slaves throughout the empire had been achieved in 1838. But that still left people enslaved elsewhere in the world, including America, and attempts went on to free them all. J.D. was joined in his determination to do what he could to free slaves everywhere by his wife Jane. She had six young children, but she helped in the only way a woman in her position could, by offering hospitality to escaped slaves. These people were brought over from America to Britain to tour the country and, by recounting their stories, help to raise funds for the cause.

Jane and her female relatives also made things for bazaars. The bazaar project did not go too well in Carlisle. Jane could not rouse the wives and mothers to think further afield than their own city and its needs. There was plenty of enthusiasm for the infirmary funds, but very little for anti-slavery. She wrote apologising to one campaigner, 'We are very sorry to send so few things but really no one seemed inclined to help us.' One of the most eminent of escaped slaves, Frederick Douglass, stayed with the Carrs and judged them 'as anxious for the emancipation of slaves as any with whom I think I have ever met'. J.D. impressed him with his obvious kindness, and by his absolute faith that right would prevail and all slaves be freed, something that Douglass himself did not always feel. Easy to be confident in Carlisle, a million miles from the reality of slavery, but much more difficult in America, where Douglass had witnessed and suffered it.

They made a strange pair walking through Carlisle, J.D., so tall and heavy and fair, and Douglass, though not a small man, dwarfed by J.D., as most people were. Carlisle had no black inhabitants. Parish records do show that 'a blackamoor' was baptised in St Mary's as far back as 1686, and four more in the next century, but in the 1840s in Carlisle there was only one black man, servant to a Captain Giles, and he died in 1844. Jane was more familiar with the sight of black people, coming as she did from the port of Whitehaven, where Cumbrian traders regularly brought home black servants from the West Indies. In Carlisle, the idea of slaves seemed unreal, so unreal that one of the Cumbrian newspapers, the *Pacquet*, hardly believed they existed or, if they did, thought their plight was exaggerated. It pronounced itself sick of 'the fuss' made about slaves and complained that far too much attention was paid to 'their so-called plight'. The working man of Cumberland, the *Pacquet* was convinced, suffered greater hardship. Its columnist announced, 'I do not believe one word of what saints say regarding the ill treatment of negroes.' By the 1840s, just as J.D. was receiving Douglass and others into his home and organising meetings at which they could speak, the *Pacquet* was working itself up into a state of near hysteria, saying, 'there is something bordering upon mania on the subject of negro emancipation' and that 'in 99 instances out of 100 negroes are better off . . . than a very considerable proportion of the population of Great Britain'.

Against such ignorance and prejudice, J.D. was determined to set an example, to show clearly where his sympathies lay. Douglass, with his help, became another speaker who packed the Athenaeum, six months after the famous Cobden and Bright rally. He gave a lecture lasting two hours and, according to the wonderfully patronising *Journal*, spoke 'with impassioned eloquence . . . for a negro he has an intelligent and even pleasing face . . .' He gave a second lecture two weeks later and yet a third two days after that. On this last occasion Douglass spoke for three hours before a select audience, giving them their money's worth for the high admission cost (one shilling front, sixpence at the back). He had many of his sympathetic audience in tears as he minutely detailed the circumstances of how slaves were treated and how they were persecuted. Afterwards, he stayed with the Carrs before going on to Newcastle. The Carr children were deeply impressed by him – their parents did not have to explain the evils of slavery to them when they could listen to Douglass. Elizabeth was ten, Henry nine, George seven, James six and Thomas four when first he and then two other escaped slaves, William and Ellen Craft, stayed with the family. They saw these people received with respect and admiration by their parents and it emphasised what they already knew: no distinction should be made between one man and another due to colour, rank or class. In the Carr household, as in all truly Quaker homes, this was unthinkable.

And yet outside their home this division by class and rank clearly existed, even if colour was not put to the test in Carlisle. The very fact that they lived in Stanwix showed the Carrs their status, and so did their regular visits to the biscuit works. All J.D.'s children were absolutely familiar with the factory from a very early age. It was their inheritance and there was no escaping this realisation. They were encouraged to think of the workers as part of their wider family and were introduced to all the foremen and as many other workers as possible so that, growing up, they would be as much at ease as their father and able to address everyone by name. It was a paternalistic illusion but a pleasant one, easy from their point of view to accept. This was a 'family' in which the 'children' would never grow up and supplant the 'parent'. That 'parent', the 'father', would in due course change, but the hierarchy would not. The workers knew this perfectly well and so they treated Henry, George, James and Thomas carefully, knowing that one or other of the boys would become their 'father'. J.D. was a benevolent despot, no matter how caring and fatherly. Upon his capable shoulders everything rested and his word was absolute law. It seemed, towards the end of the 1840s and the beginning of the 1850s, that he could do no wrong, that there were no limits to his successful ventures, upon which the livelihood of his numerous real family and his factory family depended. The *Carlisle Directory* for 1847 trumpeted his fame, calling Carr's 'the most extensive biscuit manufactory . . . in England' and Harriet Beecher Stowe, passing through the city at this time, remarked that what Carlisle was famous for was 'a celebrated biscuit bakery'. Carr's was growing with almost frightening speed and those who worked there were considered lucky – so long as they did not drink, they had a place for life, and the advantages went far beyond a clean place in which to labour and amenities like a school-room, a library and a swimming bath.

The most prized advantage of all was the annual works outing. J.D. began these outings as early as 1840, and by 1850 they had become so celebrated in the city that they caused great jealousy among those who worked in other factories, where no such treats were regularly given. On one summer's day during the year, usually at the end of May, the entire work force plus the Carr family set off to enjoy a day in the country, all expenses being paid by J.D. The 1850 outing was one of the most memorable of all. One hundred and eleven people – all the workers and their wives, together with the entire Carr family – gathered at the railway station at half-past four in the morning, the younger ones wildly excited because this would be their first trip by train. It took an hour for the train to chug along to Cocker-mouth, thirty-seven miles away, where ten large carriages were waiting. There was just enough room for everyone to squash in, though the carriages seemed dangerously over-full, and then off they trundled along the side of Bassenthwaite Lake to the village of Portin-scale near Derwent Water. Arrangements had been made at the Blucher Hotel for breakfast. Provisions had been brought from Carlisle in big hampers, which were now unloaded and spread out on tables in the garden. The bread, baked by a volunteer night-shift just before setting off, was still warm. It was eaten with ham and cheese and boiled eggs, and there was plenty of tea to wash it down. No alcohol, of course, but nobody wanted any (or if they did, they kept quiet about it). Then came the complicated business of finding out what everyone wanted to do. Behind them Skiddaw loomed, huge and forbidding in the morning sun. Who wanted to climb Skiddaw? All the Carr boys, for a start – Henry fifteen, George thirteen, James twelve and Thomas ten lined up with the thirty-one men who were game and off they all went, taking lemonade and biscuits to eat on the top (which they reached in four hours).

Meanwhile, the older members of the party split into two groups. Forty of them got back into four of the carriages and went on to the nearby small town of Keswick, stopping just beyond it at Castle Rock, where there was a magnificent view over Derwent Water to the fells known as the Catbells. They could just make out the second group, who had elected to take to boats and were rowing right round the lake, stopping at the various small islands, where some of the more daring jumped ashore and paddled. They did a circuit of the lake, making a good deal of noise, what with the splashing of inexpertly handled oars and the laughter that greeted the worst of the attempts at rowing, passing Lodore Falls on their way back. The climbers and the Castle Rock party were waiting for them when they returned, and then the whole lot of them took to the water and spent the afternoon eating cakes and drinking more lemonade. The time passed in a haze of sunning themselves and exclaiming at the beauty of the scenery, and then it was back to the Blucher Hotel, where a proper high tea had been laid on. A long day, but the excitement was still not over. When the carriages trundled back to Cockermouth station, with half the occupants asleep, the local people were lined up along the street and the church bells rang out to greet them, so that they all felt like royalty and practised dignified waves. It was nearly midnight before the train drew into Carlisle, but next morning every single worker was at the factory on time, to J.D.'s immense gratification. The whole outing had cost him £40 and was worth it five times over in goodwill. There was no such phrase as 'labour relations' in common currency, but good labour relations, with all that would result from them, was what this was about.

It was no wonder that by the early 1850s there was the feeling in Carlisle, and especially in Carr's biscuit works, that J.D. could do no wrong. But he could. He had arrived at a point that was tricky for all Quakers, the point when, through his own endeavours and as a result of absolutely fair trading, he was reaping the benefit to the extent of having money to spare. There was nothing in the Quaker religion that held the making of money to be evil, or the accruing of profits wicked, so long as complete honesty had been observed. But at the same time a Quaker was supposed to know when he had made enough money and must not consider a further increase of wealth for its own sake. Wealth was to be obtained (if at all) by labour, by the following of temperate habits so that it accumulated and by the practice of thrift. This had been easy advice for the eighteenth-century Quakers to listen to, for none of them became seriously rich, but in the nineteenth century as a result of obeying these tenets some of them amassed substantial capital, which gave them opportunities to increase their wealth still further, and not by their own 'honest trading'. They were not supposed to indulge in speculation, but they *were* supposed to make the most of every opportunity presented to them, if it could be taken advantage of honestly. For a man like J.D., who had made his money by taking risks and having a sense of vision, it was apparently possible for him to reconcile his religious beliefs with what was undoubtedly speculation: he was merely using opportunities presented to him and, if more money resulted, it would all be put to good use. Money was power, power to ameliorate social wrongs.

At any rate, in 1850 he engaged in a bit of speculation, which had nothing to do with his business or advancing his own particular interests. Reputed to have done so at his brother Henry's suggestion, J.D. speculated in a Cornish tin mine, and because of his involvement other people followed suit. He did not seem to suffer any crisis of conscience, but it was the only evidence that success and the making of large amounts of money had led him into the kind of venture most business people would call a shrewd, if risky, investment, but which a very strict Quaker could just possibly condemn as greedy. The tin mine crashed in 1853 and everyone who had backed it lost their money. A local solicitor was sent to a meeting convened to investigate the causes and made a report, in which J.D. was exonerated from any blame. The fifty Carlisle shareholders who had followed his example passed a resolution saying they fully acquitted him of any want of integrity, and his reputation for honesty was held to be untarnished.

Except by himself. He felt not only tarnished but directly responsible. If he had not lived up to the high ideals of a sincere Quaker in making this unwise investment, he did live up to them after the disastrous crash, resolving personally to reimburse the other investors who could not afford, as he could, to lose their money. It took him four years to do so and meant drastic cutbacks in his own life. First, he sold The Villa, the beautiful home in which he had spent only seven years, for £5,900. This left him and his family homeless and there were too many of them to move back to the Castle Street premises. But he had no intention of building or buying another house; all the Villa money would go towards recompensing the other fifty tin-mine investors.

Instead, J.D. rented Coledale Hall in Newtown, then a rural area, just beyond Caldewgate but still uncomfortably near it and most definitely on the wrong side of town. It had been built in 1810 for Henry Fawcett (then MP for Carlisle) and was the sort of house that The Villa had copied in a much more splendid way. Like The Villa, it had only two storeys, with a rear more impressive than its modest front. It was an attractive enough house but, though it had a generous garden, it lacked the spacious rooms and grounds of The Villa and was right on an increasingly busy road leading to a heavily polluted industrial area. Inside, it was actually more impressive than it looked. The owner from whom J.D. rented it (George Mould, a railway contractor) had made some interesting alterations and it now had a stone staircase leading from the hallway, which had very pretty and graceful wrought-iron balusters and a moulded wooden hand-rail. Most of the doors were panelled, and the hall and the main ground-floor room had elaborate moulded ceilings. The fireplaces were splendid – made of black and white marble, very striking as one entered the rooms – and all the windows had internal shutters, keeping out the draughts and giving a welcome extra warmth when used with the curtains. The site of the house had a rather distinguished history too: there had once been a house standing there owned by a merchant called Richard Coledale in the reign of Henry VI.

From Coledale Hall, J.D. could walk to his factory in ten minutes and the house suited him very well, even if it appeared to everyone else that he had come down in the world. He never owned another house in his life. It was as though he intended to do penance for a piece of uncharacteristic vanity. Why had he wanted a magnificent house at all? Much better to rent and protect himself from delusions of grandeur.

There was another reason in 1853 for being cautious financially. J.D. was then in the process of taking on the mighty Earl of Lonsdale and other local landowners, though not on his own and not for purely speculative reasons. He had been acting according to his liberal principles ever since he came to Carlisle, but that always meant liberal in the broadest sense. He was never a Liberal, never joined any political party, however political some of the movements he supported were, and so he had never clashed with the Tory landowners. He backed Carlisle's Liberal MPs, as did those other manufacturers, the Dixons and Fergusons, when they were in favour of his own causes, but otherwise he stood apart.

What now persuaded him to do otherwise was his conviction that Carlisle needed another railway line. Its manufacturing potential was growing all the time, but it was hampered by the difficulties of importing raw materials in bulk and even more in the exporting of finished goods. The canal had seemed exciting in the 1830s, but it was now obsolete. It was filled in and a railway line laid along the same route in 1853, but the new railway line went nowhere useful. What was needed was speedy access to the western ports by means of a railway running directly there. It was far too slow and cumbersome to send goods to tiny Port Carlisle, where they had to be transferred to other ships in order to reach Maryport or Whitehaven. Once, the bigger ships had been able to go directly from Port Carlisle to Liverpool but now, because of silting, they could not get that far up the Solway Firth.

So a scheme had been hatched at the beginning of the 1850s to find an independent rail outlet for Carlisle's goods traffic. This was something new for J.D. It was quite different from being part of a campaign to help the poor and deprived. Now, his own business interests would be seen to be the motive and there was nothing altruistic about that, however much he might argue that he was advancing the prosperity of the city as a whole, at the same time as increasing his own markets. And where railways were concerned, conflict of interest was inevitable. If, as J.D. and his partners (the Dixons, the Fergusons) hoped, a new port could be created at Silloth, twenty-two miles from Carlisle at the mouth of the Solway Firth (Port Carlisle lay ten miles up it), then a railway to it, an essential part of the scheme, would have to run across country owned by Tory magnates, who did not in any case want their own ports, Whitehaven and Maryport, to be threatened. The Earl of Lonsdale (who owned Whitehaven) and the Senhouses (who virtually owned Maryport) were rich, strong opponents. They had no intention of allowing J. D. Carr and the other new upstart manufacturers to ruin their vested interests.

J.D., surprisingly for such a peace-loving man renowned for his gentle nature, gave every indication of relishing the fight. He saw the contest not simply as one between two groups of powerful people wanting to make themselves even richer, but between one group that had no concern for the community as a whole and the other which, while not denying the personal benefit to themselves, recognised the enormous benefits that would follow for the whole working population of Carlisle. A company with the grand title of the Carlisle & Silloth Bay Dock & Railway Company was formed in 1852, and J.D., together with the Dixons, was the principal proposer, aided by the Liberal MP for East Cumberland, William Marshall. The first meeting of the 245 shareholders was held in 1854, with J.D. on the platform. Then followed the tricky part of preparing a bill to go through Parliament (a procedure necessary for any railway). J.D. played a large part in the drafting of it, taking a keen interest in the dimensions of the proposed new dock. It was to be a 'wet' dock, with its own pier and a railway running the twelve and three-quarter miles to link up with the existing Port Carlisle–Carlisle line (built on top of the canal). It was well known that Lord Lonsdale alleged that Silloth could never provide a safe enough harbour, because the sand-banks that were reputed to protect it were not reliable enough. J.D. came up with a most ingenious way of proving that they were. He organised a game of cricket on Robin Rigg, the most crucial of the sandbanks, between the rise and fall of the tide. The game was played, watched by delighted witnesses including J.D., and the sandbank thereby proved stable.

Gathering other evidence was not so much fun. Lord Lonsdale rested his case on Port Carlisle being perfectly adequate to serve Carlisle. His representative, called before a select committee of the House of Commons (he did not deign to appear himself), said that his lord-ship had no desire to be competitive. It was the Carlisle manufacturers, with their thrusting ambition, who were the aggressors, proposing this new and unnecessary railway and dock for their own ends. It was suggested that the proposers had little care for the future of the people of Carlisle, whatever they said, and that their virtuous claims masked their own commercial interests. Why, was it not a fact that all the major shareholders were to use the proposed line and dock for their busi-nesses? Yes, it was. It was no good John Dixon, who appeared for the proposers, pointing out that a survey had shown Carlisle's population was 'pretty near unani-mous for it [the Bill]'. He pointed out, too, that the proposers 'only ask to spend our own money' and vigor-ously refuted the sneer that pure speculation lay behind the proposal. 'I never speculated in railways in my life,'

Dixon asserted. He and his fellow-investors were merely making 'an investment of the capital which we think will be invested advantageously to all'.

Except to Lord Lonsdale. The committee grew impatient with the hordes of witnesses called by both sides to argue their case and dismissed the proposal without reaching a conclusion. It was difficult for them to know whom to believe: those who said that Port Carlisle was adequate had 'facts' to prove it (but so did those swearing it was not). The same convincing case was made on both sides for Whitehaven and Maryport. Lord Lonsdale thought he had scuppered the chances of the Carlisle manufacturers and their bid, but he underestimated their stubbornness and determination. The following year they returned to the fray, confronted the committee with irrefutable evidence, collected in the interim, that the people of Carlisle did indeed support their proposal and that Silloth would be safe as a port, contrary to Lord Lonsdale's opinion. They baffled the committee with science, producing every possible measurement and statistic to demonstrate Silloth's suitability and in the end their persistence paid off. The Bill was approved.

Work began on the new railway line in August 1855, but the building of the new dock and of the small town to go with it were far more of a problem. J.D. was personally very interested in the creation of Silloth itself, because he envisaged it as a holiday resort to which those living in Caldewgate and the other unhealthy districts of Carlisle could escape, if the railway fare was kept cheap enough. But there had to be something for people to go to apart from sea air – they needed hotels and boarding houses to stay in and places to eat, and amusements other than breathing in the ozone. Silloth was hardly even a village – just a few cottages scattered among sand-dunes – but now streets were laid out, on a grid system, and cobbled, and building plots were sold cheaply to tempt hoteliers. Within four years there were four hotels and thirty-eight lodging houses available for the hordes of Carlisle people, almost entirely working-class, who flocked there. And flock they did, right from the opening of the railway line in 1856.

It seemed as if the whole population had turned out to see the first train leave for Silloth, just after noon on a fine August day. It left from Caldewgate, carrying the Dixons and Fergusons, the Mayor and the corporation, J.D. and another 1,500 passengers, all eager to sample the delights of the new resort. A public dinner was held in the new Solway Hotel, but J.D. was not present. He never went to public dinners – too many alcoholic toasts of three times three, too much feasting of a kind that was anathema to him. But he enjoyed seeing so many of Carlisle's working classes taking the sea air, able to afford a healthy day out because fares were, as he had hoped, kept low (too low, in fact, for the line was soon running at a loss). In July and August every year from now on the number of passengers going to Silloth, the majority on day trips, averaged 1,450 a week. The holidaymakers loved the green, where they could ride donkeys, and the esplanade, where they could walk along the sea-front for miles.

It was a victory for the new company, but an expensive one. The new dock, vital to the whole future of Silloth, did not open until 1859, three years after the railway was ready. Almost at once it was realised that the flow of freight was well below what had been antici- pated and the major shareholders became extremely nervous, J.D. among them. He had no regrets about his involvement and no qualms about the correctness of it, but he did not want to be liable for any more financial disasters. Hasty deals were done with big railway com- panies, principally with the North British Railway

Company, which took over the whole line from Silloth to Carlisle and on to Edinburgh, saving the Carlisle and Silloth Bay Company from bankruptcy. It was a close call for J.D. and the other leading investors, but one he was able to justify. He had never envisaged the line to Silloth making a substantial profit. Its intended purpose had been to open up trade for the future, and as a by-product to create a holiday resort, and this had been achieved.

His own business continued to expand with almost frightening speed. The annual output of biscuits in 1844 had been 350 tons, in 1851, 702 tons, and by the end of that decade it had almost doubled again. Carr's had obtained the contract for supplying the refreshment rooms of the Royal Exhibition in 1851 and instantly J.D. had created an Exhibition biscuit – 12 lb flour, 42 lb sugar, 24 lb lard, 4 oz ammonia, 4 oz soda and 20 gallons of milk went into the recipe (how many biscuits this mixture actually turned out is not noted). The new biscuit actually started off in the Carr family kitchen, as did many biscuits, before being handed over to the factory to experiment with on a large scale. Such recipes were written out on every kind of scrap paper – the back of bills, pages torn from what looked like school exercise books, envelopes – giving the impression that anything coming to hand would do because, at first, this was a kind of game. Some of these bits of paper had the children's signatures scrawled on them, suggesting that they were enthusiastic helpers, and little messages saying, 'if this recipe proves successful some biscuits would be greatly appreciated when ready.' Henry certainly had fun concocting a recipe for caraway-seed biscuits – 'take two pounds of flour, two ozs of butter, rub the butter in, add ½ lb sugar, 103 carraway [sic] seeds, ½ oz corriander [sic] seeds, ½ teaspoon carbonate of soda, one tablespoon of arrowroot, mix to a stiff paste with warm milk, then roll out, cut thin, prick, bake slowly.' A few of the instructions were a bit vague, but it was the job of the factory to sort them out and improve upon them, to the point of putting any new biscuit into production.

To keep the consumer interested, and faithful to Carr's, new biscuits had to be thought of all the time, but of course few of them were really 'new' in the true sense of the word. The adaptations to so-called different varieties were often minimal – a little more sugar, a little less fat, a slightly stronger flavour, and a biscuit could be pronounced 'new'. The trick was to give it a new shape if possible and, even more important, a new name. By the 1850s a biscuit was not just a biscuit. It had to have a personality all its own and this was expressed in its name. The Exhibition biscuit – really a perfectly plain biscuit, hardly differing from at least six others already in existence – was an event biscuit, its romance contained in that one word, which at the time meant 'excitement'. Plenty of biscuits sought to sell themselves through association, especially the royal biscuits such as Balmoral, Albert, Prince of Wales, Osborne. The nibbler was thought to be seduced by visions of Queen Victoria eating the very same biscuit at Balmoral, or wherever, and there was (it was hoped) the delicious pleasure of having made the same choice and thereby proving oneself a person of indisputable taste. It worked – Balmorals were very popular – even if there was no proof that this was because of the name alone.

Equally cunning was the giving of a collective name, like Rich Desserts, to biscuits of many different shapes with one thing in common, in order to tempt the palate. There were twenty Rich Desserts, ranging in shape from a boat to an intricate treble loop called a scroll, and all of them had nuts and icing, sugar crystals or jam on top. A pound of Rich Desserts, picked by the grocer from the big tins in which they were stocked, could include a random selection, but children would beg their mothers to ask for whatever was their favourite shape, and it became a kind of competition to see how many of one type the grocer, obliging or not, could be persuaded to put into the bag. The Iced Routs, of which there were four kinds, were especially popular, each Rout differentiated only by the colour and style of the icing on top. But no grocer wanted to be left with his box of Rich Desserts full only of, say, the modest Freiburg, which had no icing at all on its plain oblong shape and only the merest scattering of sugar crystals.

Shape had been a gimmick right from the beginning, when J.D. had made his first alphabet biscuits, and there was always keen interest whenever a new shape was contrived. As better cutters were invented, and types of biscuit dough that would hold designs better, these shapes became more ambitious. Carr's had a great success with their Kennel range – twelve dog's heads ranging from Labrador to greyhound (though one had to look very closely indeed to see the difference between the Alsatian and the terrier). The trouble here for the grocer was that the prominent bits, the noses and ears, upon which the recognition of the dog often depended, were easily knocked off. Then the customer would complain they had been cheated, so gradually these troublesome biscuits were phased out. Easier to deal with were the biscuits distinguished by what was engraved upon their open faces. Queen Victoria's head (though rather badly drawn) appeared on the Small Change Penny biscuit, and there was another called The Wreath, which had a highly complicated and successful design of flowers and leaves all round its surface. Faces were always hard to do, but the Duke of Wellington, the Prince of Wales and Shakespeare each had his own biscuit.

Plain biscuits had Carr's name stamped on them, but most of these were varieties of biscuit common to all the firms – everyone made their own version of the original ship's biscuit, for instance, all of them with names still linked to the sea (such as Cabin, and Captain's Thin). It was often hard to tell the difference between some of the plain biscuits (those without icing or chocolate coating, but containing sugar). The Tea biscuit looked and tasted uncommonly like the Social biscuit – both were round, both the same size, but one had more tiny air-holes on the surface and the letters Carr's of Carlisle. But customers increasingly, from the mid-century onwards, were connoisseurs, and could and did tell the difference, especially where flavour was concerned. Any manufacturer putting a little more lemon in his Lemon Drop, a little more almond essence in his Almond Finger, a little more ginger in his Ginger Nut would be called to account. The old favourites had to stay the same to maintain standards.

J.D. was well aware of this and did not meddle with the basic biscuits, while endlessly trying out others, though not too many. Quality was vital in his opinion, and he did not want to be tempted into overreaching himself. Improving the means of production was, to him, more important than producing new types of biscuit and he kept abreast of the times, constantly introducing new machines into the factory, often to the apprehension of his workers. John Irving (the same man to whom J.D. had given the spectacles) entered each new machine in his diary: one for 'what they call Excursion biscuits', 'one for Pic-Nic biscuits' and one of which he confessed himself scared, 'a Dessert Machine for making Rich Desserts . . . a great mass of metal it is. How it will do I cannot say.' How it did was badly – it broke a finger on John's right hand.

By this time, the late 1850s, there were 170 employees

working for Carr's and seventeen ovens operating, a big growth in labour from the beginning. The premises had grown, too. There were now two separate factories, known simply as No. 1 and No. 2. Bread was still baked, but biscuit production was far more important, and the biscuit export trade was the biggest growth area of all. The biscuits were packed in four sizes of tin, then the tins were soldered before being despatched to Silloth by rail, and from there by sea to various European destinations. The Belgian and Dutch trade was the most profitable, but every year Carr's biscuits were creeping into markets further and further away. There was now a London office, in the Strand, and a depot in Liverpool (where Carr's had their own shed in Victoria Dock).

Obviously Carr's of Carlisle was an outstanding success story. Equally obviously, as the new decade began, their success was presenting their founder with new dilemmas. His was a family firm, rooted in a relatively small community. He was proud of this. But if the business continued to expand, as it showed every sign of doing, it could hardly stay a purely *family* firm, controlled by one man. J.D. would have to delegate more, and this was something he found very hard to do. The future of Carr's was going to depend on how he adapted to the necessity of doing so. But the economic climate was healthy enough for him to have, as yet, plenty of time to adapt. The Great Exhibition of 1851 had ushered in an age of prosperity that was to last twenty years. Virtually all duties on food had been abolished and Britain could with justice claim to be a Free Trade country. Everywhere, throughout the country, trade boomed – the industrial unit was expanding, industry was becoming more mechanised, and for energetic figures like J.D. Carr there seemed no limits to what could be achieved.

Chapter Five

THE SONS AND
THE SCHISM

A MAN OF fifty was, as we all know, considered quite old in Victorian times, certainly old enough to be entitled, even forced, to look over his shoulder to see who was coming after him, however good his own health. In this respect J.D., by the time he reached that age in 1856, felt very secure indeed. He had four sons, all big, strapping boys, who would inherit the business he had built up and assume those responsibilities they had been taught it involved. All his aspirations lay in securing the future of Carr's of Carlisle. He had none socially. He had never been interested in breaking into the county set, with all that entailed and signified – his set was the Quaker set and remained so. His social life revolved, as it had always done, round his home and the meeting-house. The only entertaining that was done was for family and visiting friends, many of whom would arrive unannounced, knowing that hospitality would be generously offered. Not too generously, though – Jane had no enormous bills for food. Sometimes, if the meeting had requested special hospitality for a large number, J.D. put in a bill for their board (small sums crop up in the accounts), but that was rare.

It was a very frugal and staid way of life for a man who was now wealthy, but it provided his children with

an admirably secure and stable environment in which to
grow up. They appeared to thrive in it and their relationship with both parents was untroubled. Of the four
sons, George, the second son, was the cleverest and
looked most like J.D. himself. Henry, the eldest, and
James, third in line, were the most religious, showing a
commendable zeal in their devotions and ever eager to
take part in communal worship within the meeting-
house. Thomas, the youngest of the sons, was most like
his mother, with her sweet face, even though he shared
the Carr build. He was bright, but lacked George's drive.
Henry and James formed one axis, George and Thomas
another, with the girls like bookends. Elizabeth, known
as Lizzie, was the typical elder daughter, her mother's
right hand, utterly domesticated and assuming from the
beginning the role of helpmeet to the others. Eliza,
the baby, was less inclined to spend her life serving
others – she was prettier, livelier and, in the way of the
youngest in a large family, a little indulged.

Since all the children, even the girls (Quakers saw
nothing unladylike in letting girls go into factories),
were accustomed to visiting Carr's from their earliest
years, they had no fear of the factory's noise and action.
It was an exciting place to them, much more thrilling
than home, and the danger – the heat from the ovens,
the sparks flying in the tin-soldering room – simply
added to the drama. Far from keeping them away from
the biscuit works, J.D. pulled them in and shared his
pride in it. The boys in particular were brought up to
feel that theirs was a wonderful destiny and that there
could be no other 'better' life. J.D. had no thwarted
ambition in him, no other career he would rather have
had and might want to thrust on his sons. He was not
dictatorial, nor did he wish to live vicariously through
them. But at the same time he did have expectations and
his children were all aware of these. Carr's of Carlisle,

the family firm he had so successfully established, needed his sons if it was to survive. J.D. expected and fully intended that these sons should take on the responsibility.

Others had also realised this. John Carr, J.D.'s youngest brother, who had come to Carlisle when he was still an apprentice, had grown tired of never being given any real power. He and J.D. had worked side by side for nearly twenty years before John decided to break away and get out from under his brother's kindly, but completely dominant, rule. John was tough, too – in fact, in worker John Irving's diary he emerges as tougher than J.D., recorded as often giving unsatisfactory workers 'a blowing up' – and could not forever tolerate the lack of equal authority within the works. He would never be in charge, not with J.D. and four of his sons blocking the way, so he left in 1856.

Family legend has it that the trigger was a practical joke played on John (all the Carrs were fond of silly pranks) and that his dignity was offended when a bucket of water fell on him, but it seems far more likely that he had planned to leave at that time anyway, tired of playing second fiddle now he had married (in 1851) and had his own family to think about. J.D. accepted his brother's resignation with surprising equanimity and gave John £7,000 as his share of the business. He still had his other brothers, Henry and George, working docilely for him so he was not bereft of brotherly support. John left Carlisle completely, going off to Ullswater, where he lived in a beautiful house, Bowerbank, with magnificent views of the fells he loved to climb. (He was not, however, finished with the biscuit trade – John's revenge, though there is no proof that this is how he saw it, was to come later.)

It was at this time that J.D. had some new office stationery printed by his friend Hudson Scott. The paper had a beautiful illustration, finely drawn, at the top, showing the biscuit works in Caldewgate, the South Vale mill (a recent addition) and the office, which was in the old Castle Street building. Naturally, the Royal Arms of Biscuit Maker to the Queen was incorporated and so was a ship, to show that Carr's now exported biscuits all over the world. Mention of the London depot (moved from the Strand to Fenchurch Street) was even worked in. The new stationery looked extremely imposing and the 'travellers' (sales representatives) especially loved it. The firm depended on remarkably few of these new professionals – only three, each of whom covered vast territories. (The whole of Wales, together with Bristol and the west of England to Plymouth, and from there to the south coast as far as Southampton was one area, for example.) Each traveller expected to be away from home for six weeks at a time, travelling in mail carts and on carriers' wagons as well as trains. However humble their transport, they looked incredibly important when they arrived in towns, wearing black coats and gloves and always, always, a topper. They had to be smart at all times to represent Carr's of Carlisle.

J.D., who was described by people in Carlisle as always looking 'quaintly Quaker', believed in the importance of clothes. He himself had stuck to the traditional Quaker style of dress even though, by the mid-1850s, there had been some considerable relaxation of the rules of the society relating to it. Having to wear only drab colours and being obliged to ignore fashions had been one of the many things that had begun to alienate the younger Quakers and they had started to rebel. Up and down the country meetings spent valuable time debating this issue, and compromise was creeping in. Perhaps some colour could be permitted, perhaps some attention could be paid to prevailing styles. But not by J.D., whose coats and trousers were still plain black and of serviceable materials and unfashionable cut. Only his brown waistcoat, made during the Anti-Corn Law days, broke up his sombre appearance – though in fact it was not so much the colour of his clothes that made him seem 'quaintly Quaker' as the materials from which they were made and, most of all, the style. His coat was much too long and much too loose: men were wearing more closely fitted coats with wide lapels, and cut away at the front. Velvet was popular and brightly coloured cravats. Trousers were narrower, and quite often striped or checked, and in an era of new prosperity the well-off man owned many pairs. J.D. did not. Another part of his 'quaintness' was the limited number and age of those garments he possessed.

But J.D. did not appear so obviously different in Carlisle as his womenfolk, when it came to dress. It was not much of a concession that they could now wear pastel colours, when they were still not allowed to accentuate their figures; it was the very shapelessness of their dresses that marked Quaker women out, even in an unmodish city like Carlisle. The skirt of the 1850s had many flounces and the waist was so severely nipped in that it required strict corseting. Quakers abhorred exaggeration – that had not changed – while dresses all around them now became more and more elaborate. At the beginning of the decade, skirts, and vast numbers of petticoats underneath, were supported by hoops, and then around 1856 the crinoline came in. It caught on even in Carlisle, among the fashionable few, and inevitably made anyone still wearing a modest gown without hoops or masses of petticoats look dowdy or decidedly quaint.

The girls and women who had begun to enter J.D.'s work force in the 1850s obviously did not enjoy the luxury of following fashion. They came to the factory in old, shabby, patched clothes with a shawl over everything and clogs on their feet. Once there, they were supplied with white aprons. These aprons had bibs on the front, upon which the woman's individual number appeared, but otherwise were absolutely plain and covered the wearer from head to toe. No one objected to the wearing of them. On the contrary, the aprons were popular and, just as J.D. had intended, made the women feel they were doing a job that mattered and for which they had to be properly equipped. Since their own garments were mostly in a parlous state, it was even a relief and comfort to slip on something so pristine.

The boys who worked in the bakehouses were also clothed in white – white jackets, white trousers. J.D. liked to believe, and there is some evidence this was true, that wearing this sort of basic uniform bound his workers together and gave them a feeling of corporate identity. So did the provision of breakfast at 6 a.m., before they started work. J.D. had discovered, after two girls fainted, that many of them were coming into the works without having had anything at all to eat or drink, so he instituted a dining-room, where anyone who wanted it was given a large mug of tea and two slices of new bread – and of course worked all the better for it. The message was loud and clear: Carr's looked after you. Already it was becoming competitive to be taken on there and already there were some second-generation workers. William Stubbs, who began in 1847, was soon followed into the factory by his son, and the Reed and McBride families had begun what was to be a 285- and 220-year record respectively.

Yet the firm had not reached anything like its full potential, nor its point of maximum growth. J.D. still knew everyone by name and could, if put to the test, recite what they did and he had worked, at some point, beside all of them, if just for a short time. He was pleased at how, entering as boys to do menial jobs like sweeping floors, his workers could rapidly advance themselves. It was noted by one observer with a poetic turn of mind, who came regularly to inspect Carr's and wrote about the conditions, that 'men come here as boys and shift here and there about the factory, twisting and turning like a small beck among the fells, until finally, reaching the main stream, they settle down in their respective channels'. Then, though the writer did not go on to say this, they were stuck. For life, if they wished, but in mid-nineteenth-century Carlisle that was no bad fate. But outside work, J.D. believed, there ought to be no limits to what his workers could achieve. It was part of his Quaker beliefs that people should strive to improve themselves and, in the case of his workers, this should be through education. The schoolroom at Carr's was only intended as a beginning, an initial, vital step in the right direction for those who were illiterate. But outside the factory walls there had to be further opportunities, and J.D. was determined to help establish them.

He knew he was no pioneer in this respect, since he was well aware that there was a tradition of self-education in Caldewgate, for all its general reputation. William Farish recorded all kinds of evening classes in existence in his time, before J. D. Carr ever came to Carlisle, commenting how well one Jemmy Wymms, who lived in the workhouse, taught, among others. Classes were held above the weaving shops, but far more popular were the reading-rooms. The Mechanics Institute had a reading-room from 1824, but according to Farish it was too intimidating for working men to use – he said their clogs and poor clothes made them feel uncomfortable beside the clerks using it. They preferred rooms like the one in Blue Anchor Lane in Caldewgate, where newspapers were made available. If a man could not read, another would read to him. Handwriting was learned by copying from the same newspapers and from letterheads on bills, all helpfully supplied by the gentlemen of the town, including J.D. By 1857 there were six flourishing reading-rooms in Caldewgate, with the John Street one, opposite Carr's, overcrowded. It had a membership of 150, all the members paying one penny a week.

J.D. had been a regular visitor to both the Blue Anchor Lane and the John Street reading-rooms and had always been impressed by what he had seen. There was a sense of order and purpose which, when he first witnessed it, had surprised him, and he had been touched by the trouble to which the men had gone to try and make the rooms seem like schoolrooms. They had made rude desks from odd bits of wood and found benches to go in front of them, not seeming to mind that crammed onto them they looked like overgrown school-children. They appeared neither awkward nor embarrassed, but were eager, keen and anxious to learn. Newspapers were spread out on the desks, with six or seven men crowding round each one, straining to see the excruciatingly small print, while one of their number followed it with his finger and read aloud. How much each of these scholars could actually see was difficult to work out, but what was not in doubt was that they *heard* every word and absorbed its meaning. The moment the reader had finished reading an item aloud, a discussion, often heated, would begin. J.D. realised that learning to read was only part of the value of these reading-rooms and that the other part, an understanding of what was going on in the world, was even more worthwhile.

But it was the observation of writing and arithmetic lessons that touched him most. Learning to read was hard, but learning to write was even harder, and only the more dedicated men attempted it. How solemn and anxious they seemed as they traced letters from bill heads, their large hands, used to so much rough labour, to spades and saws and hammers, clenched round pencils, which suddenly looked impossibly fragile. Pencils, provided by J.D. and other interested gentlemen of the city, were a luxury (charcoal was used more often) and pen and ink very rare indeed. The particular dexterity needed to shape letters seemed unaccountably lacking in most of the men and J.D. could only conclude it was something that ought to be practised in infancy. If it was not, then the adult hand seemed reluctant to adapt itself. The men laboured in silence over their writing, which was an individual effort, made with flushed faces and outbreaks of temper, whereas learning to read seemed to be collective, binding them together. Arithmetic was different again. Many of the men had a natural aptitude for it and learned quickly. There was one man from Cockermouth who was adept at algebra as well as arithmetic, and yet he had not been able to read or write when he first came.

What fascinated J.D. was that no one person ever seemed to be in charge. The men simply came and appeared to organise themselves, according to who could do what. There was no fighting about it. Newspapers would be produced and the groupings round them seemed to form naturally. The only threat of violence came outside the reading-rooms, as far too many men tried to get in. There was nearly always a queue and it was obvious that larger premises and better facilities were desperately needed. J. D. Carr was seen as the man to approach.

He did not disappoint. But he wanted to do more than help to provide a better reading-room. He saw this as an opportunity to do something for the temperance movement. Drunkenness was still the greatest threat to advancement facing a man living in Caldewgate and J.D. knew that, although his own workers had signed the pledge, they were exposed to constant temptation once outside the factory, living as they did in the midst of so many pubs and beer shops. What he therefore did was to offer land he owned, upon which a building could be erected in which a temperance hall as well as a reading-room could be housed. In May 1860 he called a meeting in the schoolroom of Carr's for all those interested. Rules were drawn up for what was to be the Caldewgate West End Total Abstinence & General Improvement Society, which would incorporate a reading-room. J.D. donated a minutes book but would not become president or chairman. He wanted a working man to have that responsibility, so that from the beginning the workers would think of the society as belonging to them. The foundation stone of the new building, on land directly across the main street from Carr's, was laid a year later and a subscription list opened to collect the £400 needed to build it (though the cost turned out to be £800 before the place was ready).

The rules governing membership were fierce. Taking the pledge was, of course, the first and most important rule, but the demands went further. Members had to vow not only not to touch a drop of alcohol themselves, but also not to provide it for others and to promise to 'go about discountenancing' it. In a fit of confidence, 500 membership cards were printed for the first meeting but only fifteen were taken up, so circulars were drawn up advertising free coffee and tea, as well as newspapers, for those who joined. When the inebriate of Caldewgate still did not flock to sign up, the next ploy was to tempt them with concerts on Saturdays. These did prove popular and brought in converts (converts for the space of a Saturday night anyway), but then there was trouble over certain songs. Bawdy ones crept in and the committee was obliged to operate censorship. But most effective of all as a measure to secure members was the opening of a quoits alley. Men crowded in to play, especially since there was a leg of lamb as a prize for the highest scorer.

The reading-room was on the upper floor, with its own entry passage and door at the north end. There was a permanent caretaker, who saw to the cleaning in return for free accommodation and 1s 6d a week. A piano was first hired for the downstairs hall then bought for £18 and a pianist engaged for three shillings to play at the Saturday concerts. J.D. did not approve of this, but he had no say in policy decisions, having opted out from the start. Almost at once they had serious problems. At first, anyone who could sing could come to a concert free, and it became a game for boys with no intention of signing the pledge to get themselves in and then disrupt proceedings. The police had to be called several times before, regretfully – because the committee wanted to catch them young – the notice 'No Boys To Be Admitted' went up. Consideration for health was evident in some of the decisions – oranges, for example, were bought as treats. Knowing how hungry most of their members would be in such hard times, the committee decided that free soup should be provided in the winter. The ingredients were paid for by J.D. and the soup made under the supervision of Dr Eliot. A hundred gallons at a time were made from 50 lb white peas, 100 lb beef, 60 lb barley, 10 lb salt, 10 lb onions, 10 oz black pepper and an undisclosed amount of potatoes and carrots.

J.D. was pleased with the success of this venture, especially since one of his sons became involved. James came to the first meeting and showed himself willing to be an indefatigable worker (in the cause of temperance rather than literacy). He turned up at every subsequent meeting and, unlike his father, was willing, when pressed, to take the chair. He was so keen to help recruit that he suggested dividing Caldewgate up into zones, so that each zone could be systematically covered without any duplication of effort. It was James who suggested inviting lecturers and who obtained the services of notable speakers in the temperance movement, such as Mr Septimus Davis from Newcastle, an orator reputed to be so inspiring that men *fought* to sign the pledge after his address. Not, however, the men of Caldewgate. After James had introduced Mr Davis and heard with pride his splendid oration, only four men came forward to sign the pledge. Nothing daunted, young James soldiered on, serving on the committee to manage subscriptions and going as the society's representative to the Federal Union meeting of the temperance movement. His enthusiasm was remarkable and surely showed that he was a worthy successor to his father, good news for the future of Carr's.

But he was not the man his father was. Nor, where the management of Carr's was concerned, were any of J.D.'s sons, whatever their other sterling qualities. It is always difficult for sons to follow in the footsteps of an outstandingly successful father, but it was particularly hard for J.D.'s sons. None of them had his curious combination of physical strength, entrepreneurial flair, ingenuity and charm. Their father towered over them in every sense and the fact that in manner he was so gentle only made his dominance more curious. He still ruled by example, not by fear. All his children were, in childhood and while growing up, content to do what he said, but once they reached adulthood they changed, as children invariably do, especially those for whom a definite path has been marked out. It was a problem for so many of the new manufacturers: their sons not only did not measure up to them, but lacked their drive and did not develop a similar passion for the business. Inheriting a factory was not the same as inheriting a house and land. A factory was not passive, its production line was never static, and it needed a constant injection of ideas and dynamism to survive and improve. None of the Carr sons either could, or was prepared to, give this.

The most promising had been George. He was the nearest in temperament and ability to his father and also looked most like him. As a child, he was capable and conscientious and it was he whom J.D. offered as a guide when visiting friends wanted to go to other meeting-houses some distance away. George would take them. But as well as being competent and absolutely trustworthy, he was also the most independent-minded – again, like his father – and by the time he could, and should, have been going into the biscuit works he had other ideas. After school at Stramongate in Kendal, he decided he wanted to be a doctor, not a biscuit manufacturer. It was a worthy enough calling, and seemed to spring from a sense of vocation that should be listened to, as divinely inspired. And, with three other sons, J.D. could afford to be generous.

George was allowed to go to Edinburgh University to read medicine – a big concession by his father, so famous for his unwillingness to compromise. (Quakers had been entering the universities and, through them, the professions for quite some time by the late 1850s, when George went to Edinburgh, but J.D. still disapproved of the affirmations required from them.) While he was at Edinburgh, George was joined by Thomas, who had come to a similar decision, heavily influenced by his brother's example. That meant two sons lost to the business, but also, very quickly, lost to medicine. Both boys studied science and then decided to go into agriculture. They went into farming together after graduation, working with Amos Cruickshank on a farm in Aberdeenshire and then, as farmers, taking on a 400-acre farm back in Silloth.

J.D. appears to have done nothing to stop these two sons from becoming farmers: he could quite easily have prevented it, simply by refusing to finance them. But he was content, at least for the time being, while still at the height of his powers, to give them their heads, showing an admirable Quaker tolerance. He had Henry and James to call on, and both of them were happy to go directly into the biscuit works. Neither of them could ever be called master bakers, like their father. They were not apprenticed in the way J.D. had been, even though they went through every department of the works, learning how they functioned. Neither of them was capable, as J.D. and his brother John were, of doing any job in the place as well as any worker. And they were from the first very much in their father's shadow, doing exactly what he said in the manner he decreed. They were not privy to decision-making and were by no means taken into partnership or groomed for succession.

Henry gradually took over the supervision of biscuit production, in a managerial capacity, and James the grain buying, so that each operated in a separate sphere but neither superseded their father. As a consequence, they never really understood the business as a whole, but this hardly bothered them. Both had a far stronger interest. Their lives revolved entirely around religion. Henry and James appear regularly in the Fisher Street meeting house minutes from the age of eighteen onwards, as representatives to monthly and quarterly meetings, as assistant clerks and on standing committees for everything from school inspections to revising lists of members. This was what made them happy, this was what aroused their enthusiasm, rather than anything to do with biscuits.

But that did not worry their father; on the contrary, it was gratifying to see his sons grow up as devout as he was himself. He was also pleased to see three of them make good Quaker marriages and start to produce Carr heirs, to whom the business would be handed on in time. George married first, in 1863, at the age of twenty-five, to Mary Brockbank, daughter of the Thomas Brockbank who had brought J.D. to Carlisle all those years ago. It was a match that made him extremely happy, as did the birth of a grandson, Edmund, a year later. He visited the new family on the Silloth farm often and was impressed by the energy and ideas George exhibited. On his farm, which was really four farms in one, he was in the process of pulling out old hedges and making new, bigger fields of thirty to forty acres, which he drained to a depth of three feet then ploughed using a steam-plough. He worked with his labourers, just as J.D. had done with his factory workers, often far into the night, using a special lamp he had invented and attached to the plough. His 300 cattle and 500 sheep, including 80 ewes for breeding, made an impressive herd and J.D. could see what a success this second son of his would be in his own right.

Thomas, at the age of twenty-five, and James, aged twenty-seven, made good marriages two years later. Thomas, who on George's marriage had parted from his brother and come into the biscuit works after all, working in the offices, made rather an impressive match. He married Elizabeth Kitching, whose father was Superintendent of the Retreat in York, a hospital with a new approach to mental illness. Its aim, revolutionary for the times, was to restore patients to full mental health by basing treatment 'on God's healing love which is unconditional'. The hospital was attractive, with a library and pleasant rooms and grounds, and every effort was made to entertain as well as care for the patients.

Coming from this environment, Elizabeth met with her father-in-law's full approval. She gave him another grandson, William Theodore (to be known as Theodore) within a year, which was some consolation because Edmund, George's son, had died aged six months, and his next child was a girl, Edith. James married Eliza Ashby, member of another well-known northern Quaker family, the same year as Thomas married Elizabeth, but she produced no children. She was 'delicate' when he married her (the nature of this delicacy unspecified) and never overcame it. These three marriages made within two years left only Henry, the eldest son, single (though Lizzie was single too, and remained so, and Eliza was not yet married either).

Henry's marriage, in October 1866, was the only one to cause trouble of an unexpected and immensely significant kind for the Carrs. Signs of approaching trouble had been there for the previous few years and had nothing to do with the woman he married, though it had everything to do with how he married her. Henry, who with his brother James had always been such a devout Quaker, had begun to question the very foundations of his beliefs. He was not alone in this. By the early 1860s Quaker membership had been falling steadily for the last two decades and a process of slightly panic-stricken reappraisal was going on up and down the whole country in the various meetings. What was emerging was a growing sense of resentment against some of the Society's stricter rules. The Yorkshire Quarterly Meeting was particularly adamant that Quakers should be allowed to marry 'out' (of their religion) and that plain dress and plain speech should be optional. Discussions about these and other proposals for change dominated the yearly meeting of 1861, which was one of those attended by J.D. as representative for Cumberland. Henry went with him, acting as a kind of usher on the doors, and listened very carefully to what was said. The meeting expressed 'earnest concern . . . that inexpediency of marriages between persons *not* of the same religious views should remain unimpaired'. But fifty rules were softened or removed, and there was a definite feeling that the rule about not marrying out could not be upheld much longer. Too many younger members, in a declining membership, were being disowned because of it.

But what was of more importance to Henry was the Quaker attitude to the Scriptures. He had been growing increasingly evangelistic in his religion and paying closer and closer attention to the Bible, interpreting it as the literal truth, as did his brother James. Carlisle Friends were beginning to find these two Carr boys rather tedious, with their passion for standing up and reading out texts whose meaning they then felt moved to expound at great length. It was true that George Fox had said that the Bible contained the words of God, and he made it his own authority for everything he did, but by the 1860s there was a feeling among Friends, due to all the scientific discoveries then being made, that perhaps every word in the Bible was not in fact meant to be literally true. Henry and James thought it was, and that this truth should be actively spread. Then in October 1866, while this conflict was brewing, without having yet been brought into the open, Henry married Sarah Forster.

She was the 26-year-old daughter of Joseph Forster, a manager at Ferguson's textile mill, and belonged to the Congregational church. The Forsters lived at that time at Grange in Borrowdale and attended the Congregational chapel in Keswick, which is where the marriage took place. Both Henry's parents were present and so was his older sister Lizzie – and three of them signed the register, as did Sarah's parents. This in itself was remarkable, since 'marrying out', though by then much more common, was still regarded in some areas as grounds for expulsion from the Society of Friends. Yet J.D. and his wife and daughter, instead of disapproving of Henry's marriage, or turning a blind eye and disassociating themselves from it, travelled to Keswick and stood by him. Naturally the news drifted back to Carlisle and there was consternation. A report was requested on Henry Carr not having married according to the rules of the Society. Rather embarrassingly Hudson Scott, J.D.'s oldest friend, who had known all the Carr children from birth, was sent as one of a committee of three to visit Henry and ask for an explanation. Henry admitted that he had indeed married in the Congregational church – he could hardly deny it – but maintained that he was still attached to the Society of Friends, still a Quaker. He did not consider, however, that this necessarily meant it was his 'duty' to attend meetings for worship and 'gave no hope of doing so'. This was rebellion and had to be dealt with. The meeting gave Henry two months to reconsider and when that time was up and he had not put in an appearance, poor Hudson Scott was sent to tell him that he was on the verge of expulsion. Meanwhile, in this tense atmosphere, Eliza Carr gave notice of her intention to marry Robert Ashby within the fold; and other Carrs were still appearing regularly in the minutes and performing their usual duties. Ironically enough, J.D. himself was particularly busy, serving on those committees of three which vetted prospective marriage partners.

But anger was increasing against Henry Carr. He had not only defied the marriage rules, but had been seen 'in another place where a paid ministry is employed', while absenting himself from worship among the Friends. And now James was following suit. He might have married according to their rules but he was no longer worshipping with them, either. (There was actually an element of relief in this: James's texts were even longer than Henry's and people were tired of them.) Things had gone far enough. The two Carrs were seen as arrogant young men who thought they could do what they liked. They had all their father's strength with none of his grace. It was decided to send another committee of three, to each of them this time, to demand an explanation.

Both young men admitted attending another place of worship, but when challenged about the minister there being paid – a heinous crime in Quaker eyes – they said that this minister had promised them it was 'his expressed intention not to receive a fixed salary in the future'. (A premise greeted with derision by the committee.) But what was more shocking was that Henry gave as his reason for not attending Quaker worship that 'the doctrine he has heard preached when he formerly attended was unsound'. This was outrageous. What did he mean? What doctrine was he talking about? Why was it 'unsound'? What was Henry Carr implying? As if his allegation were not insulting enough, his brother James then sent a letter to the meeting. He gave as his reason for not attending that he had been ordered by an elder to stay away if he could not keep silent. He wrote that he had not known elders had this power but that he had obediently stayed away, as instructed, even though he had wanted to attend. Both he and Henry objected to being visited by a committee without having previously had, according to Quaker custom, the 'benefit of private advice and admonition'.

It was all extremely unfortunate and very difficult for J.D. He had been a pillar of the Quaker community in Carlisle for over thirty years, serving it faithfully in many capacities, and now here were two of his sons on the verge of disgrace. They were not, as he knew, hotheaded youths shouting defiance for the sake of it, but extremely sincere and serious in their religious faith, men who would not do anything lightly but always weighed the consequences as they had been brought up to do. Things got even worse. In March 1867 it was alleged in the meeting that both Carrs had indeed been given that private advice of which they claimed to have been cheated. Neither had heeded it. As for the slur about 'unsound doctrine' being preached, this was met with a sorrowful dignity in the best Quaker style. It was 'regretted' that the Carr brothers 'should make a charge of so general a character, so much opposed to Christian charity'. Then the elder to whom James had apparently alluded by name (though it is not recorded in the minutes) 'entirely disclaimed' ever having requested him to keep silent in meeting. Three other Friends also declared that they each had had a private word of warning in James's ear. Everyone expressed disappointment in both Henry and James and there was unanimous agreement: both of them were to be expelled. If their father and other family members objected, none of their objections were recorded. Testimonies of disownment were prepared forthwith. Henry and James stuck to their original statements and so the ugly situation came about of one Quaker virtually calling another a liar.

In June, it was recorded 'that Henry Carr is no longer a member of the Society of Friends', though it would be 'glad to receive him again when he shall see it as his duty to conform to the religious principles and practices we profess'. James's expulsion followed. He was swift to retaliate in a long and passionately written letter of defence, littered with texts. His own great desire, he wrote, was 'to seek the Glory of God in the salvation of souls'. These souls could be saved only by making them pay close attention to the Scriptures, in which 'the truth is revealed to us by the Holy Spirit'. In his opinion, the Friends were no longer paying close enough attention to the Scriptures, or making the truth evident in them central enough to their religion – and as for going *out* to save souls, they were not doing it.

James's wife took until December to resign but meanwhile his immediate family had reacted more swiftly. Thomas and his wife resigned a month after the disownment of Henry and James, in another long letter, which did not echo the same reasons but took a different line. They said it was 'not right for us any longer to have membership in any body of which every Christian is not a member, seeing no Scriptural authority for names and sects'. But they were more specific about doctrinal differences than Henry had been. 'We have been led into this step', they wrote, ' . . . primarily because we have found that the doctrine of the substitution of Christ is not generally accepted by Friends and that the preaching of it cannot be permitted in your meeting. Believing that without Christ as our substitute we have no hope of eternal life . . . we feel it incumbent upon us . . . to uphold the doctrine of justification by faith in a substitute.' The last criticism was of 'the exclusion of the Bible from meetings, composed as they necessarily are in part of unconverted persons, in which we could not feel satisfied'.

The brothers' elder sister, the unmarried Lizzie, resigned the same day as Thomas and his wife. She wrote a surprisingly strongly worded letter of her own, conveying a good deal of anger that Henry and James had been disowned 'with an absence, as it seems to me, of that Christian love and patience which they might have expected from you'. Jesus Christ, she reminded the Friends, died for all sinners, as her brothers had preached in meeting, and she could not condone objections to this preaching. The Friends were no longer loving and 'by their disuse of the Scriptures in their meetings seem to me to hinder the latter'. There was no suggestion that Lizzie had meekly agreed to show solidarity with her brothers. She had thought everything out for herself and had come to her own conclusions. There was no mention in her resignation, or Thomas's, of that other problem, Henry's marrying out, or of the brothers' protest that they had not been given private advice. She concentrated on the doctrinal differences.

Lizzie's resignation left only her sister Eliza, her other brother George and her parents still belonging to the Society of Friends. Eliza, who had just married (strictly according to Quaker rules), no longer lived in Carlisle and neither, of course, did George. Now that they had moved out of the sphere of the Carlisle meeting, neither seemed to think they should resign, suggesting that in their own meetings the same doctrinal problems either had not arisen or did not trouble them – the Carlisle situation was simply a localised difficulty.

But what about J.D. and his wife Jane? They were still in Carlisle, still attending the Fisher Street meeting-house. They had had to witness the expulsion of two of their children and endure the censure of them by the Friends, among whom they had worshipped for over thirty years. They took a long time to decide what to do and when, in April 1869, they finally decided to leave too, theirs was the simplest and gentlest letter of all, containing no criticisms, flaunting no superior knowledge of the Bible and entering into no arguments. They had, they wrote, been praying long and hard about what they should do. While remaining 'individually attached to you with whom we trust to be ever united in the bond of Christian love', they had realised, sadly, that 'we do not see alike with you on some important points of doctrine and practice and therefore believe that it is not well to remain nominally what we are not in reality'.

So they resigned, but ended, 'we would wish ever to remain, with love, your friends'.

It was a time of agonising significance in J.D.'s life. His entire career, which had been so enormously successful and had made him, in Carlisle, an important and wealthy man, had been founded upon and guided by Quaker principles. His religion, and his worship within it, was the cornerstone of all his work. Take it away, and what would happen? Things looked ominous, especially since it appeared that he had resigned to support his noisy sons, out of some kind of pique, unworthy of a man of his standing. To those who knew him, his decision seemed to go against his nature – J.D. was a leader, not a follower, a man who influenced, not one who was influenced. It was inconceivable that he should copy Henry and James, or that he should put family before faith. And indeed it was barely credible, but it was true all the same that, for the first time, Henry and James had come out from under their father's shadow and made their own way. Though they might not have been moved to do this in business, they had done it in leaving the Friends, or rather in bringing about the circumstances that caused them to be disowned. The moment they had done so, they were happier young men. Freed from those constraints that membership of the Society of Friends had imposed, they emerged as ebullient evangelists, following the style of a man who had recently come to Carlisle, a Scottish Presbyterian minister of some fame within his own Church, called William Reid. He was a powerful preacher, as fervent in his belief in the literal truth of the Scriptures as Henry and James, who became his devoted disciples.

Reid had written a book called *The Blood of Jesus*, and Henry became its chief distributor. When he was not at the factory he was, from now on, scattering *The Blood of Jesus*, and another tract, *The Herald of Sal-*

vation, throughout Cumberland. Sundays he devoted to preaching, at the village of Todhills near Carlisle, where another Presbyterian, T. H. Hodgson, had begun conducting evangelical meetings. Henry took these over when Hodgson's health failed, and also opened his own home for small prayer meetings. James did the same kind of missionary work and was actually the better preacher, drawing large crowds. His voice was loud and deep and carried over considerable distances in the open air while he proclaimed 'the Good News'. He dared to go to fairgrounds and to race-meetings to preach about sin – 'Flee from the wrath to come!' he boomed – and he did so with such conviction that he worked himself into a lather, having to cast off his jacket and roll up his sleeves, as though engaged in exhausting physical labour. He was often laughed at, especially on Carlisle racecourse out at Durdar, but he was also listened to, and he terrified many a horse-betting gambler and drinker into seeing the light and repenting.

But their father was not happy once he left the Society of Friends. There was no relief for the quiet and dignified J.D. in ranting and raving to crowds. Without his regular attendance at the Fisher Street meeting-house he felt displaced. He was removed from like-minded companions such as Hudson Scott and had no new mentor to whom he could attach himself, as his sons did. From the start his enthusiasm for the Presbyterian Church was limited. He did not like the steeple-house itself (though the Warwick Road building had a tower, not a steeple): it was exactly what a Quaker derided, self-important, with a dark and solemn interior. Instead of the silence he had been used to, J.D. had to put up with hymns and psalms and church music, mostly dreary, and with thunderous sermons. He was never comfortable there and eventually left, joining a small religious community akin to the Plymouth Brethren (and therefore to the Society of Friends he had just left). They called themselves simply The Brethren and at first met in a room in Bank Street. Among their number was John Laing, the builder who, like J.D., had established a successful business in Carlisle, from nothing. The study of the Bible was important in their devotional meetings and great emphasis was laid on converting sinners (which was mainly done from tents at camps set up outside Carlisle). There was no officially appointed ministry – J.D. had found this part of Presbyterianism hard to take – and members took it in turn to lead prayers. The Brethren suited him better than the Presbyterians, but nevertheless something had gone out of his life: that certainty he had always had as a Quaker had vanished and he missed it.

It was, as it turned out, not a good time for J.D. to have a crisis of conscience. The biscuit world had changed and a crisis of a more prolonged sort was approaching. By 1860, Huntley & Palmer had become the largest biscuit firm in Britain and was acknowledged by the industry to be the leader. At first this did not particularly worry J.D., because he thought there was room for everyone in the prevailing excellent trading conditions; but then, after 1870, things began to change. There were indications, soon to be confirmed, that the boom was over. Export trade, which in the previous two decades had grown phenomenally for Carr's, as well as for the other biscuit firms, began to slow down. The reason was not difficult to find. Other countries, especially the United States and Germany, were catching up with Britain's early industrialisation. Not only were they becoming formidable competitors, but they were protecting their own goods with high tariffs, whereas Britain was a Free Trade country. In order to compete, and maintain the level of export trade, prices would have to be lowered and the only way to do that was to take a cut in profits – either that or, unthinkable to J.D., reduce the quality. His factory produced 72 different kinds of fancy biscuits by 1861 (compared with the two he had begun with), but they were all still top-quality.

In the home market it was beginning to be obvious that there was after all a limit to how many tons of biscuits could be sold – competition, from new as well as old rivals, increased all the time. Robert McVitie's Edinburgh firm was expanding rapidly in the 1860s; John Macfarlane's and James Lang's partnership was proving successful in Glasgow; William Crawford was operating now in Liverpool and London, as well as in Edinburgh; William Meredith and William George Drew were manufacturing biscuits independently of each other in London, but both were doing well by the mid-1850s; and in 1857 Peek Frean's began manufacturing biscuits, tempting J.D.'s brother John to join them five years later and make them even more successful: so the market was crowded and as a result far more aggressive. If one firm produced a new biscuit all the others tried to compete, but where the rivalry was most intense was in new forms of advertising. J.D. had always appreciated the value of letting people know what you had to offer and he had never failed to trumpet his successes. But now other firms were beginning to prove sharper still. Huntley & Palmer, for example, had the brilliant idea of handing each passenger boarding a train at Paddington a small packet of their biscuits wrapped in paper bearing the company's name – a ploy that was far more likely to keep customers loyal to their brand than a staid advertisement taken in a newspaper or periodical. What was equally worrying for Carr's was the way all the biscuit firms were beginning to spread themselves right across the whole of the country, whereas before each had had its own principal area.

So just as J.D. had left the Society of Friends, and

was feeling more displaced than he could easily confess, his place as a leading biscuit manufacturer was about to be threatened. A series of disastrous harvests was approaching – 1873, 1875, 1876 and 1879 – which would mean that 70 per cent of the country's wheat would have to be imported at considerable cost, and would affect, among many other things, the price of biscuits as well as the profits to be made from them. J.D. needed his religious faith more than ever in the ruthless fight for markets. His guideline from the start had been not to make money for its own sake, but to *serve* a need, not to take advantage of it; but if his firm was to flourish in this new economic climate, these were standards that would be put to a severe test. He was no longer a Quaker, no longer bound by Quaker obligations, but instead of this being a relief, freeing him to operate without Quaker restraints, it was instead more a cause of anxiety. He was obliged to make his own rules for business conduct and it became a question of how much baggage he was going to carry with him from the Society of Friends to the Brethren. In the event, it was a great deal, but as he entered his sixties he was by no means sure of that. Certainty had departed along with his strict Quaker membership.

Chapter Six
•
DEATHS AND DUTIES

IN HIS SIXTIES, J.D. was still a strong and very healthy man, with no fears of declining powers. His success had always depended on keeping his eyes open and aware – he had never been content to stand still, knowing very well that the success of a business depended on adapting to changing times. He understood the dangers of being a relatively small family firm and how easy it would be to be squeezed out by bigger, more adventurous firms once the boom ended, as it was now threatening to do. It was important to try new methods and test new machines, just as he had always done, and he continued to do this. But he made some poor decisions, such as investing in expensive new machinery that had not proved itself sufficiently, and he took some risks that did not pay off. This is where his sons could have come into their own, but they failed to do so.

Henry and James were still completely obsessed with their religious activities in the late 1860s and so far as the biscuit works was concerned, though they were diligent and worked hard, they simply did what they were told. Their father did not take them into his confidence or ask their advice (not that they had any, in a technical sense, to give) and they did not demand a true partnership. They were perhaps too reliant upon him, except for George, who had distanced himself both by choosing a career that had nothing to do with the family firm and by moving to Silloth. Yet even George did not seem to want to remove himself from his father's influence because he found it suffocating: there was never any suggestion that he found J.D.'s dominance frustrating and wanted to escape for that reason. He did not so much rebel as simply choose another path, and, since his father gave him the financial support he needed at first on the farm, J.D. cannot have disapproved. If he was disappointed, he did not show it, but remained close to this second son who had not wanted to follow in his footsteps.

Thomas, who was now in charge of the running of the office since his uncle George's death in 1864, was equally obedient and lacking any real initiative. So there was no one to cry caution when J.D. bought a machine supposedly able to raise dough without yeast and make 'aerated' biscuits, which would be absolutely pure because there was no fermentation in the process. It was an expensive failure and within two years had to be scrapped. Only one machine, only one mistake, but others followed, and J.D.'s total control made these errors more likely to happen.

But no one, then, really worried about J.D.'s failure to consult or delegate. His sons were all too busy with their rapidly growing families as well as their new religion to fret about the future of the biscuit works as their father aged. The grandchildren came thick and fast in the 1860s and 1870s, with plenty of sons among them. By the time J.D. was sixty-five in 1871, he had twelve grandchildren, of whom nine were boys. Henry by then had three sons, George had four and Thomas had three, and none of these families showed any signs of being complete. J.D. saw most of Thomas's brood because they lived across the road, in Newtown House, a mere three minutes' walk away. Because George's eldest had died as a baby, Thomas's son Theodore, born in 1866, was the eldest, and from the start his grandfather knew that he was promising. Theodore had a passion for finding out how things worked, clearly indicating a practical turn of mind. When J.D. took him round the biscuit works, Theodore was transfixed by the machines and had to have every detail of their workings explained to him when he was still a very young child. Thomas's next two boys, Bertram and Ernest, one born at the beginning of 1868 and one at the end, had nothing like Theodore's curiosity, and neither did Henry's sons, Arthur, Henry and Laurence.

It looked as if Theodore would prove a natural heir in the next generation, until the birth of Dodgson, George's sixth child and fourth son, in 1871. He was of course named after his grandfather, long before anyone could tell whether he would look like him or be like him, but by the time he was three the similarity was said to be striking. Mary, his mother, commented that Dodgson's fair complexion was the same as his grandfather Carr's and so were his features, 'to his rounded forehead and nose, his eyes bluish-grey, his mouth and chin perfect'. Then there was his remarkable height and strong build. He was taller, at three, than his older brothers Wilfrid and Fred had been, and level with his cousin Henry who was nearly two years his senior. But it was not just Dodgson's appearance that reminded the family of his grandfather – it was his disposition. His mother described him as extraordinary, in that he was 'of a wonderfully heavenly turn, never quarrelling, always perfectly amiable and loving'. Even though this grand-child lived at Silloth, J.D. saw a lot of him. He was a popular grandfather, not at all terrifying, and he liked to take his grandchildren for walks round the fields opposite his house to see the cows being milked. Rather surprisingly, considering his pacifist views, he did not object to his grandsons shooting bows and arrows in his garden, so long as they did not aim them at birds or animals. He would amuse them by using his strength to shake the pear tree in his garden so that it rained pears upon them, and he would push them on the swing that dangled from its thickest branch.

There were regular teas for all the family at Coledale Hall, with strawberries in the summer from the huge bed in the garden, served on a Coalport dessert service. But best of all the children liked him to give them rides on the pony that the gardener used to mow the lawn – a very odd pony, which wore leather boots. Lizzie, J.D.'s eldest daughter, did all the arranging of these family tea-parties, which was hard on her because she had no great fondness for children. She did not go out much, remaining almost entirely at Coledale Hall with her mother, running the household and greatly depended on by her parents. She always wore a cap, oval in shape, and trimmed discreetly with lace, and the children used to be fascinated by her cap basket, vying with each other to carry it about as though it was filled with precious stones. But though Lizzie appeared so staid to her nephews and nieces, and old before her time, she was a strong character, not in the least submissive or timid. She was very direct in all she said, like her father, and though she had left the Quakers she never discarded the Quaker outlook. James Jordan, a boy who started at Carr's in 1858, always remembered being sent to Coledale Hall with six quarts of milk and while he was in the kitchen being asked by Miss Carr, 'Boy, canst thou eat a tart?' James said no, out of politeness and because he was shy, but looked forward to being pressed, when he fully intended to accept. But Miss Carr did not ask him again and the cook laughed and said, 'With Quakers, lad, yea is yea and nay is nay.' That was how it remained with Lizzie, and indeed with all the family. The Quaker influence permeated Coledale Hall still and all the grandchildren were aware of it, even though only George's children still belonged to the Society of Friends.

It had always been remarkable, ever since they came to Carlisle, how healthy the Carr family seemed to be. They all lived in areas reckoned to be the safest from disease but even so, up to the mid-1870s, they had been lucky, considering that Carlisle's mortality statistics in the mid-nineteenth century compared unfavourably with other manufacturing towns in the North. (The percentage rate per annum in Carlisle was 2.69, whereas nationally it was 2.17.) There had been regular epidemics of cholera, diphtheria and scarlet fever in the city, but the Carrs were not affected. The family grew and grew (only James was childless) and, with the exception of George's first child, they remained untouched by the killer plagues that swept through other families. But then their luck ran out and J.D. was obliged to witness the deaths of four of his nine little grandsons. He had always thought George's family the most protected because of where they lived, at Silloth, on the shores of the bracing Solway Firth, a long way from the fever nests of Carlisle; but it was Dodgson who died first, followed by his brother Wilfrid and then by his cousins Arthur and Henry. Not long after J.D.'s sixty-eighth birthday in December 1874 the promising Dodgson, who was so like him, caught what appeared to be an ordinary cold, although he complained of a sore throat and his mother was instantly on the alert. George had to go to Carlisle that day, so she asked him to drop a note into the doctor's on his way, asking him to call.

Meanwhile, Mary was taking no chances. Like all Victorian mothers, she knew what a sore throat in a feverish young child might mean and she took every precaution, applying a linseed poultice to Dodgson's neck in the hope that it would reduce the internal inflammation of his throat. She was angry that the doctor took six hours to turn up, obviously thinking she was merely fussing, and said to him, 'I am always so anxious when anything ails the throat, I think about diphtheria.' She was bitter that the doctor 'did nothing except give the child an emetic'. He thought it might simply be a case of a suppurating tonsil, a diagnosis that Mary did not for one moment believe. She sat up all night with poor Dodgson, but by dawn, when she was sure he was worse, she made George go for the doctor again. He arrived grumbling, but one look at the boy's throat and he was at last all concern: he could see, and so could Mary, 'the white leathery growths'. These increased rapidly and since the first doctor had given her no confidence, Mary sent George galloping off to Maryport, twelve miles away, for another. This one at least tried to do something, acknowledging that Dodgson was in grave danger.

Mary held her little boy's head, soothing him, though he was obedient and docile enough in spite of the pain, and the doctor applied 'a caustic pencil' to the growths, which were now giving off a horrible foul stench. Dodgson then fell asleep, to Mary's relief, and slept on and off all the next day, waking only now and again to ask for water. Concerned that his strength would ebb away if he took nothing else, Mary beat up raw eggs in brandy and managed to spoon some into his mouth. He swallowed a little, though only with a great effort since every swallow was agony – 'he was a good boy to the last'. But then his nose began to bleed heavily and Mary did not need the doctor to tell her that this was a fatal symptom. So it proved. Dodgson died three days before Christmas, the coldest day of the year, 'all white with snow and keen frost'. The house, instead of being full of merrymaking, was utterly silent. Aunt Lizzie had come from Carlisle and had taken the other children – Edith (eight), Fred (seven), Wilfrid (six) and Mary (four) – back with her to Coledale Hall to their grandparents. Mary had listened to the excitement as they departed and knew that none of the other children had realised what death really meant. She had told them that Dodgson might soon be needed by the angels, who would come for him, but the reality of the sad event had not registered.

The funeral for Dodgson was a Quaker one – George was the only son still a member of the Society of Friends – so the family was spared the mournful extravagances of the day. It was a quiet, simple ceremony, of which Mary was glad.

But hardly were they all together again at home before Wilfrid began complaining, just as Dodgson had done, of a sore throat. This time the doctor thought 'it might only be a relaxed sore throat'. Mary was contemptuous, knowing at once this was diphtheria. But Wilfrid did not seem as ill as Dodgson had been, even though he was more feverish, and since he was three years older, he was likely to have more resistance, or so she consoled herself. Yet again, the Maryport doctor was brought in, earlier this time, and he 'urged stimulants . . . and brushed the throat with a camel's hair brush in a solution of caustic'. She tried to take Wilfrid's mind off his throat by reminiscing about all the things he had enjoyed, reminding him of the large fir cones he had loved to collect and the brilliant-coloured fungi. He had always been a thoughtful child and had liked to walk behind with her, while the others ran on. He had told her, after one trip through rowdy Caldewgate on the way to Coledale Hall, that when he was grown up he was going to close all the nasty drinking shops – his grandfather's influence most clearly demonstrated, Mary had felt. Once, on one of the days when he had been round the biscuit works with his grandfather, Wilfrid had broken his leg running down a steep hill on his way home with his father, after they got off the train. Mary reminded him how he had got better then, how he had passed the time learning to spell and had enjoyed it. He had feared he would never be able to run around again, but he had, he'd been able to pick bilberries soon after. He was an intelligent boy and she tried to distract him with story-books and with stories from the Bible, but he was listless and fretful and much harder to amuse than Dodgson had been. And, of course, he knew that his younger brother had also had a sore throat and that soon afterwards, while Aunt Lizzie had taken him and his brother and sisters away to Carlisle, the angels had come for Dodgson. Death was no longer an abstract concept for Wilfrid, and his mother guessed what he was thinking.

Wilfrid was not as co-operative as Dodgson had been – he hated the horrible procedure of applying the caustic pencil and struggled against it. Mary managed to hold him still long enough for it to be carried out, but she failed entirely to get him to take any of the eggs-in-brandy by which she set such store. All Wilfred would sip was weak beef tea and 'sometimes he voluntarily took milk, but it came back'. Lacking nourishment, he began to grow weaker and weaker, and the doctor said that an operation was his only chance. He was going 'to remove the white growths with a little instrument'. This was painful and messy and Mary could hardly bear to assist, but without her help Wilfrid could not be treated, so she had to steel herself to endure the torment of watching him be put through it. The operation was successful, but afterwards Wilfrid would not open his mouth to swallow anything at all, so he was fed by injections. He asked to see his brother Fred but, fearing infection, Mary could not allow this last remaining son to come into contact with his dying brother. Seeing him so near death she tried to calm the restless boy by telling him that the Lord Jesus was going to take him to Heaven soon, and 'he assented, as if resigned and satisfied'. His father joined Mary to sit by him all night and Wilfrid died a mere seventeen days after Dodgson, on 8 January 1875, aged six years and four months.

Mary, who was pregnant again throughout this double ordeal and loss, wrote down an account of her sons' suffering because she could not bear to let it pass unrecorded. She knew perfectly well that what she was describing was commonplace, but that did not make it any easier to bear. A month later, Arthur and Henry, Henry's sons, died of that other prevalent disease, scarlet fever, and Mary grieved for her nephews too. She struggled hard to remember the good times they had all had, the Carr excursions and picnics when the various branches of the family had come together, and the gatherings at Coledale Hall presided over by the benign J.D. She sat beside her sons' graves, in the graveyard of the nearby Beckfoot meeting-house, so close to the sea that 'the waves on the beach are quite in unison', and listened to the lark 'which seems to sing . . . through the livelong day, making a solemn, melancholy sound'. She visited the graves often that winter and spring until the birth of another son, Reginald, eased her pain. She still had two healthy daughters and now Fred had been joined by another brother to compensate for the two who had died and she knew she was lucky.

So was the Carr family, in spite of these four deaths so close together. Thomas's children had escaped both diphtheria and scarlet fever, even though they lived nearest to Caldewgate, and two more sons, Sydney and John, had been born, bringing his total to five by the time J.D. was seventy in 1876. But it was Thomas's life that was to be devastated by that other Victorian tragedy: his wife Elizabeth died in childbirth in 1880 bearing twins. Elizabeth was only thirty-five and had borne six children already in the fifteen years of her marriage, with no apparent difficulty. Before she became pregnant with twins she had had the longest respite yet between babies – John was born in 1876, four years before this last and final child-bearing. The twins, Harold and Hilda, survived after their mother bled to death forty-eight hours later. Thomas was left the father of eight children, the eldest, Theodore, just fourteen. His aunt Mary moved in to take charge for a while – Lizzie, his sister, who usually filled that role, was ill – and there were three nursemaids, a cook and two other servants to help the distraught bereaved father. But Thomas, never a masterful man, had looked entirely to Elizabeth to run his household and preside over the upbringing of his many children. Without her he was adrift and the makeshift arrangements of his sisters, nursemaids and servants only increased his feelings of being lost and displaced. He was fortunate to have his parents living across the road, and to have so much help from other members of his family, but he became a deeply unhappy man.

Work was hardly any comfort to him. On the contrary, by 1880, when this blow fell, there was a great deal to worry all the Carrs working in the biscuit factory. The wheat situation, upon which the manufacturing of the flour for the biscuits depended, was potentially disastrous. The repeal of the Corn Laws in 1846 had not, as some people anticipated, caused the immediate collapse of English agriculture, but by the end of the 1870s wheat was coming in from America, where the invention of a mechanical reaper had made the production of wheat in the vast prairies possible. The railways could now carry these huge quantities of wheat to the ports, where steamships were waiting to convey it across the Atlantic. This flood of good-quality wheat at low prices meant that English flour millers were forced out of business. J.D. had three flour mills of his own, all in Carlisle, and had always been glad of them – they had made him independent – but they were now becoming liabilities instead of assets. Cumbrian farmers no longer found it worthwhile to grow wheat, so if he wished to keep on milling his own flour J.D. was going to have to buy the imported American wheat. This meant that to keep the whole operation economical he would have to scrap his existing mills, because they were not located at ports, and concentrate on building a larger one on the coast to avoid the increased transport costs.

This would mean choosing a port site, probably Silloth, where land was available beside the dock. But there was another problem: ready-made flour was also being imported, from Hungary as well as America, and this flour was finer and whiter than any that his own mills could produce. Should he, therefore, give up being a miller entirely? It might be sensible, but it went against the very philosophy upon which he had founded his success. If he let the mills go, he would be no different from any other baker and would, like them, be subject to the fluctuations of foreign suppliers. So throughout the 1870s J.D. stuck by his mills, though he had read the warning signs correctly, but by 1880 he finally faced the inevitable. He would have to sell his inland mills and build a large, modern milling plant at Silloth. It was either that or get out of milling altogether, and he still could not bring himself to take that much more drastic step. Silloth, as he had realised, was the obvious choice, because it was the nearest port with a railway connection to Carlisle.

But then J.D. had a stroke of bad luck. No sooner had he made his decision than the walls of Silloth dock collapsed; the great stone walls of the entrance to the dock simply gave way and the gates fell in, leaving ships previously anchored in deep water now stuck in mud. Facing up to this natural disaster was hard for a man of seventy-four, who had finally begun to feel intimations of mortality and wished to have all his business affairs tidy, but J.D. acted promptly. He bought a mill at Maryport instead. Modern machinery was installed and milling, with the new type of rollers, began.

All this was expensive, but then J.D. had always ploughed back profits into his business and seen this pay rapid dividends. Equally expensive had been the purchase of ships to form Carr's own fleet. One was a ketch, the *Swallow*, and the other four steamers, *Swift*, *Surprise*, *Eden* and *Nith*. These plied backwards and forwards between Liverpool, Maryport and Silloth, giving Carr's further independence. Henry and James, and more rarely Thomas, went regularly to visit the ships and enjoyed going on board and meeting the captains. As far as these sons were concerned, the ships and the new, modern mill were all signs of the continuing affluence of their father's business. J.D. had once again surmounted the difficulties all on his own, without any consultation with them, and they were grateful to him.

Thanks to their father, Henry and James were now living in a style to which J.D. had only briefly aspired and then discarded. Henry was actually living in The Villa, which he began to rent in 1874 (changing its name to Edenside), and James lived in equal splendour in a large house, Cavendish Mount, also in Stanwix. Neither of them had any financial worries and their houses showed that they were living very comfortably indeed off the business. What they were unaware of was that a huge proportion of the profits of the last decade had gone into the new mill, the ships, new offices on the Viaduct (built over the north end of Carlisle's Citadel

Station) and other modernisation within the biscuit factory itself, and all this expenditure at a time when the boom of the 1870s was over and competition had increased.

Everything depended, as it always had done, on J.D. himself. He still walked every day to the factory, continued to supervise everything himself and as long as his venerable figure was there, walking more slowly now but still strong and purposeful, everyone had absolute confidence in the business. Then, in March 1884, he went to a lecture about Martin Luther – a man in whom he was very interested because of his courage as a reformer – and was observed to be looking not quite as hale and hearty as he usually did, although people reminded each other that he was seventy-seven years of age. A week later he had a stroke from which he never recovered. The end was slow in coming and for his family shocking, as well as sad. They were all there with J.D. when he died on the morning of Sunday 6 April. The Bishop of Carlisle was preaching that day in Holy Trinity Church in Caldewgate, right beside the biscuit works, and referred to J.D.'s death in the same breath as that of the Duke of Albany (Queen Victoria's eighth child), who had also died that day, aged thirty-one. 'It is not only to the Royal Family death comes,' he said, giving listeners the distinct impression that Jonathan Dodgson Carr's death was the more important. The Bishop said that J.D. had 'caused a light to shine' and added that he personally had always been struck by his 'kindliness of manner and his wish to do good to his fellow creatures'. He saw J.D.'s business life as being 'closely identified with the commercial prosperity of Carlisle' and praised his 'practical philanthropy', which had been a potent influence on the local community.

The funeral, attended by 500 people, took place on Thursday 10 April. J.D. was buried in Carlisle cemetery, his coffin carried by his four sons. He left behind him, as well as his middle-aged sons (aged forty-nine, forty-seven, forty-six and forty-four), his wife Jane, two daughters and seventeen grandchildren, of whom twelve were boys. Theoretically, the business succession was secure. Each son was left in his will one-fifth interest in Carr's (his wife having the other fifth). They were the trustees and were given clear instructions as to how they should conduct themselves. The welfare of the business was to be paramount: 'My desire being that all the members of my family should assist each other as far as possible in maintaining and keeping the Business which has cost so much care and expense in developing.'

J.D. left them a considerable amount to maintain and keep – four flour mills (he had not yet actually sold the Carlisle mills, though he had bought the new Maryport one); a bread bakery (now across the road from the factory, in its own premises) with a shop; three other shops; offices on the Viaduct; five ships; two depots (in London and Liverpool); and of course the biscuit works itself. The varieties of biscuits being produced were now up to 128, and the 1,000 workers employed there were turning out 950 tons a year. It was a substantial inheritance, and for the sons both alarming and even frightening. They were all conscientious and wished to honour their father's trust, even George, who was still farming and had never had anything to do with the business. They felt their collective responsibility deeply and had no desire to evade it, but it nevertheless daunted them. The calamitous effect of the removal of their all-powerful father could hardly be exaggerated and it was only their passionately held religious faith that gave them any confidence at all. 'Trust in the Lord' had to become their motto, even more than it had always been, because they no longer had J.D. in whom to trust.

At first, once the initial shock was absorbed, there

was the comfort of feeling that the business ran itself. Everything carried on as usual, to their relief. People did the jobs they had always done, since they were all stuck in well-oiled grooves and hardly had to think. Margaret Ann Brown, who had started working for Carr's in 1876 in the packing department, hardly noticed the death of the Founder (as J.D. was known). She went on packing cream crackers just as she had always done, standing with a line of other women at a long trestle table surrounded by tin boxes full of straw, into which the biscuits went. Twenty of them worked in that room, so it was quite a small section and pleasant enough to be in. The room had whitewashed walls to give it some feeling of brightness, because there were no big windows, only a skylight. The women all wore the regulation long white aprons and had their hair tied back, though they were not required to wear hats because there was no baking going on.

Isabel Hetherington, who had started work a year earlier than Margaret Ann, worked in the icing and decorating room and had never even seen J.D. in the factory. So far as she was concerned, the most important person was Miss Nixon, her supervisor. Isabel went in fear of her – mistakes were easy to make if one's concentration slipped, and Miss Nixon noticed them all and could be extremely severe. The job Isabel had to do was tricky. She squeezed prepared icing on to each biscuit, through a muslin funnel with a tin spout on the end. Exactly the right amount of pressure had to be applied at exactly the right point, just enough for each biscuit. It was a matter of squeeze/stop over and over again, and if the correct rhythm was not maintained, threads of icing were carried over from one biscuit to another (there were 140 on a tray), ruining the whole batch.

The men in the factory were rather more aware of

the handover from father to sons. J.D. had continued to go often into the fitting shop, where all the spare parts for the machines were worked on and repaired, and all twelve fitters had known him well. Those in the export department had been familiar with the sight of him too – theirs was a very important department and visits from all three sons, as well as J.D., were frequent. The export trade was so competitive that the pace was hectic and everything was done at speed. William Morrison, who started off pushing a barrow (as so many boys did) was by this time a clerk in the department and noticed no slackening; on the contrary, at the time J.D. died, the Belgian and Dutch trade was enormous and everyone was working flat out to keep up with it. One constant problem was getting enough wood to make crates (Scots pine wood, grown on the Netherby estate of the Grahams, was used). The crates were huge and had to be securely fastened with strong cords. Carr's were anxious, in the depressed economic climate and the new intense competition at home, to keep up their lucrative export trade, and it was given priority.

This put particular pressure on the tin shop, which was located in the oldest part of the building. Here six different sizes of tins were made, all with hinged lids, and another specially large one to hold 60 lb of Captain's Thin. The bins for export had to be soldered, then tested in a water tank, before being rubbed dry with powdered chalk. The final stage was the application of a coat of fine lacquer. The tins had fancy linings, frills of paper lace, with little cushions of softer paper placed between the contents and the lid. All the linings were cut by hand and it required great dexterity to fit them. But it was a job that everyone engaged on it enjoyed: anything to do with the export department felt exciting. Willie McCormick, who never left Carlisle in his life, loved marking the wooden crates with their destinations –

'every country in the world,' he boasted. Sometimes letters from far-away countries would be received and posted on the wall, causing great amusement. One customer wrote from Accra on the Gold Coast:

Dear Carr!
I have the honour most respectfully to inform you that I beg do no be anger about this my letter. Please I and you be correspondent as the follows. Everything I want in England I send money to buy it and I will also buy small tin of your biscuit. Put the thing in it and send it. Anything you want in Gold Coast lucky stone, telisman, etc. Ask.

Less amusing, but more pleasing, were the letters that came saying that biscuits packed years ago were in perfect condition when opened. A member of a geological survey team in Southern Rhodesia wrote to report that a box of Carr's biscuits kept in the tool-box of a car for two years had just been opened and that the biscuits were crisp and delicious.

The workers were as anxious as the Carr sons that everything should continue to tick over after J.D.'s death, just as it always had done, and they played their part admirably. This, after all, was a family firm and, with the disappearance of the head of the family, another took his place. Henry, as the eldest, was the new leader, a position unchallenged by James or Thomas. He walked around the factory, just as his father had done, and was there for people to turn to. But it was an indication of how very different things were going to be when Henry's first act was to call the entire work force together, not to raise morale by assuring them that the business would carry on as usual, but to get them to pray with him and to order them to take care of their souls above all else. J.D.'s faith had been strong, but he had never presumed to lecture his employees about the condition of their souls. Would Henry, and James and Thomas with him, be *practical* enough to take the helm and steer a judicious course in the way their father had done?

Nobody watching the May Day procession in Carlisle the following year could possibly have doubted that the transition from father to sons had been made smoothly and that Carr's as a business was still rock-solid and prosperous. The parade was a big event in the city, a showcase for all the manufacturers and tradesmen, with prizes awarded for the best displays, many of them regularly won by Carr's, which greatly added to the firm's prestige. J.D. had always encouraged participation in these May Day events. Flags were hung from all the factory windows and Carr's horses and wagons were superbly groomed and decorated when they emerged through the gates, taking their places behind the Artillery Volunteers, who marched at the head of the parade playing a lively air.

Carr's horses swept the board that year – Jock, Captain, Dick, Tom, Sally, Maggie and Fanny (a particularly fine chestnut with a prancing air) all winning prizes in the four most important classes. It was Henry's first triumph. The stables had always come under his jurisdiction and now he had made them better than ever, visiting them every day, keeping a close eye on how each horse was treated, and never without a sugar lump in his pocket for them. He would not allow any horse to be whipped and took it upon himself as soon as he was in total charge to break over his knee some whips that he found. He would not even allow whips to be carried in the important procession just for the look of it, and was delighted when this did not prevent the drivers winning. The conditions in which the twenty-four horses were kept were immaculate at all times and they were beautifully groomed. The heavy dray-horses carted flour from the mills to the factory, took refuse to the Corporation dumps and collected empty tins and wooden cases from the railway depots, while the light horses did the bread and flour deliveries. It was the men running the stables who liked Henry best. The men in charge of the machines simply wished that he would show as much knowledge of, and concern for, things mechanical.

Meanwhile Henry had a family matter to distract him from getting to grips with the business. Thomas was causing his brothers concern, by apparently being smitten with a young woman called Mary Laurie, who had come from Scotland to work in his house as one of the three nursemaids who cared for his eight motherless children. His aunt Mary had long since gone home to her own family and Thomas had managed with the nursemaids, supervised by his sister Lizzie and his mother, who were so near at hand just across the road. The three older boys, Theodore, Bertram and Ernest, were all away at school, leaving only the younger ones. Mary Laurie's particular concern was the twins, Harold and Hilda. She looked after them almost exclusively and wheeled them in a big, ungainly pram along the road to a point where the railway to Port Carlisle could be seen. Here she would hold the children up to wave at the trains and the train drivers, and would wave herself. She was a pretty, cheerful girl and popular with several of the men who worked at Carr's, a couple of whom had walked out with her. She was popular with her employer, too. Thomas had been without a wife for seven lonely years when, on 10 January 1887, he left Carlisle and went to Edinburgh with Mary Laurie, his servant, and married her.

It was all done in great secrecy. Thomas was, as his brothers were, highly religious, but he married Mary in a register office. No member of his large family was present. Mary's brother, Peter Laurie, a railway inspector, and Rebecca, her sister, signed as witnesses. Thomas described himself as a biscuit maker, and Mary's father's occupation was given as signalman. There was plenty for the Carrs to take exception to if they wished, and they did so. Thomas was forty-six to Mary's twenty-four, but that was perhaps not as offensive as the difference in rank and status. The Carrs were only manufacturers, but in Carlisle at least they were of some standing, if in a category that some might choose to classify as *nouveau riche*. Mary was not only a servant, and a lowly one at that, but the daughter of a working man. When, on the bridal couple's return to Carlisle, the bride moved from the attic to the master bedroom, Henry and James made known their disapproval and displeasure – without, unfortunately, leaving any written record of precisely what their reaction was based on, but forcing the conclusion that it came from snobbery. Brought up as they had been as Quakers, this was an unexpected response but there seems to be no other explanation. There could be no justifiable objection on other grounds. But Thomas clearly guessed how these two brothers would react, so he took care to marry away from Carlisle, a secrecy that would further offend them. He acted like a guilty man, although he had no real need to. He was a widower, he had waited seven years to remarry, and Mary was perfectly respectable and well liked, a woman to whom the younger Carr children were devoted. If she was a gold-digger, a common accusation in these cases, picking a man with eight children who lived modestly was not an obvious choice.

Harder for Thomas to bear than the censure of his brothers was the reaction of two of his sons. Theodore and Bertram promptly moved out and went to live at

Coledale Hall with their grandmother and Aunt Lizzie. They were now aged twenty and eighteen, not much younger than their new stepmother, an embarrassing and awkward situation for all of them. They were old enough to remember their own mother vividly, which the younger ones were not, and to contrast the dignified and serene Elizabeth with the cheerful but very ordinary Mary. Doubtless a kind of prurience came into it too: young men of this age find it distasteful to imagine their middle-aged father going to bed with a girl their own age. It would seem all wrong, and the easiest course was for them to move across the road to their grandmother's. But Ernest, almost eighteen himself, did not leave. If he felt any embarrassment or repugnance, he conquered it and stayed. The following year, on 14 July 1888, a full eighteen months later, Mildred was born. Three years later her sister Agnes Marjorie appeared, bringing Thomas's family to a total of ten.

The birth of these two daughters seemed only to widen the rift that now existed between Thomas and two of his brothers. George and his sisters thought the second marriage was Thomas's affair and there was no split there, but Henry and James persisted in their self-righteous disdain. In a family firm this had serious consequences, not just for the present – Thomas, always on the sideline, was now squeezed more and more out of control of the business – but also for the future. But the future, frankly, was Theodore, and Theodore was Thomas's son. There was no open and official parting of the ways: Henry and James needed Thomas's signature on too many important documents, so they could not alienate him entirely, and Thomas had ten children dependent on him, so he could afford no grand gestures. They were all locked together in the business left to them, with all the onerous responsibilities it entailed, by their father. They were obliged to pull together. J.D. had never been in such a situation; he never had to handle anyone carefully. Those who did not agree with his total dominance could leave (as his brother John did). But he had bequeathed a system which was, from the beginning, highly unlikely to work smoothly. Four brothers with equal shares caused a situation that was likely to give rise to arguments and weak leadership. It was a fair and just division, but it presumed a level of co-operation and a belief that the business could be run as a co-operative that J.D. himself had never condoned. His legacy ran contrary to his own ideas on how a business should be run.

But in other ways the legacy was much more likely to be honoured. All of his sons were indefatigable workers in their respective churches, all of them so sincere and passionate about their faith that they held prayer meetings in their own houses. Where religion was concerned, there were no doubts that they would fulfil their father's expectations. Similarly, all four cared about social reform of one sort or another and were determined to involve themselves, just as their father had. Temperance, health, good housing, reading-rooms, all these causes were supported by one or other, and sometimes all, of the Carrs. They were equally conscientious about looking after their employees and seeing that the excellent conditions their father had created and maintained for fifty years were made even better. No one could fault them on diligence in this respect. But all this took money, lots of it, coming in constantly, and money was what Henry and James now discovered, to their own surprise, they did not have in the abundance they had believed.

Chapter Seven

'. . . FROM DARKNESS INTO LIGHT'

Henry Carr walked to work most days, just as J.D. had done, though his progress through Carlisle was not marked in the same way as his distinctive father's had been. This was partly because his clothes looked perfectly conventional: unlike J.D., Henry did not look 'quaintly Quaker'. Since he was no longer a member of the Society of Friends, he could wear what he wished. But the difference was not just one of dress. Henry, although also tall and well-built, lacked his father's presence. There was nothing striking about him. He was ordinary and melded into the crowds.

In Carlisle these crowds had grown enormously by the time Henry became head of Carr's in 1884. The centre of the city had always been busy, especially on market days, but now the crowds there could be so dense that a man had to push his way through if going from one end of English Street to the other, as Henry was obliged to do. The city seemed to be bursting at its seams, its population continuing to rise dramatically, up to 40,000 when J.D. died, twice the figure it had been when he arrived. Carlisle looked different too. The Mayor in 1859, Robert Ferguson, had remarked, 'Carlisle is becoming a handsome town,' and he had been right. The following two decades had seen several handsome buildings go up and the effect was marked. The County Hotel was built in 1853, designed by one of the leading architects of the day (Anthony Salvin, who refurbished Windsor Castle); the Great Central Hotel, right next to Carr's offices on the Viaduct, was even more impressive when it was completed in 1880; and in English Street itself the White Swan Inn had come down, to be replaced by a shop of magnificent proportions. Other new buildings on both sides of the street had made it look far more gracious, because instead of uneven lines, architecturally there was now a symmetry. Carlisle was still a market town but it looked far less like one.

But what had changed the city most of all was the construction of the large main-line railway station. When the first railway companies came to Carlisle in the 1840s they had their own small stations in London Road and Crown Road, neither of them near the centre, but when the main north–south route began to operate in 1847 the two big companies involved agreed to build a joint station. The Citadel Station, designed by Sir William Tite, was a beautiful building which quickly became the pride of Carlisle, looking more like a palace than a railway station. People went there just to look and marvel at the endless trains steaming through, their very passage making Carlisle seem important. But many of them also went there to work. The railways employed a large proportion of the male work force in Carlisle from the 1860s onwards. Outside the Citadel Station stood horse-drawn cabs and luggage porters with hand-carts, each porter licensed as a street trader and wearing his City of Carlisle licence plate, with his name painted in white on his cart. The station dominated the city, the shrieking and whistling of the engines echoing right across it and the huge mess of railway lines spread out over the whole western side, beyond the old city wall.

Yet walking through Carlisle, Henry Carr was nevertheless observing many aspects of its life that remained unchanged from his father's day. Not all the old landmarks had gone, nor had all its peculiar features been swept away. Building was soon to begin on a vast covered market, into which all the traders massed in front of the Town Hall would be obliged to move, but as yet the stalls remained there, just as they had been when Henry was a child. In fact, there were even more of them, crammed into what was a relatively small area round the town cross on Wednesdays and Saturdays. Everything from vegetables to fruit, pottery and even guns was sold there and the bargains were generous. The Rudd women were still there, sitting on the steps of the cross, wearing men's flat caps and selling the soft red stone (hence their name), which came from the bed of the River Caldew and was used to give a red finish to doorsteps and window-sills – no self-respecting Carlisle housewife could manage without it. 'Five-fingered Johnny' in his strange, floppy hat still appeared, selling eggs; Jimmy Dyer played his fiddle; and Blind Lizzie sold newspapers – all the real characters were still there and known, by sight at least, to Henry and all the other local people.

Most enduring of all, and a measure of how old traditions went on, even in a city developing and changing so rapidly, were the hirings. Men and women stood beside the cross twice a year, at Whitsun and Martinmas, offering themselves for hire on a half-yearly basis. A deal was struck between employer and employee by the giving of a sixpence. J.D. had never liked the hirings. The scene was not a pleasant one, with many of those who offered themselves being already drunk, or spending their sixpences, when they got them, on more drink. The women dressed inappropriately, and according to the Carlisle *Patriot*, their besetting sin would seem to be a love of dress 'unsuited to their station in life . . . rough country girls . . . do not render themselves more attractive by acres of crinoline and nutshell hats and red feathers'. On top of that, the manners of the women were labelled 'coarse'. But the hirings were a part of Carlisle life and could not, as yet, be banished just because the city was moving into a new era.

Henry was perfectly aware of what was happening in Carlisle – he was as much involved in charity work of one sort or another as his father had been – but perhaps not quite so aware of the overall picture in the country in general. Trading conditions were still fairly buoyant in the late 1880s in Carlisle, but the way in which the economy was going from boom to slump and back again in the country as a whole was not so easy for a biscuit manufacturer to grasp. What Henry did realise was that there was a new threat in his world, from shops, with big chains like Sainsbury and Liptons opening their own factories and making their own brand products, which undercut the prices of the established biscuit firms. The first ten years after J.D.'s death in 1884 were crucial ones for the business. Henry, with James at his side, had to make some important decisions long before he was in any position to make them wisely. When he became head of Carr's, by virtue of being the eldest son, he had very little idea of the financial situation and yet had to decide more or less immediately whether to go ahead and build the new mill at Silloth, together with a warehouse, once the dock had been rebuilt. He knew that his father had intended to do so and therefore had the feeling that he was only following instructions and did not have to weigh up the pros and cons for himself. Told what such a project would cost, he was shocked, but what really threw him was the discovery that the money to cover it was not neatly piled up in the bank.

Too much had been spent immediately prior to his father's death to leave a large surplus. The only thing to do was borrow from the bank, which he did without too many qualms, confident that since business was good it would quickly be paid back.

The Silloth mill was soon in production, but unfortunately it was slow to show any profit at all. Henry had failed to realise that the importation of the new white flour from abroad, which had caused J.D. such concern, meant that this new mill started up at a time when the country had never been in less need of home-produced flour. But what made the overall financial position of Carr's truly perilous was that Henry and James chose, at this delicate time, to expand the biscuit factory and increase the number of lines. Under J.D. there had been no attempt to compete with the several hundred varieties of biscuit offered by Huntley & Palmer, but now his sons were sure that future prosperity demanded this. They borrowed more money from the obliging Clydesdale Bank and started building an additional factory in 1890. The *Carlisle Journal* announced excitedly in February that 'extensive additions are about to be made to one of the most important of our local industries. Messrs. Carr & Co., having found their biscuit works totally inadequate to carry out existing orders . . . have decided to build a new biscuit manufactory . . . a large block, four storeys high, covering 15,400 sq. ft.'

This was a far more ambitious scheme than any their father had contemplated. People came from all over the city to watch the new building go up and, when it was finally completed, there were gasps of astonishment because the whole place was lit by electricity. This showed, on the one hand, that indeed they did not fully understand the turbulent British economy, unlike their father, who had distrusted it; but, on the other, that they had in them more boldness than had yet been apparent.

They did not want simply to mark time. They were prepared, now that they were in charge, to make major decisions and show themselves equal to the challenge of inheriting the family firm. They wanted to show what they could do. They also wanted to be modern and move with the times. Lighting the new factory with electricity was an example of this: at the time it was still unusual for large buildings to be converted to electricity (which had only been introduced in Britain in 1875). The smell of gas, lingering throughout the old buildings, which were lit by gas jets, had always been disliked (and the jets feared by those who had to light them, because it was such a fiddly business). Electricity was clean, smell-free and involved no labour – the joy of simply pressing a switch was a daily delight. The dynamo that produced the electricity was powerful enough to supply 350 lamps of 16 candle-power, as well as a 'sunbeam' lamp of 300 candle-power to floodlight the entrance to the new works. In a city still lit by gas (the Electric Lighting Station was not built until 1898), Carr's works were now a showplace.

No expense had been spared, a fact appreciated by the workers who reaped the benefits. The new packing and forwarding rooms were opened in 1892 and those who worked there commented without even considering the electricity, 'It was like changing from darkness into light.' There was a tea-party to celebrate, given by the Carrs for all the employees – a knife-and-fork 'do' for those over eighteen, while those under eighteen got cake and biscuits in a paper bag. The new dining premises, now in Morton Street across the road from the factory, had two halls, one just for women, where there were cloths and flowers on tables for four, and one for mixed company, where there were long, bare tables. The fact that there was now a special dining-hall for women, and that it was the largest and by far the most pleasant,

showed not only a desire on the part of the new management to please and show concern for the female work
force, but also how their numbers had grown.

The entry of women in the nineteenth century into
the genteel labour force, for example as teachers, caused
little controversy, and the resistance to their working in
shops had given way without too much struggle, but
the appearance of women as factory workers was heavily
resisted. The Victorian doctrine of 'separate spheres'
meant that manufactories were seen as definitely a male
sphere. They were simply not suitable for women and
in any case men needed the work more, especially in
the nineteenth century when they had large families to
support. It was the explosive growth of the textile
industry that first brought women into this kind of
labour – young, single women, that is. This prepared
the way for the acceptance of women in other manufactories, but it was still unusual in the 1850s when Carr's
began to employ a few for specialised work thought
appropriate for women (such as icing the biscuits). At
least in Carr's factory there was no worry that the female
worker would be the victim of unscrupulous foremen,
since it was a well-regulated place and still heavily under
J.D.'s own Quaker influence. Once employed, the
numbers of women grew every year, until by the time
Henry took over slightly more than half the work force
(which now numbered just under 2,000) comprised
women. All of them were single or widows – married
women were still barred.

There was also a garden for the workers to walk in
during their dinner hour, half an acre of ground
adjoining the new dining-halls, which had been laid out
and planted with shrubs and trees, 'a veritable oasis in
the midst of bricks and mortar', as the *Carlisle Journal*
admiringly reported. Even the factory cats were well
looked after, all fourteen of them. The storeman saw

that Blossom (of the chocolate department), Darkie (of the cream room) and all the others got their three quarts of milk each day. The traditions established by J.D. were certainly being maintained, but at a cost he would not, at that juncture, have sanctioned. More workers had been taken on and many more varieties of biscuit were being produced. Henry and James were not worried, but the bank was concerned enough to say that if the loans could not begin to be paid off soon then drastic action would be demanded. The Carr brothers had been advanced money on the reputation of a firm, and a father, understood to be rock-solid. Henry and James might be of irreproachable character, but they had overreached themselves and must pay the penalty.

This penalty was that they should sacrifice total independence by becoming a limited company. There were several meetings between the brothers – all four of them, George coming up from Silloth – and the Clydesdale Bank officials, at which some basic facts of financial life were spelled out. It was explained how becoming a limited company would be the answer to all their problems, as it had already proved to be for so many small family firms. The conversion from family companies into limited companies had been going on since 1856, when the Joint Stock Companies Act was passed, but J.D. had never been tempted, or obliged, to follow suit. The point of becoming such a limited company was, of course, that it limited liability, but the drawback to men like J.D. and others of his generation was that doing so effectively divorced ownership from management. As far as J.D. had been concerned, to own *was* to manage, to possess was to undertake complete responsibility. If Carr's became a limited company, power would then begin to pass to shareholders more concerned with dividends than anything else and, once that happened, patriarchalism of J.D.'s type would be defunct. But

Henry and James had very little choice. They had to take the bank's advice. They were not happy about agreeing to become a limited company, realising perfectly well that there was an element of betrayal of their father's wishes in so doing, but they soon got over their uneasiness. After all, times had changed, and everyone was doing it.

Unexpected opposition came from George, which was particularly irritating for them, considering that he had never had anything to do with the business. He came from Silloth with his elder son Fred and was very determined about certain concessions and alterations that he wanted made before he would sign the necessary papers. What these were is not recorded, but Fred wrote to his fiancée that his father had shown 'a most uncompromising front of no surrender . . . we managed to carry the vital alterations . . . it will be a great advantage to us as it will obviate the probable necessity and danger of an arbitration . . . it has taken us just about two years to get our rights recognised, though there are still some considerable faults . . . I am thankful the fight is now over.'

Any kind of fight was something J.D. had hoped to avoid, but then he had not anticipated either how relationships between his sons might change under financial pressure, or how existing personal antagonisms might in any case lead to difficulties. Henry and James formed a united front, which easily dominated Thomas, who had already suffered from their displeasure, but George was a different matter. He had always been strong and independent and he could not be browbeaten. Thomas, made so unjustly to feel inferior, could be depended upon to sign anything within reason, but George, cleverer than either Henry or James, could not. Whatever it was that he got out of those 'alterations', he soon left Silloth and moved to Wolverhampton, where he bought the estate of Aldersley. The harmony that J.D. had seen as essential to his firm's prosperity had been broken. George, though never an active participant, had entirely opted out.

This left the other three brothers heading what was now Carr & Co. Ltd. The first board meeting of the newly named company took place on 7 March 1894, almost exactly ten years after J.D.'s death. Henry took the chair, with James and Thomas as the other directors. They were all in sombre mood, uncomfortably aware that their father had never held such things as board meetings. He had decided everything on his own, controlling every minor detail of how Carr's was run. Henry's first task was to choose a room in the offices on the Viaduct to be the boardroom. He chose the room on the first floor at the front, a natural enough choice since it was the largest and was in fact his own office, easily adapted to accommodate a meeting of the other directors. Henry had spent some money on his office, so it was by no means merely functional and was quite imposing enough to be a boardroom. He had one oak table there already, but had another larger one brought in, with an inlaid leather top, big enough for eight people to sit round. The straight-backed oak chairs that matched it also had leather seats, and there were two more comfortable armchairs near the windows, which now made the room just a little crowded. The carpet, an expensive Axminster, was dark green with a pattern round its border; the curtains were made of good-quality plush and were also green. The windows were large, but nevertheless the room was rather dark. Not much sun came into it, partly because the tall buildings opposite cast long shadows, and partly because Henry very often had the Holland roller blinds pulled halfway down. He kept the windows tightly shut, sunny weather or not, because the noise of trains pulling in and out of the Citadel Station and passing under the Viaduct was loud and constant. Even more irritating were the coal smuts from the trains, which made it hard to keep these windows clean. Henry saw that they were washed every week, but that was hardly enough to keep the glass shining. The pigeons annoyed him too – not their cooing but their droppings, which smeared the window-sills and could quickly become encrusted. Henry was sensitive to noise, but it is doubtful if anyone else noticed either the trains or the pigeons. They were more likely to be aware of the chimes ringing out on the hour from the mahogany-cased clock, which had come from Coledale Hall and which they all remembered from their childhood teas there.

The three Carrs – James, Thomas and Henry – had met often enough before in this room, but it seemed different now that it was graced with the title of boardroom. Henry, overcoming any hesitation, reported that Mr Bremner, manager of the Clydesdale Bank, had granted them further credit of £70,000. The capital of the new company was £253,000, divided into two different sorts of shares. Of these the ordinary shares (1,530 of them) were divided between all four brothers, but with George getting fewer because he had had the farm (given outright in lieu of more shares). The other shares went to 200 members of the public, and there was a rush to apply for them the moment they were available. The first annual general meeting saw a Board of Directors consisting not just of the Carr brothers but also of four of their sons – Theodore and Bertram (Thomas's sons) and Laurence and Frank (Henry's sons). As far as the chairman, Henry, was concerned, the crisis was over and everything now sorted out satisfactorily. Their overdraft with the bank was reduced by the sale of shares to the public and all that was necessary was for the wonderful new factory and the new Silloth mill to start making the expected profits.

Henry and James were now in excellent spirits. Henry felt he had shown true leadership and was properly in charge, while James was happy not just because all the worry about forming the new company was over, but for personal reasons. His wife, the invalid Elizabeth, had died in 1883 and he had remarried. His new wife, Margaret (known as Maud) Mitchell of Elgin, had just borne him a son, Ronald. He had been a widower for nine years, just as Thomas had been for seven, and, as with Thomas, his wife was half his age – only twenty-six to James's fifty-four. But there was none of the moral outrage that greeted Thomas's marriage to Mary Laurie, confirming that it had been snobbery alone which had caused the family reaction to Thomas's match. Maud Mitchell was of impeccable social standing and was absorbed into the Carr family without difficulty. The birth of Ronald did indeed cause some astounded comment within the family, but once the shock was over everyone was very glad. It evened things up. James now had a vested personal interest in the future of the firm, too. It had been hard for him, witnessing all his brothers spawn big families, and being the only one not blessed. Maud had no more children, but James was content at least to have one son.

It was obvious to any dispassionate observer, however, just as it had been to J.D., that there was one grandson who showed himself the most able of the next generation: Theodore, Thomas's eldest, who was eighteen when his grandfather died, and twenty-eight when Carr & Co. Ltd was formed. Theodore had been committed to the family firm from the moment J.D. had first taken him by the hand round the factory and explained how all the machines, which so fascinated him, worked. Even before that, he had realised what being a Carr meant. When he was in bed, recovering from measles at the age of five, his nurse had given him some of the labels, which were at that time routinely stuck on biscuit tins, to cut out in order to amuse him. There were eight different colours, starting with red for types of biscuits beginning with A or B, and as he cut them out Theodore concluded that the word 'Carr's' was synonymous with 'biscuit' and that nobody but his grandfather made them.

He loved the biscuit works; the excitement of going round them never wore off and it became his playground. When any of his toys broke and he could not mend them (though he always tried to and often succeeded), he would run to Charlie Wild in the tin shop. And Charlie would not only put right whatever was wrong, he would explain what he was doing so that the next time Theodore could do the mending himself. Even at this level, Charlie saw, just as J.D. had done, that the boy had a natural aptitude for all things mechanical. The joiner's shop was another favourite haunt of Theodore's, because here he could persuade John Forsyth to give him some long wooden bars to make tracks for his model railway set. But the place that drew him most was the fitting shop, which housed one of the first gas engines invented, and its workings completely fascinated him. It was unfortunate that it was Mr Mac-Gregor in charge there, who did not share John Forsyth's and Charlie Wild's patience with small children. Nor was he in the least inclined to welcome Theodore just because he was a Carr – out he went, once discovered, every time.

Living as he did so close to the biscuit works, Theodore was never away, once he was old enough to cross Newtown Road and make the ten-minute walk down past the infirmary and into Caldewgate himself. On weekends and holidays when he was at home from school he haunted the place and became utterly familiar with its geography. He ran about freely, sometimes with his brothers, sometimes with his cousins, but mostly alone. Like his grandfather before him, it was the power of the factory that gripped him. He had an intense interest in the mechanical, rather than the human, processes by which it operated. Workers remembered him alone of J.D.'s grandchildren standing mesmerised by some machine, watching it work, scrutinising each part he could see, as though indeed memorising it. When a machine broke down Theodore did not get bored and move away, the spell now broken. On the contrary, he became even more absorbed and got in everyone's way trying to follow how it was put together again. No Carr, not even J.D. himself, had ever accumulated such mechanical knowledge so young, and Theodore's education had encouraged rather than stifled this passion.

He started off at Stramongate in Kendal, even though his family were no longer Quakers, but was then sent to the Old Hall School at Wellington in Shropshire. Carlisle's own very ancient Grammar School (mentioned as early as the twelfth century) was not considered for any of this generation of Carrs, any more than it had been for their fathers. The children no longer *had* to be sent to Quaker schools, but the schools now chosen for them were those middle-class schools where the sons of manufacturers were not looked down upon. None of them, as yet, went to the prestigious public schools (though in the next generation that leap was duly made). In choosing the Old Hall and rejecting Carlisle Grammar School, Thomas Carr was not unusual – the reputation of the grammar school still had not recovered from a period at the end of the previous century and into the early nineteenth, when it was so bad that there were fewer than fifty pupils. Later, by the time his younger sons were of an age, the grammar school had improved so much that it was considered safe to let them go there for a year or two. But, as with many former Quakers, the sending of children to minor public schools was part of a social transformation. It was going on all over the country. George and Samuel Palmer had gone to a Quaker school, but they sent their sons to minor public schools (and they, in turn, completed the transformation by sending theirs to Eton or Harrow).

The Old Hall was an odd but inspired choice of school for Theodore's father to have made. Founded in 1845, twenty-one years before Theodore was born, by Joseph Cranage, it was doing well by the 1870s. Cranage was a scientist who believed that education should be a joy. He was only eighteen when he opened his school with just five pupils, but by 1862 his reputation had flourished to such an extent that he was invited to be an Inspector of Schools, although he declined. He was happy teaching, laying great emphasis on his own subject but also believing in a broad-based curriculum that included Greek. He was a bit of an inventor himself and when Alexander Graham Bell invented the telephone in 1876 Cranage promptly installed one in his school, to Theodore's delight. (Theodore had made one himself at home, out of collar boxes, but this was the real thing.) Instead of letting sports monopolise the non-academic side of his teaching, Cranage preferred to focus on natural history and archaeology. His pupils got their fresh air and exercise through exploring the countryside. It was exactly the right school for Theodore, even more so than for his brothers Bertram and Ernest, who followed on in due course. When he left, Theodore did not go to Edinburgh University as his father had done (and as his two younger brothers, Sydney and John did, to read medicine) but to Owen's College, Manchester, where he took a degree in engineering. Owen's, opened in 1851, had at first, according to the *Manchester*

Guardian, been 'a mortifying failure' but in 1880, two years before Theodore went there, it was incorporated into the Victoria University of Manchester (intended to be part of a federal university of the North) and, with a new constitution and new buildings as well as new status, it rapidly improved.

By the time Theodore left Owen's and came home to Carlisle to go straight into the biscuit works, the year his grandfather died, he was better qualified than any Carr had ever been to be put in charge of the practical side of production. Nobody else in the family, in any generation, could touch him for expertise – certainly not his Uncle Henry – and he had, besides, retained his extraordinary enthusiasm. There was no need for any discussion about whether he wanted to go into the business, for his keenness was apparent to all. The only thing he found tedious was having to start off in the forwarding department, as all those destined for managerial positions (that is, all Carrs) had to do. Clerking was not to the practical Theodore's liking. He spent every day, all day, laboriously copying out orders into enormously heavy leather-bound books in a building across the railway from the factory, a place not nearly as congenial to him as the factory itself.

From the forwarding department Theodore went on, with some relief, to the packing room, where he was supervised by Mr Picton, who was very particular. This was no more to his liking but had to be endured, until at last he was moved into the factory itself and came under the general manager, William Tremble. Mr Tremble was, according to Theodore, 'hard as nails' and did indeed make even a Carr tremble. But Theodore was happy to be near the machines and enjoyed his time moving between the various sections of the factory in which they operated, feeling confident from the first. It seemed to him that he really was treated like any other employee, starting at 6 a.m., just as all the workers now did, and finishing at 6 p.m., clocking up a total of fifty-five and a half hours a week. There was only one gate for everyone to come and go by and Theodore's punctuality was checked, just as every other worker's was, by old Patrick Reed, the ex-army gateman who had served in India during the mutiny (and wore his medals on occasion to prove it).

Theodore settled in well, followed by his brother Bertram two years later. Bertram, too, appeared happy enough automatically to go into the business, but he was a more restless soul than his older brother. There was not much scope at first for his wanderlust, but his flair for languages suggested that he might be useful later in dealings abroad, and so would his charm. He loved clothes and dressed smartly, and was good-looking and better with people than Theodore, who, as he grew older and began to be given some real responsibility, could be rather tough and abrupt in the exercising of command. But both of Thomas's older sons were well liked and highly thought of, and Henry was obliged to recognise this. His own two surviving sons, though clever and dutiful enough, had nothing like Theodore's and Bertram's involvement in the business. Laurence, five years younger than Theodore, wanted to be a doctor. His cousins Sydney and John were allowed to become doctors by their father, Thomas, and so excused from entering the business, but Henry was having none of this. He had only two surviving sons, after all, and he wanted them to succeed him, so both Laurence and Frank, who fortunately showed no such undermining ambitions, had to go into the biscuit works at eighteen and work their way through all the departments, just as Theodore and Bertram had done.

Nevertheless, by the mid-1890s, Henry had accepted that Theodore was likely to become the chairman of the new company in the next generation. He was fully confident that when the time came he would be handing over a thriving business and that the problems he had inherited would have been dealt with. This optimism, as Henry ought to have known, was not really justified. Very few other manufacturers were feeling it after another volatile decade of trading conditions. Indeed, so worried were the successive governments of both the Liberal Gladstone and the Conservative Lord Salisbury that a Royal Commission on the Depression of Trade and Industry was set up in 1886 to investigate the economic situation. It came to the unsurprising conclusion that there was indeed a depression in progress, defining it as 'a diminution . . . of profit'. It recommended a cheapening of the cost of production, so far as was consistent with maintaining quality, and greater activity in the search for new markets. No mention of this report appears in any minutes of Carr & Co. Ltd's board meetings and it gave rise to no recorded discussion as to how Carr's might follow its recommendations. But then Henry may have thought he was already doing so: from his point of view, the family firm was surviving the depressed conditions well, and before he retired he expected it to do even better, after all the investment he had made in new buildings and equipment.

But retirement, he trusted, was a long way off. He was not yet quite sixty and his father had been active and vigorous right up to his death at the grand age of seventy-seven. However, Henry's faith that he had a long life still ahead of him was badly shaken in 1895, when his brother Thomas died suddenly, aged only fifty-five. Thomas had not been well for some months, but since Henry and James saw little of him – socially, the rift caused by his second marriage was still apparent – they had not appreciated that his indisposition was a symptom of heart trouble. He had a heart attack on his way home from town, where he had gone to record his vote in the election. He was in a carriage, with his wife Mary and one of his daughters, when he was taken ill on Caldew Bridge, only a few hundred yards from the biscuit works. The carriage stopped and some passers-by carried Thomas into the nearest building, which happened to be a public house in Milbourne Street – a very embarrassing place for a teetotal Carr to die.

Henry and James were shocked, but when the shock wore off they were also exasperated. Their brother's widow, Mary, had been left the shares in Carr & Co. Ltd held by her husband. She was still only thirty-two, and had two daughters of her own, aged seven and four, in her charge as well as her fourteen-year-old step-children, Harold and Hilda. It was natural enough that she should inherit Thomas's shares but it was also awkward. Mary now had 374 of the ordinary shares, a significant holding. It had been easy enough dealing with Thomas, who had never tried to exert any power within the business, but they feared Mary might prove trickier (though they had no grounds for believing this). The truth was that they did not know Mary and were embarrassed to realise there would have to be some regular direct communication with her. For Theodore and his brothers (the three of them already in the business) there was also some sense of dismay, as well as great grief. They had been left, during Mary's lifetime, hardly any shares of their own and yet two of them were on the board of the company. Ernest did not mind so much (he already had other plans, though he, too, had started off in Carr's) but Bertram and especially Theodore could hardly believe they each still held only fifteen of the vital ordinary shares. Mary also inherited Newtown House and all Thomas's goods and chattels, but that did not concern them, since they had been living comfortably in Coledale Hall ever since their father's marriage to her. Their grandmother Jane was dead by the time of Thomas's death (she had died in 1891) but their spinster aunt, Lizzie, was very happy to go on housing them.

George, whom Thomas had appointed as his executor, obviously worried about the fairness of the will. It could hardly be contested, nor was it right that it should be, since Mary needed the income (her only income) from her shares to bring up her daughters and maintain a home for them and the twins. But he could understand how difficult the lack of bargaining power was for Theodore and Bertram on the board. It was no good consoling them with the reminder that, on Mary's own death, her shares would be divided among all Thomas's children. She was young, after all. So George acted like the good Quaker he still was and divided his own remaining shares between his nephews. Theodore and Bertram each got forty-four, which, together with the fifteen they already held, improved their position (and their incomes) considerably.

The increased income was especially appreciated by Theodore, who in 1893 had married Edith Hobbs, daughter of a colonel who was Paymaster at Carlisle Castle. Their first child, Dorothy, was born a year later. Theodore could not afford to live in Stanwix, as his uncles Henry and James did, but with his finances a little more healthy he was able to buy a pleasant property in Dalston, a village five miles to the west of Carlisle, taking his Aunt Lizzie with him. Coledale Hall had only ever been rented and now that Lizzie would have been alone there it was wasteful to keep it on.

The Dalston house, Sunnycroft, had an orchard and a big garden, and was altogether an ideal family house. There were plenty of trees for children to play on – crab apple, nut, copper beech – and a big vegetable patch. The River Caldew, that same river which made its way into Caldewgate, ran along the bottom of the grounds. Theodore turned a small cottage near the river into a reading-room for the working men in the village and here he occasionally gave hugely popular magic-lantern shows. The house was only ten minutes from the railway station, on the Maryport–Carlisle line, and it was highly convenient for Theodore to get to work, though he preferred to drive. Everyone, both in his family and at the biscuit works, knew what a genius Theodore was with machines, but he excelled himself by building, in 1896, the first car ever seen in Carlisle. He got Mr Fendley, who had a bicycle shop in Mary Street, to make the wheels and axle, then he put these together himself with an engine (of the combined inverted type, with cylinders $1\frac{1}{2}$ and $2\frac{1}{2}$ inches in diameter and 3 inches stroke) and a boiler made by Leyland and Co. It was a very odd-looking contraption, with the carriage part mounted on the specially strong wheels – only three: one at the back and two at the front, all with pneumatic tyres – but it worked. The fuel was ordinary petroleum (the running-cost was less than a halfpenny a mile), which was burned under air pressure, generating clouds of terrifying steam. Observers expected it to blow up any minute but it didn't, though if it cornered at more than 5 m.p.h. it tended to tip to one side and throw out the passenger. The roads around Dalston were not yet all surfaced with tarmacadam, and many smaller roads had a good portion of manure mixed in with the surface soil and stones, so that being tipped out could be very unpleasant indeed. Theodore, as the driver, usually escaped this fate.

He decided to test his car on a long run to prove its reliability and took his youngest brother, Harold, and his doctor brother, John, on a tour of Scotland in September. The car created a sensation as it puttered along at 8 m.p.h. Told even before they had left Carlisle that a man should be walking in front of this dangerous contraption with a red flag (though in fact the law had just been changed and this was no longer required), Theodore offered the job to anyone who objected, but his offer was not taken up. They did not get far on the first day. The car came to a stop just before the Metal Bridge (which crosses the River Esk, on the border with Scotland) and though Theodore was able to repair it – in fact, he rather enjoyed any mending that had to be done – it was nearly dark by the time Ecclefechan was reached, so they stayed the night there. Next day, when Beattock had to be tackled, came the real challenge. Would the car cope with the long, very steep gradient? It did, though Harold and John had to do a good deal of walking. Driving down the other side was easy and they reached the car's maximum speed so far (a grand 10 m.p.h.). They spent a night at Abington and the next morning there was a delay of another sort: all the people in the hotel where the Carrs had slept were gathered round their vehicle, and there were so many questions to answer that Theodore virtually delivered a lecture lasting an hour, explaining exactly how the car had been made and how it performed.

They reached the Braids Hill Hotel in Edinburgh that same day but not until ten o'clock at night, by which time it had been dark for nearly three hours and it was nerve-racking, even for Theodore, to have the road lit only by the bicycle lamp perched on the front of the car. But they got there safely, feeling triumphant to have negotiated their entry into such a big city. Elation evaporated the next morning, however, when they had a crash, straight into a street lamp, which smashed and scattered glass everywhere. The car fell over onto its side and all three men were flung out into the road. None of them was hurt, and as usual Theodore was not in the least put out and treated the whole thing as a joke. It was not so funny when he discovered the damage done to the car – the rooftop condenser was bashed in and the front dented, though luckily the boiler was intact. A crowd had gathered and under Theodore's direction some of them were only too willing to help right the car and push it to a blacksmith's. Some quick work with a hammer patched the car up, though it now looked much less impressive and far less roadworthy. But Theodore would not be put off. He made Harold and John help him push the car on to a coach-builder, who could improve on the blacksmith's efforts – a humiliating journey, with tram-car drivers and cabmen (of horse-drawn carriages) yelling out facetious comments and roaring with laughter. The Edinburgh police piled the indignity on by suddenly catching up with the car and claiming compensation for the broken street lamp. All very well to be pioneers, and admired, but being jeered at strained even Theodore's enthusiasm.

The coach-builder did a good job, however, and spirits picked up again during a beautiful and uneventful drive to Queensferry, Kinross, through Glen Farg, Dunkeld and Pitlochry. From Pitlochry onwards no mechanically operated carriage of any kind had ever been seen and there was great excitement in the villages through which they passed. But there was also a good deal of consternation and even fear – horses were terrified both on the road and in the fields, and unfortunately lots of chickens, used to roaming freely, were run over. They stayed in Kingussie on the Sunday, doing no driving at all out of respect for the Sabbath, and relished the fact that they had only their own bills to pay without the extra charge for stabling a horse. After Kingussie, the roads became rougher. Theodore checked his tyres repeatedly, but though the rubber was slightly cut by the sharp stones they were passing over, there were, miraculously, no punctures. Coasting into Inverness, a steep downhill ride, the primitive braking system was rigorously tested, and proved adequate. The people of Inverness were as amazed by the car as the inhabitants of Edinburgh had been. The same sort of crowds gathered, and Theodore, though he loved talking about his invention, was glad to get the vehicle stowed away in the back yard of the Victoria Hotel. He wanted some peace and quiet to check the car over, but decided to wait until he reached Beauly – the planned terminus of the journey – before doing a complete overhaul.

By the time it reached Beauly, the car had been driven 300 miles, so it was not surprising that various nuts and bolts needed to be tightened and certain parts of the engine adjusted. The ride back took the scenic route, along the shores of the Beauly and Moray Firths, and it was on this stretch that the three brothers felt utterly relaxed and at ease. This, they agreed, was the life, bowling smoothly along without physical effort, no business worries and with time to look at the beautiful views. The fact that the noise the car made shattered the peace of the countryside failed to trouble them. At Grantown, feeling magnanimous, Theodore graciously treated some of the inhabitants to joy-rides before moving on to Kingussie again. They anticipated no problems between Kingussie and the next intended stop, Amulree, but the road had been badly affected by rain and there were deep ruts in it. All three Carrs were obliged, at times, to get out and push the car, but the fatigue of this was made up for by the ease with which they were able to drive from Amulree to Crieff and eventually, by way of Ardoch, to Dunblane and Stirling. John and Harold parted company with Theodore after that at Airdrie and went home by train, though not because they were tired of driving: they both had reasons for needing to be back before the time Theodore estimated the car would reach Carlisle.

Once on his own, Theodore was able to indulge his taste for speed, especially on the stretch between Lanark and Carlisle where he knew the road. He did the seventy-five miles in less than nine hours, but was travelling as fast as the car could go, nudging 14 m.p.h some of the time. It had been a terrific adventure and he felt he had more than proved the worth of his car. The future belonged to motoring and he was right there at the outset. This was absolutely true on both counts: it was only ten years since Gottlieb Daimler had put the first light-engined motor-car on the road, so Theodore was truly one of the first to build and drive his own car, and nobody could doubt, after the first London–Brighton trip in 1896, when fifty-four cars took part, that horse-drawn carriages were on their way out (though at a lecture, given the year Theodore made his marathon drive, there was loud laughter when the lecturer said that he hoped to see the horse abolished and found only in hunting fields and parks). There had not been a single puncture on the whole trip and, driving back into Carlisle, Theodore was triumphant – but eager to build a better car. That first one had only three wheels, but he promptly built a four-wheeler, which was more stable and comfortable. Cars and motor-bikes continued to be his great love and the countryside round quiet Dalston echoed to his noisy experiments, frightening cows and horses and making him as unpopular with local farmers as he had been with Scottish ones on his first trip.

But Theodore's prodigious energies went not only into his cars, but into the biscuit works. Just like his grandfather, he was always looking for ways in which new mechanical developments could be adapted to improve the production of biscuits. And, because he was primarily an engineer, he was able to incorporate his own ideas into existing ones. He took someone else's invention for an icing machine, added some refinements of his own, and produced what became known as the Baker-Carr machine, which iced biscuits in one-tenth of the time it had taken human hands to do it. Then he invented a biscuit to appeal to more sophisticated tastes, the delicious Café Noir, to demonstrate how well his machine worked. An oblong, thin plain biscuit, iced with coffee-flavoured icing, the Café Noir proved a tremendous success when it was launched in 1891.

Even quite apart from machines, Theodore was inventive. It was he who improved upon the Captain's Thin, that standard of all the biscuit firms from the beginning (and developed of course from the original ship's biscuit). What he did was to experiment with the thickness of this popular biscuit, trying to make it thinner and crisper, until it would seem almost like a new variety. In 1890 he succeeded in turning out what became known as the Table Water biscuit – the Captain's Thin, reduced to one-third of its normal thickness and almost twice the size (though later a smaller version was also produced). It had a delicate texture and was paler in colour (because it was not baked for so long). It seemed far more elegant (if that word can be used for a biscuit) than the existing variety, and was sold for sevenpence a pound.

Carr's employees noticed Theodore's flair and were impressed by it. He was the Carr who was forever in the factory, very hands-on, very familiar with the way in which everything worked – even more so than his grandfather, who was still remembered by the older workers. But Theodore's time had not yet come. It was Mr Henry who was still in charge, and he kept his bright young nephews and his own sons away from the decision-making, just as his father had shut him out. The Directors' Minutes Book for the first ten years of Carr & Co. Ltd gives the impression that everything was ticking over nicely again, now that the upheaval of the bank forcing them into becoming a limited company was behind them. Sometimes Henry took the chair, sometimes James, but meetings were perfunctory. Henry could be high-handed with the younger generation, although not so much with Theodore and Bertram as with Ernest, whom he tended to treat as an office boy, and he could be unexpectedly tough if he felt it was required of him.

In August 1896 he certainly felt a firm hand was needed when, to his astonishment and alarm, there was the first ever threat of a strike in the biscuit works. Henry should not have been quite so surprised at the threat. The labour situation was now very different from the way it had been in his father's time: throughout the manufacturing industries the relationship between employer and employee was being called into question. The slump that had begun in 1873 and had continued off and on for twenty years had changed everything. Unskilled workers, upon whom factories were dependent, had learned that in a slump they were the first to suffer; and out of this growing realisation came the formation of the new trade unions. Up to the time when Henry took over at Carr's, the Amalgamated Societies (sanctioned by Acts of 1871 and 1875) had tried to protect their members by negotiating with employers. In good firms like Carr's, this kind of negotiation was fairly successful, and indeed negotiation had existed there, if of limited scope, ever since J.D. had initiated regular meetings with his foremen. But in those days there were far fewer employees – everyone knew everyone else – and the employees had not appreciated their own power. The new unions had little faith in negotiation alone. Their long-term policy was to obtain better working hours, wages and conditions of employment that were agreed to and enshrined in law for the whole work force. Negotiation would never bring the concessions that the unions wanted from the employers, whereas the threat of a strike, of a complete stoppage in production, could do so.

Seven years before this little incident at Carr's, effective action by the new unions had already taken place. The Gas Workers' & General Labourers' Union, one of the first to be formed, won an eight-hour day in 1889 for its members, without actually calling a strike. They merely threatened to call one and that was enough. The dockers followed their example the same year, and when they did not enjoy the same success, went ahead and fulfilled their threat. The dock strike that followed alerted the whole country to what was happening and what could happen in the future. It took place in London and affected the food and other vital supplies of the capital. What was even more alarming was the way in which public opinion was in their favour – subscriptions collected to help the strikers reached £49,000. The dockers were eventually successful and almost all their demands were met. The stimulus this gave to the formation of other unions and action by them was immense. In 1888 the number of trade union members was 750,000; by the time Henry had to deal with the first murmur of strike action at Carr's, it had grown to 1,500,000.

The Carlisle newspapers as well as the national ones had reported all this strike activity, but clearly Henry thought Carr's exempt. He, and in fact everyone else involved, except for the strikers, found it unbelievable. This was Carr's, the family firm, where such things did not happen. Why would they? What could possibly cause discontent when the employees had always been looked after so well, and listened to at meetings with their foremen? It was a wholly impertinent idea and Henry was outraged. Told that four apprentices had dared to present the formidable Mr Tremble, the works manager, with a note saying they would strike if those among their number who had just been 'let go' were not reinstated, Henry, quite frankly, could not believe it. The fact that there was a case to answer – it was true that, upon serving their time, some young men had indeed been paid off and it was also true that others of their age and status had nevertheless been hired – was beside the point. Henry had, he believed, the right to hire and fire as he wished and it was no good these four trouble-makers saying it was not fair to let apprentices go the minute they were fully qualified and entitled to a full wage. They complained that his action meant that none of them had security of employment any more. Of course they did not, no apprentice ever could have; what were they thinking of?

So Henry did not hesitate. He had the four ringleaders taken before the magistrates at the Town Hall. They were fined ten shillings each, on the grounds that their note had declared their intention to leave their jobs without giving notice, as their indentures made them bound to. Since their weekly wage was twelve shillings, Henry was judged magnanimous when he graciously agreed to accept one shilling only from each of them for damages (though no damage had taken place). There was no further trouble and Henry did not even see this incident as particularly significant for the future. But Theodore did. He worked with the men, which Henry did not, and was aware of the resentment among the apprentices, who feared their apprenticeship was worth nothing if at the end of it they were not assured of prospects. Carr's had always been fair: there had been that famous saying since the 1840s that if you were once in their employment and behaved yourself, you could be there for life. Now it appeared you might not be. You could be paid off because overnight you became too expensive and others were cheaper. There was a good deal of muttering, and Theodore, hearing it, though nothing was said directly to him (much too dangerous, he was a Carr), had the first seeds planted in his mind that there ought to be a more efficient system of airing and hearing grievances. It was not enough merely to depend on foremen to report them in weekly meetings with the management.

There was nothing, at that stage, that he could do about it. Henry was happy for Theodore to put into operation new methods for packing tins into crates (he made it into a hydraulic process and did away with the use of the big black horse called Bob, which had shunted them), but he kept all details of the running of the business to himself, confiding only in James. Theodore, Bertram, Frank and Lawrence were all on the Board of Directors but none of them knew what was actually going on overall. Perhaps Henry, so heavily involved in his religious activities, did not know, either. It seemed to come as a shock to him to discover towards the end of 1897 that baking bread was no longer profitable. Bread might be the most basic of foodstuffs, which it had pleased his father to make cheaply and well, but there were not now the returns on bread that there were on biscuits. Bread production would have to go, he decided, and with it the retail shops which had sold Carr's bread right from their very beginnings in 1831. At a special meeting of the shareholders of the company, Henry told them, 'It is desirable to discontinue and sell and dispose of the retail bread business now carried on by the company and also to discontinue the manufacture of bread.' There were no objections from the shareholders – no one stood up to plead the case for continuing to bake bread as a service, as part of a long tradition.

The subsequent 'disposal' of the shops and the bread

business brought Henry and James into a revealing dispute with one of their nephews, but it was not with the strongly placed Theodore. Instead, his younger brother Ernest stepped forward to say that he thought he could find a buyer for that part of the business. If his uncles were agreeable, he would act as middleman, although of course he would require a commission for his helpful services. Henry and James were furious that any Carr should want to be paid for this, and they were also suspicious. Theodore and Bertram had integrated themselves very well into the business, but Ernest showed less dedication and was known to aspire to start a business of his own that had nothing to do with biscuits. He was cheerful (some said cocky) and not in the least in awe of Henry. Ernest had some spirit and he was clever; he refused to be browbeaten. The uncles demanded to know for whom Ernest was acting as agent, but their nephew would only refer to 'an undisclosed principal' who was willing to pay £22,500 to take over the bread side of Carr's and another £3,500 for one of the shops. For this Ernest would require a $1\frac{1}{2}$ per cent commission on the whole deal. His uncles, anxious to get the whole thing over, grudgingly agreed, but said that the lowest figure they would accept was £30,000 and that did not include any of the shops. The deal concluded with Mr Jackson Saint buying the bread business (including the four shops) for £44,000. He was given the right to use the name Carr for twenty-one years.

It looked like a satisfactory deal from everyone's point of view, but Henry and James had heard it rumoured that young Ernest, as well as acting as middleman for the new company, was also going to work for them, so they sent a letter to Mr Jackson Saint, stating, 'We must stipulate that . . . no person of the name Carr having any interest in *our* company should appear in any prospectus, or become an official, or hold office as Director, Manager, or Traveller, or other officer in *your* proposed company.' The letter was actually signed by Theodore on behalf of the company – an unbrotherly touch, suggesting (wrongly, as it turned out) a possible rift between this generation of brothers, just as there had been in their father's generation, with significant consequences for the running of the business. Mr Saint accepted the terms and Ernest was excluded from the new bread company. He was not in the least put out. All he wanted was his $1\frac{1}{2}$ per cent commission, then he would take himself off, using the lump sum to set himself up.

He wrote a jaunty but perfectly polite letter to Henry, pointing out what a good deal he had secured for them and asking for his commission. Henry refused to pay it, taking the moral high ground by declaring that Ernest could not expect 'to act at the same time as broker and buyer and receive commission from both parties'. Carrs did not do that. They were, above all else, honourable men. James felt it should be explained to Ernest, face to face, exactly what being honourable meant and summoned him to his house.

It was fortunate that Ernest had such natural confidence and that he was impossible to intimidate, because Cavendish Mount, where James lived, might have been designed to overawe. The drawing-room where the confrontation took place was vast and gloomy, with an enormous sideboard occupying the whole of one wall and a black horsehair sofa most of another, with a huge harmonium, decorated with fretwork texts, standing opposite the window. James, believing as he did that every word in the Bible was true, had made sure that as many of them as possible adorned the house – texts were everywhere on the walls, and over the harmonium was one gigantic HALLELUJAH! embroidered in white on a blue background. Any young man (Ernest was not yet thirty) would have felt at a disadvantage in such a setting, faced with an uncle of such passionate religious conviction. James never allowed alcohol or tobacco in his house (though, curiously, rum butter, a local speciality, was allowed on picnics) and his domestic life bristled with restrictions. To James, the whole world was evil and it was his duty to try to reform it.

But as far as Ernest was concerned, he had nothing of which to be ashamed. He maintained that if he had gone on, as he had indeed planned, to work for Mr Saint's new bread company, he would not have claimed any commission on brokering the deal, but the fact was that he had been prevented from doing so and therefore thought it justifiable to claim his commission. Nothing James could say changed his opinion that he was being unfairly treated. But the uncles were adamant – no commission – and so, with a final letter of protest, Ernest took himself off to start his own tea and coffee business. He was going to shift for himself, just as his grandfather had done, and indeed showed something of the same entrepreneurial spirit. He soon moved eleven miles away from Carlisle, to Wigton, where he bought a jam factory with an adjoining piece of land, upon which he built a lovely house for himself and his new wife, Louisa Ashby. There was no break with his own brothers, though his subsequent relationship with his uncles was never again cordial. He continued to visit his brothers often, and Theodore and Bertram, both still under Henry's thumb, rather admired him.

Yet this mild altercation had revealed the dangers inherent in a family firm: everything was fine while the family agreed and while there was one capable and inspiring leader under whom the rest were willing to serve. Splits within the family had never been envisaged by J.D. – that would have been heresy – but in the argument with Ernest there were indications of what could happen in future. It was essential now to close ranks and ensure that solidarity was maintained. But, in fact, this very solidarity was being threatened in another way. Almost as soon as J.D. died, outsiders had been brought into the management of the business. Ernest Hutchinson came into the firm in 1885 from Gloucester (where he had been apprenticed as a printer). He was a devout Quaker, which was in his favour, even if the Carrs were no longer Friends. His department was clerical – buying, costing, looking after advertisements. Although not a Carr, he very quickly impressed with his dedication, and James and Henry sought his advice more and more frequently. That close little circle of family power was beginning, at the turn of the century, to weaken slightly, if almost imperceptibly. Already, in the sixteen years since J.D.'s death, Carr & Co. Ltd had become a very different firm from the one he had bequeathed.

The workers certainly noticed this difference. John Sanderson, whom J.D. had taken on as an apprentice, was shocked to be given notice by Henry as soon as the bread business was sold off. It was true that his speciality was as a baker of bread, trained by J.D. himself, but he also baked biscuits and had not expected the sack. His pride hurt more than his pocket: he had been loyal to Carr's for fifty years. He tried to find work baking bread elsewhere, but could not. For five weeks he was out of work. Then Henry heard about his failure to secure alternative employment and did what he doubt-less judged the decent thing – he sent for John and offered him work back at Carr's, as a labourer. His wages were naturally lower than before, when he had been a master baker, but it was the humiliation of labouring, rather than the loss of income, that made Sanderson low-spirited. He worked to support his family for a year or so, then one morning he didn't go into the factory. He got up, lit the gas fire, dressed, except for his boots and topcoat – and then he hanged himself. His GP, Dr Murphy, told the coroner that John Sanderson had become very depressed. A verdict of 'suicide during temporary insanity' was recorded. The death of one of their employees was not necessarily, or wholly, the fault of Carr's, but the fact that it proceeded from the sale of the bread business was significant. Carr's was a family firm, Carr's cared about its workers, but Carr's was also a business, and business interests must come first. It was a foolish worker who forgot that.

•
MACHINES, MILLS
AND MISSIONARIES

THE NEW century began peacefully in Carlisle as well as elsewhere in Britain. Queen Victoria was still on the throne, if old and very frail, and people had become used to the stability she represented. The only whisper of war to be heard in almost fifty years came from a long way off, in South Africa. In October 1899, the Boers had declared war against the British and the progress of events was being watched with some excitement, as well as anxiety, by the Carlisle newspapers. Carlisle might be a long way from the seat of action, but it was as jingoistic in attitude as much of the rest of the country. People wanted the Boers to be 'given a good thrashing' and what the Carlisle *Patriot* called 'our shameful capitulation at Majuba nineteen years ago' wiped out.

But the Carrs themselves were not jingoistic. J. D. Carr had been opposed to all militarism and, though his sons were not Quakers and did not have to adopt this pacific stance, their father's influence made them against war. They were worried about what was happening in South Africa though, for reasons that had nothing to do with pacifism. Their concern, as might be expected, was to do with the effects war might have on their particular trade. They had a healthy trade to South Africa (begun in 1896, in Cape Colony) at this time and most certainly did not want it interrupted. When the British Prime Minister, Lord Salisbury, rejected peace offers in March 1900 from Paul Kruger, the Boer leader, the Carrs were anxious, and remained so until May 1902 when the Boers were forced to surrender unconditionally. None of the Carrs were military men, none of them had gone off to fight, but they were as pleased and relieved as anyone when this war was over. But before it ended, Queen Victoria had died (in January 1901) and so, eleven months later, had James Carr. His was the first of three deaths in the family that greatly affected the family firm.

James died on 28 December 1901, his ninth wedding anniversary, of a heart attack, leaving a seven-year-old son, Ronald, and a young widow who inherited his shares. George was the next to go the following year and, though he had nothing to do with the business, his influence as Thomas's executor had been felt by his nephews, who still regarded him as someone to whom they could turn for advice and who would give it impartially. This left Henry in sole charge and well aware that, as his three younger brothers had all died of heart trouble, he, too, might succumb and share their dramatic end. Thomas had been just fifty-five, James sixty-three, George sixty-five, and he himself was by then sixty-seven. Perhaps realising that it would be sensible to start preparing his nephew to take over, he allowed Theodore to take the chair for the first time at a board meeting in August 1902. Two years later, Henry was walking up Scotch Street on his way to the Viaduct offices from his home in Stanwix when he, too, had a heart attack. He was seen to stagger, clutching his chest, and passers-by helped him into Marshall's, a china shop. His sons and nephews were sent for, but by the time they arrived Henry was dead. At least there were no problems about who should succeed Henry as chairman. Theodore was not only the eldest of the next generation but indisputably the best qualified to take over. Nobody did dispute it. He was appointed chairman immediately at the first board meeting on 2 February 1904. He was thirty-seven years old, still living in Dalston, and by then had three children – daughters Dorothy and Aileen, aged ten and seven, and a son, Stanley, who was eight.

But once he had been made chairman of Carr's, Theodore had little time either for his family or his beloved cars. He quickly discovered, on taking over after Henry's death, that the company was in debt and called for an auditor's report. He was shocked when it was presented to him. It recorded many errors and discrepancies in the books, which had not been properly kept, and reported that large losses were bound to occur between the supposed and the real value of the various mills if, as Henry appeared to have been planning, they were sold. These mills, and the whole flour-milling side of Carr's, had been a problem throughout Henry's twenty years of heading the firm, but he had never quite decided to stop milling altogether in the way he had stopped baking bread. The mills, especially the Maryport one, were not profitable and it would have been sensible to close them down, or to close three of them and make Silloth bigger and better. Henry had actually brought himself to the point of preparing to sell Maryport when he died. This left Theodore with major decisions to make. Feeling a rising sense of alarm, he called for a report on the Silloth mill. If he carried through the sale of Maryport, could Silloth be expanded? That report came as an unpleasant surprise, too. The Silloth mill was only twenty years old but it was already outmoded and, if Carr's were to stay in milling, a completely new mill would have to be built, at vast expense. The estimated cost was £25,000.

Theodore acted boldly, in a way that was to become

characteristic. He relied on his own instinct, after judicious studying of the relevant facts and figures, and took the whole weight of responsibility on his own shoulders. Unlike Henry, he did not try to keep all the details of the company's finances to himself. Board meetings immediately became long and minutely documented. There was his brother Bertram to consult, and of course his cousins Frank and Laurence, but everyone knew whose opinion counted. And Theodore's opinion was that Carr's should not only stay in milling but that they should *expand* that side of the business. A bank loan would be necessary but he did not expect that to be a problem. Unfortunately, however, it was. Henry had died on 28 January 1904. The company's accounts for the previous year were announced on 31 January. These showed a loss on the flour-milling side of £15,000 and a drop in profits on the biscuit-manufacturing side, which meant a net loss altogether of £5,000. The bank was not impressed by these figures. But Theodore was extremely energetic and persuasive, and he won over the Clydesdale Bank manager with his frankness. The bank agreed to advance a loan 'to re-equip your Silloth mill' and credit of £40,000 was arranged.

Building on the new Silloth mill began in July, with the hope that it would be finished by the end of the year. It was not, in spite of Theodore's best efforts. He went anxiously backward and forward to Silloth, appalled at the slowness of the building work and even more at the constantly rising costs. He was never off the site, endlessly pushing the builders and negotiating with the suppliers, but still the work proceeded slowly and ruinously expensively. The original figure was lost sight of and it was now far too late to back out. Unlike his grandfather, Theodore was not a quiet, calm man whose determination was hidden from view; he was much more volatile and, under this kind of pressure, bad-tempered, making his presence felt in a way that could make him feared. But he managed to control himself sufficiently to write some honest and dignified letters to Mr Wilson of the Clydesdale's head office in Glasgow. He explained that 'the actual cost of the re-equipment proper will not now fall far short of £50,000 instead of the £40,000 expected, to which must be added the cost of the new silo granary, the new Provender mill . . .' On and on he was obliged to go, meticulously listing all kinds of 'unexpected expenditure' and having to end with the dreadful news that the total cost was likely to be £72,000. He said he 'much regretted' this, 'especially under the special circumstances attending our agreement with you', but then tried to pass on a confidence that he was very far from feeling by assuring Mr Wilson, 'We now have a mill second to none in the country.' If he could just be given a little more time, then the huge overdraft would begin to be paid off in no time at all, really it would. He trusted that 'we may count on your continued co-operation'.

Remarkably, this was forthcoming, to Theodore's intense relief. In June 1905 the new Silloth mill was at last opened, six months behind schedule. It had been particularly complicated to install the magnificent new Carel engine to run it, built in Ghent and imported with great difficulty to Silloth. This engine had been developed as a showpiece by a Belgian company, and Theodore fell in love with its mechanised beauty when he saw it in action. He insisted on having it, despite the prohibitive cost (and in fact it proved worthwhile, since the engine ran without interruption for the next sixty-one years). The mill itself, a huge, grey construction of five floors, with a silo 125 feet tall, dominated the small town of Silloth. From the Green and the seafront it was not exactly unattractive, looking rather like a castle, but from the sand-dunes on the west side it appeared uglier and much more threatening. It announced uncompromisingly that Silloth was not a sweet little seaside resort but a place of industrial activity.

Theodore, with all his grandfather's flair for publicity, took half of Carlisle to Silloth to see his new mill open. He made the most of the gala opening, using it to boost the company's image and to convince everyone (especially any spies from the Clydesdale Bank) that Carr & Co. Ltd was a supremely prosperous company. Special trains conveyed 1,500 guests to Silloth and a splendid lunch was laid on for the VIPs, while the rest were given souvenir boxes of biscuits. All memories of Carr's being a Quaker firm, with the emphasis on plainness, were forgotten. The menu for the lunch was sumptuous. The wine flowed (temperance, too, was forgotten and so was tea) and there were three kinds of roast meat; boiled hams and tongues; huge veal, ham and steak pies; pastries and apple tarts; and cheese with Carr's biscuits of course (the newly famous Table Water biscuits). There seemed no doubt about it: Carr's must be doing well.

Theodore prayed this would be so, but the first month was worrying. The mill was working well, producing thirty bags of flour per hour instead of the previous sixteen, but the flour itself was proving unpopular. Theodore, though a wizard with machines, was woefully inexperienced when it came to choosing wheat. He bought the wrong sort and bought it expensively. Meanwhile, the long suffering bank began to press for repayments to begin, hardly surprisingly since by August the overdraft stood at £90,000. Not only could Theodore not begin repaying, but he actually needed more money to meet the bill for that month's wages. It was a desperate situation and he faced it bravely by hopping on a train to Glasgow – to the Clydesdale Bank's head office, to plead his case. Quite how he managed it, he never recorded, but he was given one more month's grace. His brothers, cousins and the other senior management members were all waiting for him on Carlisle station platform and knew by his face that he had pulled it off, for the moment anyway. The very next week the new flour mill began to show a profit and disaster was averted.

Theodore was able to relax a little. Another son, Ivan, was born (nine months after his return from Glasgow) and for a short while he spent more time with his family than he had done since Henry died. But even at home he was energetic, ever restless and wanting to be doing things. If he was not messing about with cars, he was making a cart for Lady, the children's pony, to pull, or helping Milburn, the gardener, pump water from the well. Unlike his grandfather and father, he was boisterous and reckless and quite scared small children, though when they were older they loved him for his daring. He had a bellowing laugh and a good singing voice, and would entertain the family with songs from musical comedies and by playing the piano. His wife Edith was a great contrast; it always surprised people that Theodore had chosen her, because she was so placid and domesticated. She read *Home Chat* magazine, liked to read Beatrix Potter stories to her children, and the highlight of her week was a shopping trip to Carlisle, where she would buy, among other things, bottles of coloured fruit drops as 'tidy prizes' for the children. While Theodore was making photograph frames in a workshop in the basement, Edith would be sewing – for she was a beautiful needlewoman. Aunt Lizzie, a member of Theodore's household since the move to Dalston, sewed too, but read the children rather more inspiring stories about Arctic exploration.

Only one element was missing from this familiar Carr picture of domestic serenity and that was religion. Theo-

dore went to church and was a Christian, but he had
none of that religious fervour that had characterised his
father and his uncles, all of whom had had chapels in
their own houses and had made the saving of souls their
primary concern. That strain in the family had shown
up in Sydney and John and, a little later, in Hilda
(Harold's twin). Neither Sydney nor John had ever been
interested in the biscuit works. They held shares of
course, but were content to take the dividends and use
them to finance missionary endeavours. Sydney, after
qualifying as a doctor, then serving with the Liverpool
Medical Mission, sailed for China on behalf of the China
Inland Mission in 1901. John, also a doctor, joined him
there in 1904. They both took on church, as well as
medical, work, and what brother Theodore did back in
Carlisle was of only passing concern to them.

And what Theodore proceeded to do after his short
summer break in 1905 was to reshape the business for
the future. None of the employees at Carr's knew
about the recent crisis, but they certainly noticed that
after Theodore Carr took over, things changed. A new
and extremely noticeable energy came into the business.
In some ways the difference was subtle. Theodore
visibly impressed the workers, as he always impressed
others, with his mechanical know-how, but he also gave
them confidence in themselves, which they had not had
since J.D.'s time, and this was harder to explain. Partly,
it was because of his physical presence – Theodore was
a big, strong man, but then so were most of the Carrs
(J.D., Henry, James, Thomas and George were all tall,
heavy men). It was more that, with his obvious energy
and strength, Theodore had a passion about him, a
passion for the business, which no one else had had
since his grandfather. He had it and he wanted to communicate it to all his workers. Just as J.D. had
appreciated that employees worked better if their

working conditions were good, and if they could see there was an obvious concern for their welfare, so Theodore realised, in different times, that a team-feeling could be promoted through sport. Carr's Football Team, Carr's Cricket Team, Carr's Swimming Club, these all bound workers together and made the works something more than just a place that produced biscuits. In addition, instead of the summer outing of J.D.'s time, there were the annual dinners that Theodore, or rather the firm, paid for and at which he was present, together with his wife. These became grander and grander occasions, with evening dress worn. Trophies were presented to the winners of the various sporting competitions – Theodore awarded a personal trophy to the winner of a swim across the Solway Firth – and there was a tremendous sense of occasion. Employment at Carr's now meant fun as well as work.

These social improvements were quite calculated, but no less beneficial for being so. Keeping his employees happy at little cost was all part of Theodore's strategy; and a strategy was definitely what he possessed, unlike Henry, who had looked no further than keeping the business going without trying to change its direction in any significant way. Theodore had what all firms, but in particular family firms, need: insight, initiative and, perhaps most important of all, the courage of his own convictions. In 1908, he did something that demonstrated all three of these qualities. He took a deep breath and proceeded to split off the flour-milling business from the biscuit works, creating another entirely new company in so doing. This went directly against his grandfather's original concept for Carr & Co. What had made J.D.'s enterprise so unusual was that it brought flour milling and bread- and biscuit-baking under one roof, or at least under the direction of one owner. It had been one of those ideas so obvious that the puzzle was why had it not been done before. But now times were different. The economics of wheat importation had changed everything and Theodore saw that, however profitable the new Silloth mill might turn out to be, it should not be tied to the biscuit works, nor should the biscuit works be an integral part of the flour milling. Neither stood to gain any longer from this mutual dependency. Both would operate better if independent.

The new company, Carr's Flour Mills Ltd, was to be run from the Viaduct offices, while the offices of Carr & Co. Ltd moved to the biscuit works (though only for the time being). The first meeting of the board of the new company occurred on 28 September 1908, with Theodore becoming chairman and managing director, as he still was of the old company. Frank Carr, Henry's son, was to devote himself entirely to the new company, becoming its sales manager as well as a director. The two companies would operate separately but, it was hoped, be mutually supportive. Harold, Theodore's youngest brother, took Frank's place on the board of the old company. Publicly everyone professed themselves happy to accept Theodore's bold move, but there were some private mutterings of unease. Theodore's own position, as chairman of both companies, struck some people as indicating that neither company could be said to be truly independent. Did independence not require some measure of privacy? Then there was a feeling that the biscuit works might lose out in a way that no one could exactly define. Might 'mutually supportive' not come to mean that profits from the biscuit works would somehow be used to help the flour-milling side, even more than they always had been?

But nobody challenged Theodore. The entire family stood meekly, even gratefully, behind him. Bertram, always close to him, had no desire whatsoever to challenge his brother. He had carved out for himself a very nice niche as export manager for Carr & Co. Ltd and was by then well established as an indefatigable traveller for the company, spending long spells abroad. The Directors' Minutes show him being given permission to go here, there and everywhere, although with strict instructions as to his expenditure. He was given the company's blessing, for example, in July 1908, to go to Canada for two months, but his expenses were to come to no more than £130 and that amount was to cover trips to Montreal, Toronto, Winnipeg, Calgary and, if possible, Vancouver. Meanwhile Ernest, though always interested in his shares, was doing very well for himself in Wigton with his new jam business and had no part in either company.

Sydney and John were still in China, both by now not so much doctors as medical missionaries. Sydney, once he had settled in Kaifeng in the province of Honan (where the people were said to be hostile to foreigners), ran a small dispensary, but his main interest was in trying to convert the Chinese to Christianity. Like his uncles, Henry and James, he believed that bringing converts into the fold was as important as being a good Christian himself. Though he was a studious, sensitive man of a retiring disposition, he worked at this with great dedication. He learned Chinese, the better to be persuasive, and mastered several difficult dialects. His younger brother John was more outgoing – he had the same hearty, booming laugh as Theodore – but just as inspired and determined. He supervised the building of two hospitals in Pingyang (one for women), a school and a YMCA institute. His energy and persistence during these building operations were reminiscent of the qualities shown by his grandfather while he was building his biscuit works, but both these worthy brothers, once they became involved with the China Inland Mission, had all too obviously opted out of anything to do with biscuits.

Harold, Frank and Laurence, however, were all on the board and obedient to Theodore, while Ronald, James's son, was only fourteen. Those others who were not family but who had positions of influence were also completely behind Theodore. He had noticed, when he took over from Henry, that two outsiders had been given permission to sign foreign bank letters, certify invoices and endorse bills. These men were E. P. Brown, who had come to Carlisle in 1904 as office manager, and Robert Hewitson. This had caused Theodore some concern at the time but he had stopped worrying, once he saw that Brown and Hewitson presented no threat, even if they had a minor degree of power that had once belonged only to the family.

Secure in his own position, and satisfied that forming two separate companies had been the best thing to do, Theodore was now free to concentrate on his plans for expansion. In 1910 he formed another new company, Bonn & Co., to take over the business of S. & H. Rakusen, whose shares he had just bought when they came on the market. Rakusens sold unleavened biscuits to the Jewish community and Theodore saw how easily and profitably Carr's could do this, used as they were to producing the Table Water biscuit based on the same unleavened principle. It meant persuading the Jewish ecclesiastical authorities that their kosher biscuits and Passover cakes (the Matzos) could be made by Carr's in kosher conditions, and allowing a rabbi to be present at the baking. A special department was set aside and the workers soon grew used to the supervising rabbi and the regular inspections by representatives from Beth Din, the Jewish Court of Justice. The profits were excellent. Theodore could afford to have a new house built.

He moved from the village of Dalston, where his

family had been so happy, back into Carlisle itself, but not to the ever-desirable Stanwix. His choice of site was odd, a corner site on the road leading from Carlisle to Dalston, just inside the city boundary and just down from the cemetery. It had little to recommend it in the way of views or amenities and neither did Greysteads, the house itself. It looked, when it was finished in 1913, rather like its name, imposing but characterless, a solid, rough-coated brick edifice with a total of nine bedrooms. Money was spent on a good deal of oak panelling and on putting leaded lights into the windows, but most of all in equipping an inner workshop with a turntable for cars and an inspection pit.

Living here, with his children now nineteen, seventeen, sixteen and seven, Theodore was just round the corner from Bertram, who lived in Goschen Road. Bertram, married since 1897 to Hannah Mabel Allen, had a son and three daughters roughly the same age as Theodore's children, which made for congenial family gatherings. Bertram also lived in a new house, though of a more pleasing design than Theodore's: double-fronted and with better proportions. The joint Carr families could be seen on Sundays walking down their adjoining roads and emerging to form an impressively long line as they filed into St James's Anglican church, which lay at the end, a mere few hundred yards from both houses. Bertram took his religion more seriously than Theodore (though nothing like as seriously as his uncles had done), not allowing his children any activities on Sundays and becoming most unlike his usual easy-going self if the Sabbath was not rigorously respected. One of his daughters, watching a fly buzzing around, and being exasperated enough to declare, 'Oh, that damned biz!' was astonished to be furiously upbraided. As this firm upholding of standards on Sundays suggests, Bertram was an active member of his church – he

was a church warden at St James's and very involved in
church affairs when he was at home.

Bertram was also the first of the Carrs to stand for
any kind of municipal office and succeed. The Dixons
and the Fergusons, those other prominent Carlisle
manufacturing families, had done so to great effect, of
course, since J.D.'s time, but no Carr had ever followed
suit, first for religious reasons, and then because all their
spare energy went into evangelistic work. But now both
Bertram and Theodore were beginning to think differently. They were prepared to take a more active part in
local politics and, unlike their grandfather, had no
qualms about doing so. They wanted influence, as well
as the opportunity to serve their community. They had
a position in Carlisle and thought they should accept
the responsibilities that went with it. None of this was
articulated at the time (it was all said later, in speeches)
but they were certainly exploring the way into local
politics. Theodore himself had no time at present to
stand for public office, but his involvement in the management of the Cumberland Infirmary brought him into
contact with Carlisle's influential people. Bertram,
however, did stand for office in 1903, and was elected a
city councillor for St Cuthbert's ward, a position he
enjoyed and was determined to hold on to.

In this decade preceding the First World War everything seemed to be going right once more for Carr &
Co. Ltd, and for Carr's Flour Mills Ltd, though Theodore neither relaxed his vigilance nor ceased looking for
ways to move forward. He was determined to motorise
Carr & Co. Ltd and, before the outbreak of war, had
bought the first two of the Ford Albion light vans that
were to become a fleet and replace their horses entirely.
He added to these vans six second-hand touring cars,
which were fitted with van bodies and painted green
with gold lettering eleven inches high on the sides. The

vans soon became a familiar sight all over Cumberland, though, with their engines of sixteen horsepower, some of the Lake District hills proved too much for them. The driver had to get out, stack most of the tins of biscuits at the side of the road, drive the almost empty van to the top of the hill, then laboriously carry up the tins. The travellers, provided with motor tricycles as soon as Theodore took over, were better off.

Carr's vans had to be very careful negotiating their way round the centre of the city, because of the tramlines that had been laid in 1899, entirely changing the look of the area in front of the old Town Hall, and because there were now also motor-buses in Carlisle. The horse-drawn buses were still in operation, too, and the congestion was becoming serious. Not only did all these vehicles drive through the city centre, but many of them started and ended their journeys there and stood stationary at times. The smell of horse manure mingled with petrol fumes and many regretted the moving of the old market stalls into the huge, new covered market: it had been more pleasant to have open stalls and the scent of fruit than to have the market square turned into a veritable garage. From being a relatively quiet place (except on market days), the city centre was now horribly noisy, what with the screech of brakes, the starting up of engines and the rumble of tyres. Carr's vans were part of this hubbub, distinctive in their green and gold livery, and even though their speed was limited to 14 m.p.h., faster and nippier than any other vehicles on the road. It was a fine sight, on Sundays, to see a whole row of vans lined up outside the factory waiting to start up the next day, their lettering glowing, their metal hub-caps shining and the bodywork of each van polished so brightly it could serve as a mirror.

These were halcyon days, with all the Carrs living well and working hard, though none as hard as Theodore. He put in long days in the various offices of both companies, as well as in the factory itself, becoming a figure as familiar as his grandfather had been. Unlike J.D., he did not walk to work, though he was no more than a brisk twenty minutes away, but drove. Cars remained his relaxation – driving them, improving their performance, messing about with their engines – but in these overwhelmingly busy, if successful, times he also had another hobby. Boats fascinated him almost as much as cars, and he found taking to the sea the very best way of rising above any business worries. He had a cottage at Rockcliffe, on the Scottish side of the Solway estuary, but his favourite place was nearby, at Kippford. He and his family spent holidays at the Anchor Inn and every day Theodore took out his boat, *Carita*, and taught his children and their cousins to sail. He believed that children should learn from experience and let them take out a dinghy, *Minnow*, on their own, laughing uproariously when they ran into sandbanks or capsized. His laugh was so loud that at night, when the children were sleeping in a lifeboat on the beach as an adventure, it would carry from the inn and make them feel secure.

Theodore's capable leadership made everyone feel secure about the business. In fact, not for a long time, not since the death of J.D., had Carr's felt so stable. There were not even any worries about the family succession. Theodore was only forty-eight and extremely fit and healthy, and there were plenty of heirs in the next generation. Stanley, his elder son, seemed particularly promising, and so was James's son, Ronald. He was a typical Carr to look at – more so than Stanley – big and heavily built (though an excellent sprinter, setting records for the 100- and 220-yard races at his school, Repton). The tradition of taking all young Carrs round the biscuit works continued, and with it the sense of duty to the family firm upon which all their fortunes were founded. There was an impression, in 1914, that Carr's was invincible.

Chapter Nine

STRIKES AND WAR

Before the First World War, Carr & Co. Ltd had experienced no labour troubles: that 'strike' by the three apprentices in Henry's day was hardly worth remembering and had been dealt with swiftly and effectively. In 1911 there was a national strike of railway workers, which had affected transport from the flour mill at Silloth for a short period, but there had been no strike action within the mill itself. Theodore felt confident that his relationships with his foremen and workers were good enough, and that the regular meetings that had always been held between management and employees could prevent the kind of problems other firms were beginning to experience as the trade-union movement strengthened. Besides, he had no economic need to be careful with his work force, since there was then an apparently inexhaustible supply of labour in Caldewgate and wages were low. If there were any problems, men could be sacked and replaced many times over. The working day was very nearly the same as it had been in J.D.'s time and there were still no official tea-breaks, though ten minutes was allowed, morning and afternoon, for standing at the machines and having a cup of tea. Nothing had changed, including the harmony.

But it was a harmony dependent on the existence

of a large available labour force outside and on fairly repressive measures within. Theodore and his managers kept an almost military discipline inside the biscuit works, with suspensions and dismissals acting as a very effective deterrent. Then there were the fines, levied at different rates for different offences. There was a fine of one shilling, on the spot, for using profane language, striking another person or damaging a machine; bringing alcohol of any description into the factory meant a six-penny fine (and the disposal down a sink of the alcohol); and wasting time (wide open to convenient inter-pretation), or not washing one's hands, was a twopenny offence. The employees were kept strictly in order by these means and Theodore was satisfied with the running of the factory, although he was not complacent. He had known for some time before 1914 that this happy state of affairs, from the employer's point of view, could not last, even if up in Carlisle everything seemed stable enough.

The first thing to alarm him, even before war was declared and he lost male employees, was the realisation that in fact the labour supply was *not* bottomless. Sud-denly, for the first time in Carr's history, he was obliged at the end of 1913 to ask the head office of the Labour Exchange for a list of towns where labour of the kind he needed was available. He had expanded the biscuit works again, a year before war was declared, and working hours had also been marginally reduced, so he needed to employ more people than ever. Since it never occurred to Theodore to raise wages, he knew how important it was to quash any early signs that the workers appreciated the potential of their collective power. The last thing he wanted in his works was rampant trade unionism and he attempted to deal with this threat on a personal level. Any trade-union official who attempted to recruit in his factory was invited to a meeting of all the workers. Theodore strode in with the official and, standing confidently before them, said, 'Now, this gentleman here thinks you're all badly done by and need him and his union to look after you. Anyone who agrees with him and wants to join his union, put your hand up.' Not a single hand went up, no one moved. 'Well, that settles that,' said Theodore and marched out. But he knew perfectly well that the abandoned union official would (and did) find recruits and that something fairly drastic would have to be done to pre-empt a decisive and unwelcome switch in the balance of power within Carr's.

Before he had put into operation a plan he had been thinking about, there was an ominous rumbling, which made him see that he had been foolish to delay: 500 girls in the packing department went on strike one Wednesday afternoon in September 1915, in protest at their treatment by Miss Smith, the works matron. As a consequence, 300 other workers had to stop work, with the result that a total of 800 were idle. Aghast, Theodore took himself down to the factory at once to discover what on earth was happening. To his relief, he quickly learned that this unprecedented strike had nothing to do with wages or working hours: it was all to do with the manner in which Miss Smith treated the girls. Three of them had asked permission to take all of one particular Saturday off and had been refused. They took the day off all the same and were sacked when they next came into work. The strikers demanded that the three girls be reinstated and the hated Miss Smith herself sacked.

Initially Theodore refused both demands, simply because he had no intention of being dictated to within his own factory, but he suggested a conference to discuss the grievances. Before this could be organised, the girls went on the rampage, sweeping out of the factory, all still in their white overalls and identifiable as Carr's employees. They marched to Miss Smith's residence (in St James's Road, far too near Theodore's own house for comfort), where they hammered on her door and yelled abuse; and as a final insult they pulled up the flowers in her garden and chucked them at her windows. All this was appalling enough, but even worse, from Theodore's point of view, was that at a meeting in front of the Town Hall the powerful Gas Workers' & General Labourers' Union declared itself proud to assist the girls. On the Friday evening, two days after the girls had gone on strike, an open-air meeting was held in front of the Town Hall, with the speakers standing on the steps of the old cross, as they had always done on such occasions. The steps gave them a bit of height, so that everyone in the crowd could see them, and the cross was an excellent focal point, somehow giving an air of authority to anything that was said. The steps of the Town Hall would have been even better, and there was a balcony where the two flights of steps met in front of the door into the hall, but permission was needed to use it. No permission was needed to speak from the cross and for centuries it had been used by every kind of agitator and radical reformer.

It was a fine September evening and the crowd was large, stretching across the tramlines right over to the magnificent new Crown and Mitre Hotel, which had replaced the old inn. From the windows of all five storeys people peered out, trying to work out what all the commotion was about. There was a great deal of shouting and laughing – since it was Friday, most of the crowd had just been paid and many had already celebrated with a pint or two. The 500 Carr's strikers were treating the meeting as something of a party, and the atmosphere was convivial. There was so much noise that the speakers, serious union men, had to use megaphones to make themselves heard.

It was obvious to the local newspaper reporters, if not to the actual strikers, that the representatives of the Gas Workers' & General Labourers' Union were using this little difficulty in Carr's factory as a jumping-off point to discuss hours and pay and the issues that really concerned them. Nobody mentioned Miss Smith or her bullying, nor did any speaker openly criticise the management of Carr's. On the contrary, they were careful to make it clear that they thought the girls should accept Theodore Carr's offer of an inquiry. Theodore was not among the crowd, but he was informed about what was happening and fully appreciated where it might lead. The Gas Workers' & General Labourers' Union was highly dangerous to employers: everyone remembered how they had been one of the first unions to show their power and how they had won their case back in 1889. They had gone from strength to strength ever since, and the last thing Theodore wanted was for them to take up the cause of his strikers and turn such a small incident into something disastrous for Carr's.

It was time to put a stop to all this. Theodore promptly accepted the enforced resignation of Miss Smith and called a conference of all the forewomen, together with six representatives from the strikers. Satisfied and triumphant, the girls went back to work. The whole affair had lasted only four days, but it was the first time such a thing had ever happened in Carr's works and was deeply significant. Theodore was disturbed enough but knew he would have been far more concerned if the strike had been about something more important, and if it had been undertaken by men. But it was wartime, a large proportion of the men were away fighting, and the wartime work force was predominantly female. All the men who joined up were assured that their jobs would be there for them when they returned, and their wives were given an allowance of five shillings a week, plus sixpence for every child. Some kind of welfare organisation, better than supervision by a matron, was clearly needed for the female workers. Miss Smith, who was a bully and had attempted to oversee the morals of the girls and their behaviour outside working hours, would no longer do. A proper system of care had to be set up, and Theodore intended to see that it was, as soon as possible.

But in those early days of the war he had a great deal on his hands. The factory had never been busier: it simply could not produce enough biscuits to keep up with the sudden astonishing demand. Export trade, which had become Carr's strength, was naturally curtailed by the war, but home trade boomed. The wartime diet quickly became so dreary that as a consequence biscuits became more and more desirable. With so many women working, eating habits were changing, too. There was little time to bake, or to make proper meals, and snacks of tea and biscuits kept people going more than they had previously done.

Theodore got permission to build an extension and the factory was in production day and night. The pressure was so great that retailers were offering bribes for more supplies – one such bribe was a piano – and travellers had never been more popular. Because of the obvious difficulties in getting sugar, Theodore tried to concentrate on those biscuits that needed less, but, of course, it was the sugary type of biscuit that people craved. He also tried to restrict production to those types of biscuits not in need of particularly skilled labour; 211 of his skilled workers were in the army and he had found them difficult to replace. The new girls he had had to take on were still being trained.

At least Carr's were fortunate in that Theodore was

in charge. He was forty-eight when war was declared and therefore, at the beginning, too old to be called up. So were Bertram, Ernest, Laurence and Frank, though Harold, at thirty-four, could expect call-up papers at some point. Laurence in fact seized the opportunity to get near to the doctoring he had always wanted to do by requesting leave from Carr's in December 1914 in order to serve with the Medical Corps in France. He drove an ambulance and did his bit for the war in that way. But the real worry for the family was over the next generation. Stanley, Theodore's son, was eighteen when war was declared and James's son, Ronald, was twenty. They both joined up immediately. This made Theodore all the more keen to help the war effort by becoming chairman of the Carlisle Munitions Committee in June 1915. Lloyd George had declared that this war was becoming 'a war of munitions' and that people must now see the production of munitions 'not as turning out something to kill the enemy but to save the life of a comrade'. Or a son. Theodore, in charge of a new munitions factory in the drill hall in Lowther Street, set out to make it the most successful in the country, applying to it the same passion he had brought to the biscuit works. It was a very different task and he had to start from scratch, without inheriting any structure as he had done at Carr's, but in many ways it was more rewarding and exciting for him. Nobody could say he had it easy, that he was merely following in the footsteps of his forebears. And, with every perfect shell that was turned out, he might save Stanley's life.

He was proud, of course, as fathers were then, that his son had volunteered instantly, becoming one of the 11th (Service) Battalion of the Manchester Regiment, raised in August 1914 at Ashton-under-Lyne and composed of the first men to come forward. Stanley did well, becoming a Second Lieutenant on 23 October, and

Lieutenant on 5 January 1915. Ronald Carr, who had joined the 6th (Service) Battalion of the Border Regiment, became a Lieutenant in September 1915. By the time his father had the Carlisle munitions factory in full production, Stanley was in the Gallipoli peninsula (as was Ronald), one of the brigade that made the first landing in Suvla Bay. In the fighting that followed, eight officers and 100 other ranks were killed, and ten officers and 330 other ranks wounded. Stanley survived and left with his battalion in December 1915 for Egypt. The news of his survival and latest destination took a long time to get through to Carlisle, but there was enormous relief that Christmas. Stanley and Ronald were being lucky so far and there was every hope that the war would soon be over.

But there was another Carr, not fighting in the army, who was in more peril than he realised at the time, and that was Bertram. In May 1915 Bertram was determined to carry on as normal and go off on an extensive business trip to South America (which he has already visited in 1910, setting up Carr's representatives from Ecuador to the Falkland Isles). He was warned that the seas were full of German torpedoes but he scorned the warning, even though the *Lusitania* had been sunk off the coast of Ireland on 7 May, three weeks before he began his own voyage. Once on his travels, he wrote that he was seeing more Germans than he was ever likely to see in England and that they were all boorish. He related with relish the tale of how four Germans in a railway carriage had stuck their legs out to stop anyone getting out and how an Englishman had climbed patiently over the outstretched legs, then paused when he reached the door to say, 'That is how it will be – four against one, but we will climb over you.' Exactly Bertram's sentiments. His knowledge of German (learned at school) was useful, and he improved his Spanish too (though mostly

Theodore and Bertram Carr in the motor car which Theodore built in 1896.

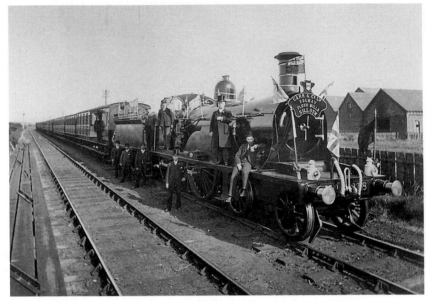

The special Carr's train arriving at their flour mills in Silloth.

*The wafer machine room, rather darker and more satanic-looking
than the rest of the factory.*

The Rudd women on the steps of Carlisle Cross about 1895. They sold a local red stone used to give a red finish to doorsteps.

A busy market scene, in front of the Town Hall steps.

An advertisement of 1904 (used in a modified form on their stationery), showing the scope of Carr's empire.

APPOINTED PURVEYORS

LONDON DEPÔT:
MIDLAND GOODS STATION, ST. PANCRAS, N.W.

LONDON SAM
19 EASTCHE

ESTABLISHED
·1831·

BY AUTHORITY

CARR & Cº have obtained the Highest Awards given for Biscuits at the following International Exhibitions :—

SYDNEY 1879
AMSTERDAM 1883
CALCUTTA 1884
ANTWERP 1885
LIVERPOOL 1886
NEWCASTLE 1887
NOVA SCOTIA 1891
KIMBERLEY 1892
VIENNA 1900
Gold Medal & Star of Honour

CAR

BISCU
C

Flour Mills Silloth.

Entrance to Biscuit Works

·Appointed Biscuit Bakers to the la

SCUITS TO H.M. KING EDWARD VII.

TELEPHONE NOS:
CARLISLE OFFICE 40
,, WORKS 33

LIVERPOOL DEPÔT:
BATH LANE, BATH STREET.

MANCHESTER DEPÔT:
SALFORD STATION, L. & Y. R.Y.

BRISTOL DEPÔT:
WELSH BACK BRISTOL.

PARIS DEPÔT:
7 RUE AMBROISE THOMAS,

R & Cº LTD

ANUFACTURERS

LISLE

Offices Carlisle

Flour Mills Maryport

Flour Mills-Carlisle

orks

een Victoria by Special Warrant 8th May 1841·

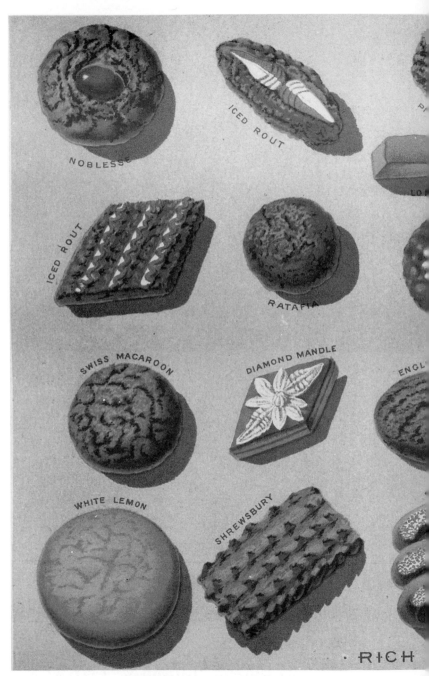

The famous Rich Dessert selection.

FIA

LE

ICED ROUT

FRENCH MACAROON

SANDWICH RATAFIA

ICED ROUT

OON

DIAMOND MANDLE

SMALL ITALIAN MACAROON

FREYBURG

QUEEN'S DROP

SSERT·

The new motorised delivery vans, with their smart green and gold livery and 16 horse power.

Bertram Carr, as Mayor of Carlisle, announces the Armistice in 1918.

through constantly getting stuck in hotel lifts with Spanish-speaking attendants, which gave him the wrong sort of vocabulary). He had had a risky enough time going out from Liverpool on the Royal Mail Steamer *Avon*, but returning was even more dangerous. There were still German submarines in the Irish Sea and he was advised to sail home on a neutral ship – 'advice I was in no way inclined to follow'. He defiantly boarded an English ship, feeling safe because the captain was a chap from Workington, in Cumberland. He slept fully dressed, knowing that minefields were being negotiated, and reached home rather proud of himself.

Mabel, his wife, who had been left with a one-year-old baby when Bertram went on his latest trip, was very relieved to see him back safely. The war, for her, was little different from peacetime. She was at home with her four daughters (her only son, Allen, was at boarding school) and, unlike the other women in the Carr family, had no chance to make something of the new wartime opportunities available. Working-class women were doing jobs in factories previously monopolised by men, and Theodore now employed almost exclusively females in the biscuit factory. Women filled the vacuum left by the men not only in the factory itself but on the roads, driving Carr's vans. Theodore, such an expert driver himself, had grave doubts about the advisability of letting any woman drive one of his precious vehicles, but there was no alternative. Women alone were available and would have to be taught.

The first to take up her duties, causing something of a sensation, was Nellie Campbell – small, red-haired and slightly built – who started in May 1916. She did well and was followed by seven other women, most of whom transferred from the forwarding department, where they had been clerks. They wore long, heavy coats, buttoned right up to the neck – the vans were open at the front, with only the goods, in the body of the van, covered over – and rather unattractive hats, a little like a square-looking trilby. Nellie was by far the best of this brave bunch, not because she was a better driver, but because she had absorbed something of how the internal combustion engine worked. If the car broke down, Nellie could often manage to get it started, whereas the other women were helpless. Fitters, who were in extremely short supply, had to go out to wherever the van had broken down and would often find the fault to be quite minor. So the women drivers, except for Nellie, were not popular.

For middle-class women like the Carrs, the way was open to serve in all kinds of voluntary but vital organisations. Maud Carr, James's widow (and mother of Ronald), suddenly came into her own, taking charge of a house on Stanwix bank, which became a convalescent home for wounded soldiers. Her sister-in-law Edith was too worried about Stanley and too given to nervous headaches to help, but Dorothy, Edith's eldest daughter, had what came to be called a 'good war', like so many young women previously existing idle at home.

Dorothy's only qualification was that she had taken first-aid and hygiene lessons at school, but that was enough. The moment war was declared, she became a member of a Voluntary Aid Detachment (Cumberland 6). Her commander, a Mrs Donald, was allocated a big house on the Scaur in Stanwix, which had been a Roman Catholic boys' school. The detachment was divided into sections of four, who took turns of duty, and Dorothy was in her aunt Maud's section. Maud had done a great deal of voluntary work at the Cumberland Infirmary since the death of her husband, so she knew rather more about the basics of nursing than most of the women, though in fact at first there was more cleaning and organising to be done than nursing. Like most of the houses taken over, this one, Chadwick, was filthy, and the women, who had always in their own homes had servants to do menial tasks such as scrubbing floors, had to set to and do it themselves. The house was not at all suited for transformation into a convalescent home – too many stairs, too few lavatories, too many awkwardly shaped rooms, ceilings so high that heating was difficult and expensive – but there was such a sense of purpose that all these problems were overcome.

There was some embarrassment, when the wounded soldiers began to arrive, about how they should be addressed and treated (quite apart from their wounds). Dorothy and her aunt had never been familiar with working men, and Dorothy at least felt awkward at first. But the men were 'wonderfully good . . . and did not use foul language in front of [us]', and soon any feelings of diffidence vanished. None of the serious cases came to Chadwick – they went straight to the infirmary, or on to better facilities elsewhere – but there was a steady progression of men recovering from fevers or gas poisoning, or amputations, and the psychological aspects of looking after them were as important as the practical. Some of the convalescents were Carr's employees and it gave both the Carr women particular satisfaction to nurse them. They felt that in these special and sad circumstances they were carrying on the family tradition of duty and care.

Dorothy, who was not the most fortunate of girls, was happier than she had ever been. She took after her father Theodore in looks, but had none of his cleverness and energy. Large and ungainly, she lived for horses and had always regretted the move from Dalston, where she had been able to keep a horse of her own and where there were ample fields and lanes to ride around. She had been sent away to boarding school, but by the time war was declared she was back at home, aged nineteen, with nothing much to do except involve herself in various church activities, helping the poor in the parish. She had been taken round the biscuit works, just as all the Carrs were, but they had made little impression on her. Theodore had absolutely no hopes of Dorothy, who, in any case, would have had a hard enough time, as a woman, breaking into the management of the firm, whatever her qualities. But now she had been given real employment for the first time and from the small Stanwix home she went on to Liverpool, to work as a nurse in Alder Hey hospital, which she loved. She worked in a male ward of thirty patients, where she came as near as she was ever to come to marrying. A captain she was nursing, who had, with Stanley, taken part in the Suvla Bay landings at Gallipoli, proposed to her but Dorothy refused him, feeling she did not know him well enough: 'Of course, I said it was out of the question, we hardly knew each other.' The poor captain, who was soon sent home to complete his convalescence, got his mother to write formally to Dorothy, asking her to come and stay; but 'realising that to accept might involve me in an awkward position, I did not accept and heard no more thereafter'.

Soon afterwards Dorothy's brief, exciting career came to an end. She was called to the matron's room and told that Stanley had been killed in action and that she must go home at once. Stanley had arrived in France in July and for two months had been one of those on the Somme, enduring the full horror of the trenches under the heaviest of bombardments. His parents knew where he was but they had no word at all from him, and Theodore, who was well aware how serious the situation had become, was desperately worried. The actual attack in which Stanley died on 27 September 1916 was a complete success, but sixty-one other ranks and one other officer died with him. His company commander wrote to his parents of Stanley's courage and cheerfulness, and described how boldly he had led his men over the top. When he was hit, his men came back to carry him to shelter, but Stanley said he was done for and ordered them to go on. He had been an exemplary officer. But then he had been an exemplary son, too, in whom many hopes and the future of a firm had been invested by his father. He was twenty years old, handsome, clever and, as so many sons were, the light of his mother's life. The shy, quiet Edith was devastated and never really recovered. Dorothy, called home – just as Vera Brittain and so many other daughters were – to look after her mother, could hardly leave her side.

Theodore, struggling with his own grief, was never there. His way of coping was to work harder than ever, both in the biscuit works and the munitions factory. Outwardly, he showed no distress, but those in the biscuit works who saw him on the terrible days following saw the change in him in all kinds of small ways. He walked differently for a start. Those like Maggie Robson, who had known him since he was a child, coming round the works with his grandfather, and those older men not away fighting, who had known him since he first came to work, remarked on how Theodore's brisk, authoritative stride had become a trudge. The works were full of women who hardly knew him at all, but they heard what had happened – Stanley's picture and a poem about him written by Canon Rawnsley were in the local paper – and they tried to show their sympathy by bowing their heads and keeping silent as he passed among them. Whether Theodore even noticed is doubtful.

He was putting in far more time now at the munitions factory than at the biscuit works, twelve hours in every twenty-four, sometimes at night as well as during the day, urging his workers on to ever more prodigious efforts. His work was rewarded the following spring, in May 1917, when King George V and Queen Mary, on a tour of the North of England specifically designed to show appreciation of the munition workers, visited Theodore's drill-hall factory. They came in the afternoon, while 'B' shift was on duty (but all the other shifts were allowed to line up outside). The King, who wore khaki, was conducted round the factory by Theodore himself and was impressed that he knew every worker by name and could give him little histories of them, without having to ask a single question. A point was made of introducing the King to the Reverend Hodgson, vicar of Kirkbampton, who, Theodore told the King, cycled the seven miles to work at noon, worked until midnight on a lathe, and then returned to his parish to do his religious duties in the morning, often getting only five hours' sleep. The King commented particularly on the excellent lighting and ventilation in this makeshift factory – he had seen a good few by then – and on the fact that he had been told by a high authority that the number of shells from this factory that had to be rejected because they were defective was negligible – below 3 per cent, and even then the defects were rectifiable.

It was horribly ironic that during this period of personal tragedy Theodore had never been more successful in everything he did. The war had not interfered with Carr's prosperity, in spite of worries at the beginning when the Government issued warnings to all manufacturers that profit margins should be kept 'reasonable'. Profits dropped automatically, because the lucrative export trade was affected, but then picked up again when home trade increased so rapidly. Excess Profits Duty was levied to 80 per cent after 1916 but still Carr's did well, in the new circumstances. Their flour-milling activities were subject to tight control after 1916 when the Government, entirely unprepared for the crisis over wheat supplies, took over the purchase of wheat. It was back to J.D.'s times, with a fixed price for bread (ninepence for a 4lb loaf) but this time no Carr tried to undercut it. Theodore was spending money and had no thoughts for that kind of altruism. War or not, he was carrying on with his programme of modernisation, determined that Carr's would come out at the other end in a position to hold their own in what he expected to be even tougher and more aggressive times in the biscuit business. Some of the new machines he bought while the war was at its height were amazingly expensive: a cutting and embossing machine for £1,280; an electric lift for the confectionery department for £800; a Mogul confectionery machine for £790; and steps were taken at great expense to prepare for the installation of a refrigerating plant for cold cream as soon as restrictions were lifted.

Theodore knew that, even without the changes the war would bring about, there was a subtle but crucial difference in his position, as head of a family firm, from his grandfather's position. J.D. had always said, as any good Quaker was bound to, that making money was not, and should not be, the main aim of his (or anyone else's) business. The main aim was to provide good service, to make the best goods possible and sell them at the cheapest prices possible. If, in the process, large amounts of money accrued, then that was incidental. J.D. had indeed become wealthy, but because he ploughed so much of that wealth back into the business and, as he saw it, accepted the responsibilities that he took to go with success – improving working conditions, treating his workers well – he had had no real crisis of conscience, even before he left the Society of Friends. Service, not gain, had remained his motive, Quaker or not. He never appeared, as other Quakers did, to see any hypocrisy in this. Arnold S. Rowntree said during the First World War that 'we live in an age of political democracy and industrial autocracy', a situation that J.D. had never experienced. In his time, in spite of the Reform Acts, there was no true democracy and his own autocracy within the works was never challenged. But now, post-war, it would be, and Theodore saw this.

Theodore was not, of course, a Quaker and he would never have been able to agree with a speaker at a Quaker conference during the war who said, 'There is no greater moral obligation of the employer than to organise his business so as to enable his employees to earn the highest possible wages.' Did J.D. believe that? The evidence would suggest not, however much he wanted to think he did. Looking after his workers had never, mysteriously, involved giving them anything but wages reasonable for the times, and only in the very early years were these better than elsewhere in the trade. Carr's employees *were* well looked after, so far as working conditions went within the factory, but their wages were never 'the highest possible'. But 'possible' for what? No profit? That would have been absurd, the firm would have gone bankrupt and there would have been no wages at all. J.D.'s attitude was that the 'highest possible' must keep in line with a profit margin big enough both to give security and to ensure improvement and progress within the business all the time.

Theodore's position was different again. Not for one moment had he ever believed that his duty as head of Carr's was to serve, rather than to work for gain. Serve whom? God, perhaps? He was a Christian, he attended church regularly, but he was never, in business, motivated principally by the worthy desire to serve. He had inherited a family business originally founded on such a motive, but as far as he was concerned gain was the driving force now and it would be foolish to pretend otherwise. Making money was all-important. If not enough money was made, relatively small family firms like his own would go to the wall after the war. The logic was as crudely simple as that.

Theodore had pressures that J.D. had never dreamed of. He did not have the luxury of operating as a self-contained little unit tucked up in the far North of England, with no need to worry about what other firms did elsewhere. Carr's trade was linked to what was happening elsewhere. There was no escaping the consequences of the new competitiveness, and it could only become more intense. The travellers knew all about this. No longer were there only three of them, covering huge areas in a gentlemanly way, secure in the certain knowledge that everyone would place orders for Carr's biscuits, just as the King and Queen had done. Now, six more biscuit manufacturers had Royal Warrants and many of the biscuits they produced were both better and cheaper than Carr's. There were 100 travellers working for Carr's and the top-hats had gone. Orders were far from automatic and had to be fought for. Addressing a convention of British and Irish millers, Theodore himself had stressed how completely everything had changed, how trade was more like warfare itself.

But this did not depress him. He felt equal to the fight and an important part of it was building on those good labour relations that Carr's had always had. At last he did something he had been intending to do since the girls' strike in 1915: he set up a Workers' Advisory Committee. This was not, he let it be known, to be a committee merely to enable workers to air grievances but was to 'help workers play together as well as work together'. The workers approached it warily. The committee met regularly, usually once a month, and consisted of representatives elected from each department, as well as the foremen and forewomen. It was a little awkward at first to find themselves sitting down with Theodore or one of the other directors, but the workers soon got used to it (though, no doubt, feelings, or instances, of intimidation never found their way into the minutes). The apparent anxiety of the management to do the right thing was impressively matched by the acknowledgement of the representatives that there were real problems to solve. Wages and hours, however, were not allowed to be among these: Theodore was not a patient man and this would have tried his patience too far, as well as turning the committee into something he had never intended it to be. There were long discussions about matters like pilfering, and what could be done about it, and others about what would happen after the war ended. The women were naturally worried that if, as had been promised, the men who returned were to be given their jobs back, they themselves would be sacked, though many of them were now the sole supporters of their families. That kind of topic was suitable for discussion at the Advisory Committee and, Theodore hoped, kept everyone happy.

And Theodore needed a happy and smoothly functioning factory, because he was about to become an MP and would spend much of his time away from Carlisle.

THE FINEST HOUR

Both Theodore and Bertram Carr became eminent men in Carlisle during and immediately after the First World War. Never, in this city, had the Carr name been more famous, synonymous with an importance far beyond that of a family of biscuit manufacturers. Bertram became Mayor of Carlisle and Theodore became its MP, and the Carrs were at last on a par with the Dixons and the Fergusons, who since J.D.'s time had occupied positions of local standing. Once the Carrs had ceased to be Quakers, the logical outcome of their place in the life of the city was that they should have a share in the control of its affairs.

Bertram was Mayor twice in succession, 1917–18 and 1918–19, and relished the role. He was elected on 9 November 1917 and took the responsibility very seriously indeed, with an impressive attendance record of 82.35 per cent for his first year, serving on the gas committee, the water and baths committee, the electricity committee and several other exceedingly dull committees, with a commendable enthusiasm. When he had to use his casting vote he showed himself always in favour of economy but also of progress. It was Bertram, for instance, who defeated the motion to bar the employment of women tram drivers. His concern for Carlisle's housing needs was in the tradition of his grandfather. Anxious that these needs should be addressed, he invited a Professor Adshead of London University to come to Carlisle and make a thorough investigation and report on exactly what the workers needed in the way of new housing, to be financed by the city council. Adshead recommended an estate of 600 houses, which was accepted by the council, which then appointed a committee to choose a site. This led Bertram into a little family difficulty. The site proposed backed on to his brother's house in Norfolk Road, and Theodore objected violently – the last thing he wanted was a council estate almost in his back garden, no matter how suitable the Longsowerby site or how urgent the need. He wrote to the church commissioners who owned the land and, much to Bertram's relief, they did a deal with Theodore: the building would go ahead on the agreed site and he would be financially compensated. (The moment he was compensated, he put Greystead on the market, although he did not in fact find a buyer.)

There was one other instance of family interest, conflicting with civic interest, but fortunately it was smoothly overcome. Carr's, that is Theodore, wanting to set up a temporary extra unit to cope with wartime demand, applied to take over a skating rink at the foot of Lowther Street to become a new chocolate and confectionery factory. Bertram, as Mayor, abstained from voting and permission was granted. Theodore's stock was high at the time – he had just been awarded the CBE after the King and Queen's visit to the munitions factory – and there was no need for Bertram as Mayor to influence the council on his brother's behalf.

Admiration for Theodore was in ready supply, and so was sympathy after Stanley's death. When he agreed to become the Carlisle Liberal Association's candidate in the December election of 1918 the Conservatives were also happy to accept him as their candidate for the coalition government. On Saturday, 28 December (the counting of votes and announcement of the results were delayed for two weeks so that the armed forces could be included), Bertram as returning officer had the immense satisfaction of proclaiming Theodore's success. He won the seat against the Labour candidate by 9,511 votes to 4,736. He made a splendid speech in which, rather emotionally (for a Carr, in public), he said, 'A friend loveth at all times but a brother is born for adversity.' It was of course a handsome tribute to Bertram, if an odd one, since neither of these two had known much adversity, beyond the death of their mother so long ago and Stanley's recent death. Ernest Lowthian, the defeated candidate, paid his own tribute to Theodore, thanking him for fighting fair and pointing out that in this election there had not been 'a broken head from beginning to end'. Carried away with his success, Theodore could not resist a final toast at his celebration dinner – 'Long live Carlisle biscuits!'

But the Carrs' finest hour came not that day but the next. Bertram had long been obsessed with planning the peace celebrations and had had an idea of breathtaking daring, way beyond medals for schoolchildren and bands playing in all the parks. He had suggested to the council that Carlisle should confer the freedom of the city on the President of the United States of America and invite him to come and receive it on his way to or from the Peace Conference in France, which he was known to be going to attend. Woodrow Wilson's connection with Carlisle came through his mother, who had been born in the city, where her own father was a congregational minister before the family emigrated to America. Wilson had come in search of his mother's birthplace several times, once staying at the Central Hotel next to Carr's offices on the Viaduct and once at the Crown & Mitre, both times failing to find the house where she had been born (not surprisingly, since it had been knocked down). His real love was the Lake District, but he was impressed by Carlisle's cathedral and by the volume of the singing at a religious meeting he witnessed in the market square. When, in 1912, he was elected President of the USA, the then mayor, Spencer Charles Ferguson, had the council send an address of congratulation to 'one who is a grandson of a citizen of this city and son of a lady born in Carlisle'. Wilson sent a sentimental reply saying that he had often heard his mother speak of her childhood in Carlisle and that he felt 'a sort of affectionate association with the place', which he hoped to visit again some time.

Bertram was determined that indeed he should. Wilson was due to come over to London for discussions with Lloyd George, so what could be easier than nipping up on the train to Carlisle? In a great state of excitement at what a *coup* this would be, Bertram, as Mayor, sent off an official invitation. To his delight, it was accepted. Wilson would come to receive the freedom of the city personally, bringing his wife with him. Feverish planning began, but then a second message came: time would not after all permit the President to visit Carlisle. There was despondency all round, and a slight feeling that Carlisle was not good enough. But then came a telegram saying that Wilson wanted to come so much that he had decided to make the trip somehow, though it would be only for three or four hours, if that. That was enough: it was the fact of his coming at all that was important. Bertram called a special meeting of the council and made a rather pompous speech emphasising what an honour was being conferred on Carlisle by Wilson. 'He will come to us straight from London. There, at the heart of the Empire, he is being entertained with great state and gorgeous ceremonial . . . He is the guest of the King . . . The contrast in coming here will be unique' (it would indeed) 'but we will give him a welcome which will be second to none in the depth of its fervour and gladness.' But it would have to take only four hours at most, and a Sunday morning in January was not the easiest of times for a city to erupt with joy.

The Carr family had never known anything quite like this. Up all night celebrating Theodore's victory, they then had to be on the platform of Carlisle station by eight-thirty in order to be lined up ready to greet the royal train, which had spent half the night waiting in a loop line near Penrith and was due at nine-thirty. It was a bitterly cold morning and the rain fell torrentially. Standing under the station's vaulted glass canopy, with the wind tearing the length of it from open end to open end, the women of the party tried to protect themselves from it by using umbrellas as shields, so that all Mrs Wilson could see when she peered out was what she described as 'a forest of toadstools'. The rain found its way through cracks in the roof and blew in great gusts along the platform, where everyone was doing their best to look cheerful. Bertram's eighteen-year-old elder daughter Eleanor tripped forward with a bouquet for Mrs Wilson, who had at least had the foresight to dress warmly in a long sealskin coat, heavily trimmed with fur. Theodore and his wife were there of course, together with the Bishop of Carlisle and the High Sheriff of the county, and sundry other dignitaries, all half-frozen from the long wait. The relief of reaching the Crown & Mitre Hotel was enormous: huge log fires were burning everywhere and the event began to be more enjoyable.

But the President himself, though gracious and polite to all those presented to him in the warmth of the hotel, was anxious to get out into the city, whatever the weather. He had not come to talk to the Carrs or those chosen to be introduced to him, or even really to receive the Freedom of Carlisle, but on a sentimental journey to see where his mother had been born and lived, and where his grandfather had preached. Out the official party went again and drove the short distance to Annetwell Street, near the castle, to see the place where the house in which Janet Woodrow had been born had stood. A surprising number of people lined Castle Street and stood in the market square to watch the President come and go, but the dreadful weather inhibited enthusiasm. Crouching under umbrellas and shivering with cold, the onlookers found cheering hard-going and there was nothing like the spontaneous combustion of delight that Bertram had envisaged.

The little tour continued to another house, still occupied, where Wilson's mother had also lived, and then on to Lowther Street Congregational church, where his grandfather had preached. As a precaution regular worshippers had been issued with tickets. Wilson agreed to speak in the church but would not enter the pulpit, which he thought would be wrong. He spoke well, paying tribute to his grandfather and mother, but the most interesting and gratifying part (from Carlisle's point of view) of his speech had to do with the end of the war. What he said was, 'And so it is from quiet places like this all over the world that the forces accumulate which presently will overpower any attempt to accomplish evil on a grand scale.' Listening to his words gave Carlisle people a sense of importance, as though, just by living the kind of quiet lives they did, they had somehow helped to win this war. No applause was allowed, since this was a church, but backs straightened and chins lifted, and the pride of it swept through the congregation. But the glory of being so commended was soon over. There was a quick visit to the cathedral, another brief half-hour in the Crown & Mitre, and then the President left. The Carrs collapsed, exhausted.

Mayor and MP alike had a lot to recover from after forty-eight hours of sustained tension.

Theodore had a new life ahead of him, a life quite unlike the one he had led previously. Becoming an MP took him away from Carlisle and from biscuit manu-facturing, with fairly predictable and inevitable consequences. He had to have a place to live in London and that meant making decisions: either his wife and family came with him, or else they stayed in Carlisle. The daughters, Dorothy (twenty-four) and Aileen (twenty-one), were all for moving to London to be with their father (Ivan, the remaining son, was only thirteen and was away at boarding school at Oundle). Edith, Theodore's wife, was not so keen, but a flat large enough to accommodate them all was rented and for a while they lived together. The girls loved it: it was far more exciting being daughters of a father who was an MP in London than of a biscuit manufacturer in Carlisle. They took singing lessons from a Miss Bush, who taught at a studio in the Aeolian Hall, and greatly enjoyed getting to know their way about the West End. Edith was not so content. It had suited her nature very well to be a Carlisle wife, living in a quiet road near her parish church, and knowing exactly where and what she was. The noise and bustle of London did not stimulate her, as it did her daughters; on the contrary, it overwhelmed and exhausted her. She found attending any sort of func-tion with her husband a strain and the headaches to which she had been subject since Stanley's death increased. Edith began going home to Carlisle more and more, one or other of her reluctant daughters obliged to accompany her, and Theodore found himself following what his uncles would have called the Path to Sin. Like many MPs whose wives stayed in their constituencies, he found consolation in another woman. Rumour thrived, then as now, and many people in Carlisle came to know of this, though it does not appear to have damaged his reputation. Fortunately for Theodore, there was no member of the Carr family breathing hellfire: of the two religious brothers, Sydney had died in 1914 of typhus fever and John was still in China.

It was a new experience for Theodore to sit in the House of Commons and not find himself in charge. The coalition government of which he was part had a mandate 'to make Britain a fit country for heroes to live in', the avowed and inspiring intention of the man hailed as having won the war, the Prime Minister, Lloyd George. He had called a general election the moment the armistice was signed. He was riding the crest of a wave of gratitude and, as expected, it had worked to his advantage. He was re-elected, but this second coalition government was different from his previous one, formed to win the war. The problems of the peace were only just beginning to be appreciated. Expectations ran high, raised higher by Lloyd George's own winning slogan. New members like the Liberal Theodore Carr, interested in a wide variety of domestic reforms, were going to expect more of the Liberal Lloyd George than the Conservative members, but of the 478 Coalitionists, 380 were Conservatives. During the war, the emergency had meant that co-operation between Liberal and Conservatives was, on the whole, willingly given. But no longer. Tension and excitement of an unpleasant sort were in the air. How long could Lloyd George hold this coalition together?

For Theodore Carr, coming to take his place in the House of Commons was thrilling but confusing. He came from a small, if ancient, northern city, where he and his family were known by everyone, and where he enjoyed considerable status. Suddenly, although an MP, he was a nobody. Entering the Chamber of the Commons was a humbling experience, and Theodore was not used to humility. In those days before television, he had no familiarity with what the place looked like, and in any case pictures and photographs could never convey the atmosphere sufficiently to set new members at ease. He was used to Carlisle's Town Hall and the Guildhall, and the Athenaeum in Lowther Street, and none of them held any awe for him. He was familiar with every room in Carlisle's halls, had spoken in all of them, and had never known the power of place to intimidate. But now he had to watch himself all the time, concerned that he might make some foolish mistake. He had so much to learn and was surrounded by many men who had learned it all before him. In Carlisle, responsible for thousands of workers and the fortunes of a business, Theodore had had no trouble making decisions and carrying out plans. He could, in effect, do what he liked, and he had been doing so for thirteen years. It suited his temperament. Now, as an MP, he could not. He was only a tiny cog in a machine, and it was the first machine he had ever encountered whose workings baffled him.

There was also the shock of coming to live in London. Theodore had been to the metropolis often enough and was hardly a country cousin overwhelmed by it, but nevertheless living there was quite different. In Carlisle, everything in the city centre was shut by six in the evening. He could drive through it an hour later and, apart from the trams and buses, find it deserted. There were few signs of life at all in the evening, and none whatsoever well before midnight. There were no night-clubs, no restaurants, no teashops open; except for the public houses, the hotels were the only establishments offering food, drink or entertainment. Once the pubs had emptied, the city was dead, its shop-fronts dark, its pavements empty. But in London after the war the contrast that greeted Theodore was bewildering. The city burst with a vitality he had never known – hordes spilled into Piccadilly and Leicester Square at all hours as the clubs and cafés disgorged them, everything was brightly lit and rarely was any street in the West End totally empty. He was not a merrymaker himself, or even particularly sociable, and he was shaken to be part of such exuberance just by passing through it. Even getting about during the day required stamina. He had expected to feel a little displaced at first, naturally, but what he had not fully appreciated, or anticipated, was how uneasy and helpless it would make him feel.

The worst of it was trying to fathom what the Government, of which he was a part, was actually doing. Debates about Ireland seemed to fill a lot of time and though Theodore knew the Irish situation was important (the militant Sinn Fein had won three-quarters of the Irish seats and in January 1919 declared Ireland independent), he was personally more interested in devoting himself to reforms in his own country. Nor did he find it rewarding to listen to endless discussions about war reparations, though again he conceded their importance. It was not until the problem of what was delicately referred to as 'labour unrest' came up for debate that Theodore felt in a position to contribute anything, and here he was in complete agreement with Lloyd George. They both took a very serious view of industrial disputes and anticipated that if matters were not handled very carefully indeed, there would be a series of disastrous strikes.

The days of work lost to industrial disputes had continued to rise since the war ended, amounting to 35 million working-days in 1919, and 86 million in 1921. The fear was that the three most powerful unions – miners, railwaymen and transport – would unite to strike for better wages and shorter hours, paralysing the country. Theodore understood just as well as the Prime

Minister that the pattern of work in industry had changed, and was continuing to change all over the country, and that they must respond to this, if catastrophe was to be averted. In Carr's biscuit works the working-hours had been reduced to forty-eight a week in March 1919 (six days of eight hours each) and were further reduced to forty-four in June 1920, as a compromise, after the Works Advisory Committee had asked for the working-day to go down to forty hours. The same kind of negotiations were going on throughout industry, but there was still the threat of major stoppages. The Government had to be prepared, so in 1920 the Emergency Powers Act was passed. By this Act, order could be restored by 'Regulation' in any 'state of emergency' that interfered with the 'supply and distribution of food, water, fuel or light, or with the means of locomotion'. The clear intention was to prevent any large-scale industrial action by the unions or, if it happened, to break the strike. Theodore was in favour of the Act.

But he was also all for carrying out election promises about new housing (in spite of his objection to having a council estate next to his own house). He had his grandfather's interest in seeing his, and everyone else's, workers given the opportunity to live in decent housing and though, in Carlisle, the worst of the slums in J.D.'s day had disappeared, many families were still living in sub-standard accommodation without bathrooms. Local authorities needed subsidies from the central Government to enable them to build housing estates of considerable size to satisfy the demand, but where was this money to come from? There had been ambitious pre-election plans, but now, with interest rates up and public spending in the Budget of 1919 standing at £2,500 million (half a million more than in 1917), housing could not be a priority. Through the Housing and Town Planning Act of 1919 Exchequer grants were made available to local authorities (and Carlisle had been one of the first cities to take them up), but not on the scale promised. Two years later the subsidies were withdrawn. Housing was too expensive, a luxury for a government struggling with unexpectedly severe financial problems.

For Theodore Carr, returning to Carlisle when Parliament was not sitting, such failures were embarrassing to explain away. True, Carlisle council had managed to get the Longsowerby houses built before the withdrawal of the subsidy, but it was a small estate which in no way satisfied demand. As Carlisle's MP, Theodore had to take responsibility for his government's decisions and it did not please him. He had always kept his own promises, and had never taken on a task he could not fulfil, but now he was badgered on all sides by constituents wanting to know why this or that had not been done. Inefficiency had always annoyed him and now he was made to feel inadequate as well as inefficient, as a member of a government unable to keep its word. It was tempting for him to believe that his grandfather, and his father and uncles, had been wise to stay out of politics for so long: they had surely done more to improve conditions for the people of Carlisle by staying at home and working at a level they understood and could control. Lack of control was anathema to Theodore (just as it had been to his grandfather) and he had a great struggle accepting that, in effect, he had virtually no control as just one Member of Parliament.

But accept it he finally did, and once this difficult transitional period was over, he took to following instead of leading rather better than anticipated, though continuing to suffer the common frustrations of all incoming new members who feel they have something specific to offer that is being ignored. Theodore's particular interest, naturally enough, continued to be in labour relations. He felt that he knew a good deal about both how these stood at the moment, in manufacturing industries anyway, and what needed to be done to meet the perils ahead. He knew that the men who had come back from the war were not as docile and manageable as they had been before and that post-war conditions could result in further and more violent changes in existing factory hours and wages. He sat on a House of Commons committee chaired by J. H. Whitley, the Speaker, to consider the setting up of joint employer/ employee welfare organisations in factories, similar to the Workers' Advisory Committee he had already inaugurated at Carr's. But he was also humane enough to be concerned about the fate of workers who suffered industrial injuries, and being in London gave him the opportunity to involve himself more in the Manor Hospital in Golders Green. This had originally been founded, with Theodore's help, as a place where injured workers could go to recover, but when the war began it took in soldiers too (Dorothy Carr nursed there for a short time). Now Theodore wanted to see it become the centre of an industrial orthopaedic movement which would take over from the old sick-clubs in factories and become a properly structured organisation, to which workers and employees paid subscriptions.

Dividing his time between London and Carlisle, Theodore was obviously not as closely involved with the two family companies as he had been, though there was never any doubt as to who was still in charge. No major decision could be taken without him, and a great many comparatively minor ones were still referred to Theodore, but he no longer regularly paced the factory floor in the biscuit works and his actual presence was no longer utterly familiar to the workers. In Theodore's absence, Ernest Hutchinson, the works manager, and E. P. Brown, the office manager, were the two men who appeared to run the biscuit works. They were both deeply respectable and responsible men, devoted to the Carr family firm. The control they assumed in this period saw a further shift in the balance of power, a shift away from family, which had been taking place ever since J.D. died, but had not yet been openly acknowledged by bringing outsiders on to the board of directors. Hutchinson, who had been with Carr's almost from the death of its founder, was allocated shares in 1915 but did not go on the board until after the war. Once he had done so – followed by E. P. Brown (whom James had brought in, in 1902) – the assumption was that he had somehow become 'family', but this was mere convenient pretence. Hutchinson, Brown and two others, Moore and Bowman, who were appointed a little later to the board of the Flour Mills Company, had all proved themselves over a long period of time as loyal and true servants of the Carrs' interests. They were reliable and important people in the two companies, upon whose expert judgement a great deal depended.

What was happening to Carr's in the immediate post-First World War period was what tended to happen to many successful family firms begun almost a century before. Outsiders were coming into the upper echelons, because the firm was becoming too big to be run purely by family members (and those 'family' who were available to run it did not always have either the necessary talent or interest, though this was rarely admitted). Shares, and then places on the board, did not make outsiders 'family'. The difference was both subtle and complicated. All Carrs were supposed to put the firm first, as their grandfather had decreed in his will, and most of them did. Apart from anything else, it was in their own interest. A collapse of Carr's meant more than failing their grandfather: it meant putting their own incomes in jeopardy. But outsiders could not be expected to feel like this to the same extent. Carr's could not be everything to them in the same way. They might at any time put themselves first. And this in turn affected how the company was thought of by others. There were those, in 1920, who muttered locally that Carr's was no longer really a family firm, but that it had become more like other non-family firms and had lost its peculiar identity.

This would change only once Theodore was back full-time in Carlisle. He lost his seat in the 1922 election, a blow that was softened simply because most of the coalition Liberals did so. Another blow, that same year, was of a personal nature. His brother John died in China, as Sydney had done. His two medical missionary brothers were hardly part of Theodore's everyday life, as Bertram and Harold were, but nevertheless he had been fond of them both, and admired what they did. Besides, as head of the family since their father's death, he had in some way felt responsible for them. John had been a delegate to a National Christian Conference in Shanghai, looking 'most distingué with his handsome grey hair and a very nicely cut suit'. He had spoken at one of the meetings and then afterwards, in the grounds of the mission, had felt faint and had to lie down on the grass. He had pains in his arms and chest and 'felt from the first it was angina pectoris' (from which so many of the male Carrs suffered). At first he seemed to be recovering, even having the energy to be 'distressed . . . to find that his pyjama jacket did not match his trousers, the one garment having been changed without the other in order to conserve his strength. And how insistent he was that his hair should be properly brushed.' But two days later he became delirious and died. He was buried in Bubbling Well Cemetery, Shanghai, his coffin borne by four Chinese and four Western friends. He was forty-six to Theodore's fifty-six.

Once he had lost his seat, Theodore was able to devote himself to Carr's in the way he had always done before 1918. Things had changed in the biscuit works, as he had known they would, and his work force now had different expectations. The atmosphere was still good, but what helped preserve it were the measures he took to improve the relationship between workers and management. One of these was the appointment of what was called a 'lady superintendent'. Miss Nora Wynne, the young woman he appointed in 1920, was well educated and quite different from the old-style matrons who had supervised the girls and women. Her job (a new kind of job for a woman) was to look after the general welfare of the female employees, and not just their physical well-being. She was in effect a personnel officer of quite a new sort to the factory. Her scope lay outside, as well as inside, the works. Should any of the women be absent from work, she was to attempt to visit them at home and find out their circumstances; if these had any bearing on their absenteeism, she was to try to do something about them.

On his return to Carlisle, Theodore was pleased to discover that Miss Wynne's appointment was working out well, with visible benefits for Carr's. She had settled in quickly, living first with a Carr relative not far from the works, and had established herself as a formidable presence, though not in the manner of the Miss Smith who had caused the girls to strike. One of her advantages was that her looks belied her strong character. She was slim and attractive, with a very direct, steady gaze (some said stare). She wore a white coat over her clothes, to give her an official appearance, and had her own office, though she was hardly in it during the first few years, since she made a point of spending as much time as possible on the factory floor acquainting herself with the actual role of the women whose welfare was her concern. This did not necessarily make her popular but it earned her some respect, which was more important.

Visits to some of the women's homes quickly made Miss Wynne realise that however good working conditions in Carr's might be, circumstances at home were often poor. Most of the girls and women working in Carr's still lived in Caldewgate, in the narrow streets opposite the factory, or else at Willow Holme, beside the River Caldew, in a development called Barwise Nook, where houses had been built by the council when the main Caldewgate street was widened in 1900. So many of Carr's female workers lived there that Mr Hutchinson (the works manager) ran a Mission there with great success (though half its attraction was the concerts on Saturday nights). Betty Brown, starting as a packer at the same time as Miss Wynne began work, lived at Willow Holme and loved the Mission, which provided her with the only social life she had. But she was always alarmed at the thought of Miss Wynne paying a visit, and took care to do nothing to invite one. Partly her apprehension was to do with embarrassment. Miss Wynne was a smart, middle-class woman and the Barwise Nook houses, though comparatively new, were thought of as 'not the sort of place for her to be'. None of them had bathrooms, and most were split into flats, with a staircase at the back leading to the upstairs apartments. A great many people were crammed into each 'house', all paying rent of 4s 6d a week.

Miss Wynne soon found out for herself that appearances were deceptive. The fronts of the houses she visited looked clean and pleasant enough, and were certainly an improvement on those in the older streets, but inside they were much the same – small, dark, badly ventilated rooms, very poorly furnished, and with few facilities. Getting into these houses was not easy for her. She was not a social worker or a health visitor, and she had no right of access to the homes of Carr's employees. She went purely as a visitor, to enquire after their welfare, and with the purpose of trying to determine why they had been absent from work. Absenteeism was not high at Carr's but there were some persistent offenders, and since sacking anyone without cause was not the policy of the firm (or not the official policy to which they subscribed), every effort was made to discover the reasons for it and to deal with it, if possible, to ensure that it never became endemic. All this was explained to the Workers' Advisory Committee, whose members in turn relayed it to the women, but nevertheless Miss Wynne's arrival on their doorsteps was greeted with deep suspicion. What was she, for all the fine talk, but a snooper, come to catch them out? She had surely come to poke her nose into their business and was therefore resented.

From Miss Wynne's point of view, the whole relationship with the women for whom she was responsible was immensely difficult. She did not want to seem a hostile inspector, but on the other hand she had facts to find out and could not afford to be in any way apologetic or ingratiating. She wanted to convince the women that the point of her position as lady superintendent was to *help* them, by understanding the circumstances that might keep them at home. But even walking down the Caldewgate or Willow Holme streets she felt at a disadvantage. She was so obviously alien, her very clothes branding her a foreign species. As she picked her way among groups of small ragged children playing in the gutters, she lost the feeling of authority she had in the factory itself. When she found the house she wanted, she was often obliged to stand in front of it for a long time before there was any answer to her knock. Two or three hammerings on the door were always necessary and even then there was often no response. She had to resort to selecting one of the children, who had gathered to gape at her, and asking him or her to go round the back to see if anyone was at home. She learned, eventually, that 'the back' was indeed where the women would be, usually in the wash-houses. Alerted to her presence, they would finally, but reluctantly, open the front door. But the door would open only a crack, and dismay would show on the inhabitant's face. However politely Miss Wynne asked to be let in, even to her the words seemed somehow offensive, an invasion of privacy.

She never stayed long, there was that to be said for her, and took every care not to exceed the requirements of her job. This was not a social call, so she never presumed to accept tea, if it was offered, or any other refreshment. Nor did she ask too many questions. In fact, she hardly asked any direct questions at all, relying on her own observations to piece together the situation. She made no notes there and then – that would have looked too much like officialdom – but later would jot down what she had noticed. She did not need medical qualifications to recognise the severity of a cough, the extreme pallor of a complexion or the existence of a rash, and would always try to establish whether a doctor had been visited (he rarely had, because of the expense) and whether a certificate of ill-health was available. If it was, her job was done. But far more common than specific ill-health was poor health due to lack of proper nourishment and care, and this was more difficult both to recognise and to deal with. The women feared to lose their jobs and did not want to reveal their own exhaustion. Sometimes, as she sat in a very cold room, with no heating, listening to the children cry, seeing and smelling little evidence of cooking, Miss Wynne knew that the reason for absenteeism here was poverty. The young woman might, for instance, be part of a large family struggling to cope and had been kept at home by her mother to look after the younger ones. Miss Wynne would rarely, in these circumstances, see the mother, who might herself be ill, and so she simply had to make it clear that repeated days off could not forever be tolerated. It was unpleasant and she disliked being so rigid.

But on other occasions she really could help and then her job took on a different complexion. Carr's had a sick-club, and many of the girls had not appreciated the help it could give them if they paid the small subscription required. She would explain the terms to them and persuade them to join, feeling that she had done some good. Then there was the convalescent home for those who had been really ill. This was at Silloth, on the sand-dunes to the west of Carr's flour mill (and where George Carr had once had his farm). Employees could spend a week there, free of charge, if they had a medical certificate, and this rest, in Silloth's bracing climate, often set the women up so well that they returned to work fortified, in a way they never did if they tried to recuperate at home. Arranging for women to go there was quite the nicest part of Miss Wynne's job and required little tact or skill. Dealing with absenteeism caused by problems that had nothing to do with illness or poverty, however, demanded a great deal of tact. Some women stayed away because they were being bullied or harassed, but they would not necessarily say so, for fear of reprisals. Miss Wynne was not a confessor, either by appointment or temperament – she was not a woman to confide in – but on the other hand she did, in time, build up a reputation for being fair, so grievances began to be reported. Women were more likely to report them when not in the factory, so home visits proved in the end to be valuable. But Miss Wynne never forgot her purpose. Her motive was clear: she aimed to get the best out of the women workers for Carr's. She was no more 'soft' than was Theodore, or any of the management. They were all sticklers for discipline and punctuality, especially Ernest Hutchinson, the works manager, who, if he found anyone clocking off even one minute early, would publicly reprimand them and make them go back to work for that one minute.

In the early 1920s business was excellent, with an unprecedented demand for two types of biscuit in particular (Club Cheese and Table Water), and the export trade was booming again. Bertram had a lot to do with this. It was he who, before the First World War, had travelled the world establishing depots and appointing agents with such success. The whole of Europe had been covered, and also the United States, South America and Canada. So had South Africa and other African countries (Gambia and Sierra Leone on the west coast, and the whole of the east from French Somalia down to Mozambique), as well as the West Indies. The Middle East had Carr's representatives in Saudi Arabia, but the Far East had yet to be opened to them. Once the war was over, Bertram decided to concentrate on India, where there were none of the tariffs that had started to make trade elsewhere less profitable, even before the war. In India, he reckoned, Empire Free Trade was likely to survive for a long time. He himself went to Bombay to establish a head office, and then left it to agents he had chosen to establish other offices and depots in all the principal cities. The success of the Indian department was the biggest single reason why Carr's recovered so well after the war.

But by the time Theodore was back in Carlisle after losing his seat, Bertram was going through difficult times and his work for Carr's was almost at an end. In 1920 his wife Mabel had died suddenly of enteric fever, aged fifty. Bertram had taken her on a trip to the Canary

Islands, where she unknowingly contracted the fever, and she took ill on the way home, on board a ship that had inadequate medical facilities. Everyone in the family was very shocked, especially since enteric fever was not one of the killer diseases they all dreaded; it should have been perfectly treatable. Bertram, an outgoing, gregarious man, cheerful by temperament and far more easygoing than his brother Theodore, was lost without Mabel. It was true that he had spent many months away from her on business trips, but coming home to her was of great importance and his letters breathe nothing but delighted anticipation at the prospect. Mabel had been essential to his need for stability and security, which balanced his conflicting need for variety and adventure. Without Mabel to come home to he seemed to lose his wanderlust. He was at home more than he had ever been, but found little comfort there.

Since 1916 Bertram and his family had been living at Burgh-by-Sands, a village on the Solway Firth coast, not far from Port Carlisle where the original canal had ended (though he kept his other house in Carlisle too). His two older daughters, Eleanor and Beryl (known as Betty), married in 1924, leaving him with Miriam and Diana, aged seventeen and ten, but they were at school and so was his son Allen. Bertram had always liked to walk and was interested in birds, but solitary rambles along the marsh did little to improve spirits, and his hobby of building model boats did not lend itself to conviviality. He still went in to work, but his heart was no longer in it and he was lonely.

The only activity that had always raised his spirits was travelling, so he tried a cruise to Madeira. And he enjoyed it, writing to his daughter Betty that he was having a delightful voyage, meeting interesting people, relishing the sun and appreciating the ship's orchestra. But he needed something more adventurous to help him recover more completely from his wife's death, and it was his brother Ernest who provided it. The same year that Mabel died, Ernest and his family had left Wigton and gone to live in what was then British East Africa, soon to become Kenya. In 1924 he came back on holiday to England and, visiting Bertram, suggested that he would surely enjoy and benefit from a trip to his new home near Nairobi. He tempted his brother with descriptions of the glorious sunshine, so different from the wild, wet winds on the Solway marsh, and of the wonderful natural life there, especially the wild flowers. He told Bertram it was like Cumberland, only with sun, and by the time Ernest left, his brother was won over and ready to leave with him. Bertram decided to take Allen with him and make a real adventure of the trip.

They sailed from Tilbury on the *Llanstephan Castle* (a very different boat from the one unable to provide his wife with the care she had needed). It was, wrote Bertram to Betty, 'like a large floating hotel which keeps to schedule time as does a railway train'. He felt better as soon as he embarked and loved the whole twenty-day voyage out to Mombasa, where they all stayed at the Manor Hotel. The next part of the journey was by train, 320 miles to Nairobi, the same distance roughly as London to Carlisle but with thrilling scenery all the way. By now Bertram was his old self, fascinated by all the new sights and sounds, and eager to learn and understand more about this new country.

Ernest's house, Woodlands, impressed him deeply – none of the Carrs had anything like this back in Carlisle. It was built of solid stone, with a red-tiled roof, and inside it was timbered with teak. The rooms were vast and airy, and there was a balcony sixty feet long on the east side overlooking beautiful grounds and with magnificent views. It was, wrote an awed Bertram, 'an earthly paradise'. He had thought Ernest ludicrous to claim to have found Cumberland in Africa, but now when he saw sweet peas in a vase on his brother's desk, and red and pink roses in his garden, and when he ate strawberries as good as those they had all once enjoyed at their grandparents' house, he realised it was true. Ernest took him to visit lakes and waterfalls and he saw that these could indeed be compared to Buttermere, Coniston or Mardale. And there were other comparisons to be made of a different kind, in which Kenya came off better – prices, always of interest to a Carr. Coffee was only threepence a pound, eggs fifty for one shilling (though it was true that imported Carr's biscuits were a great luxury, at six shillings for a mere two-pound tin).

Ernest had not finished showing off the delights of his adopted country. He took Bertram and Allen on an expedition up Mount Kenya, not to the top, which was four times the height of the highest Lake District mountain, but to within the last 2,000 feet. Ernest had actually had a rest-house built at 10,000 feet and a pathway had been cut all the way to it, with the twenty-eight-mile stretch from Chogonia becoming known as 'Carr's route'. They drove to Chogonia together with African 'boys' to help with all the camping equipment and then began the ascent. It pleased Bertram to find that at fifty-six he was well able to keep up, and that the physical strength on which the male Carrs prided themselves was still evident. He and Ernest might not be able to lift those twenty-hundred-weight sacks their grandfather had swung on to his back – not that they had ever had occasion to try – but they could tackle mountains without getting breathless. Bertram, as well as loving the exercise, remarked constantly on the vegetation. It struck him as amazing to see, growing in parts of the forest on the mountain, gladioli, delphiniums, red-hot pokers, thistles and heather. He was beginning to think his younger brother had been very clever after all to break away from the family firm and do so well for himself.

Ernest had yet another excitement to offer: a safari, into what was described as 'the heart of tropical Africa'. But before they went on this expedition they were invited to a garden party for the visiting Duke and Duchess of York (the future King George VI and Queen Elizabeth). Bertram, always the most sociable of the Carrs (who were not known as gregarious or sociable people), loved it. He was most taken with 'the little Duchess . . . she wins all hearts wherever she goes . . . with her smiling winsome ways'. Being a bit of a dandy himself, Bertram cared about clothes and noted her 'very simple and dainty gown' and her pretty pink straw hat. He thought the Duke very smart in his white naval captain's uniform. Also present was the Mayor of Nairobi, whom the Carrs were delighted to find was a Maryport man, and a reverend gentleman whom Bertram had last seen in a railway compartment they had shared between Penrith and Carlisle – oh, it was a small, Cumberland world. It impressed him, too, that Ernest knew so many people at the garden party and that he was a person of note in Nairobi, just as he and Theodore were in Carlisle. Whatever status Ernest had had within the family (rather an uncertain one), it was now undoubtedly enhanced – 'We have enjoyed to the full the advantages my brother has been able to give us by means of his liberality and hospitality, his acquaintance with so many people in the colony and his considerable knowledge of the country.'

The safari, into Uganda, was full of danger as well as thrills, but Bertram thrived on it all. Part of the journey was made in canoes and as he sat in the dugout, being paddled through lakes lined with reeds and beautiful purple lotus lilies, watching the wild duck skim the surface, Bertram turned philosophical. The life he had led, selling biscuits all over the world, had not been conducive to the kind of thinking he now did. There was one particular occasion, on a night when the moon was full and he was drifting silently through the water, watching an enormous moon rise 'majestically cold and calm above the mists which had gathered', when 'I thought ... the span of human life seemed a very little thing.' Mabel's was over and his own, even at the most optimistic estimate, was three-quarters gone.

By the end of the safari, Bertram had reached a decision that he revealed to no one. But saying goodbye to Ernest was hard. He had come to admire his younger brother in a way he had never expected to do, especially for what he described as his 'coolness', which had been amply displayed during the collapse of rickety bridges as they drove over them. Ernest was never daunted, for 'he is so accustomed to running risks of all kinds that nothing seems to affect him'. And Bertram admired, too, Ernest's ardent Christianity. He and his wife were taking an active part in missionary work and ran their household on exemplary lines, with set family prayers morning and evening, during which there were readings from religious tracts (shades of uncles Henry and James). Boarding the little steamer that was to take him and his son to the bigger ship, Bertram was truly sad to say farewell to his brother – 'he shook hands and turned away. As we cleared the quay and slowly made upstream he could be seen reaching the rest-house alone and then I saw him no more. The companionship of months had come to an end and I knew that thousands of miles must divide us and that it must perforce be a long while before we could meet again.' They never did.

The return to England on a dreary March day in 1925 was grim, though Bertram was grateful for the sight of 'the familiar green fields', which made him give thanks to God for protecting him and Allen throughout their trip – 'I had scarcely suffered so much as a headache.' Back in Burgh-by-Sands, with the rain lashing against the windows and the mist seeming to hang permanently over the sea, he soon felt low again. It was time to act on the decision he had made during that moonlit African night, but bringing himself to that point was very difficult.

—————————— • ——————————

Chapter Eleven

CHANGING TIMES

Bertram's absence had served one useful purpose. It had temporarily stopped the gossip about him. One of the penalties of a family firm was that devotion to them went hand-in-hand with what was reckoned to be a legitimate interest in their personal lives. Carlisle was a small, compact city, its population 57,000 now, in which it was virtually impossible for anyone in the public eye to escape observation, and for the Carrs there was no hope at all. The workers in the factory and the employees in the offices all watched and discussed and, in general, relished keeping a gimlet-eye on their owners and bosses. They knew of Theodore's mistress in London, during his days as MP, and of Bertram's interest in a certain young lady. Nobody was fooled. Everyone knew about Miss Little, to whom Bertram gave a lift from Burgh-by-Sands. She was a secretary in Carr's offices, and what could be more natural than for him to drive her in to work?

The decision that he had come to in Kenya was that he would marry Miss Little and put an end to the gossip. It was not the decision other members of the family had anticipated. They had thought Bertram would see the unsuitability of such a match and drop her, once the gossip was reported to him and he was told that his behaviour reflected on the good name of Carr. Keeping a woman in London and managing such a liaison discreetly was one thing, but 'carrying on' with a secretary in his own firm in full view of all Carlisle was another. Something had to be done, and Bertram did it. But first he rented a house a long way from Burgh-by-Sands, a long way from Carlisle, a long way from any of the Carrs. This was Threlkeld Leys, on the outskirts of Cockermouth, some forty miles west of Carlisle. No Carr had ever lived in this vicinity. Whereas the house at Burgh had been part of the village, Threlkeld Leys was quite isolated, standing alone among fields, with no other habitation in sight and the nearest village miles away. The house had the appearance of a retreat, which was precisely what Bertram intended it to be. He wanted to retreat from the censure that his second marriage would inevitably provoke: his bride was not only of a different social class but very much younger, just as his father's had been.

On 10 June 1925 he married Eva Mary Little (known as Mary), aged twenty-six to his fifty-seven. He married her by special licence in Mosser parish church, a tiny old church perched high on the side of the fells, with no one from his own family present or signing the register. Mary's mother signed, together with a friend. There was nothing for Mary to be ashamed of – unlike Mary Laurie's father, hers was listed as 'a gentleman' – but her marriage was found no more acceptable by the Carrs than Thomas William's had been so long ago. Times had changed since the war, but they had not changed enough for Bertram to have any confidence as to how his new wife would be regarded. She was, after all, the same age as his elder daughter. But he had anticipated this and prepared accordingly. Soon after their marriage, he and Mary moved, but only a mile away, to High Dyke. It was a house in a similar position to the first, extremely secluded and not near a village. Here

Bertram tried to make a new life for himself, attending Mosser church diligently and acting as governor of a local school. He had a great deal to reflect on at High Dyke, including memories of how he himself had reacted to his own father's second marriage, but he seemed happy enough to have left Carr's.

Bertram's retirement left Theodore far from contemplating his own. He was older than his brother, but he had lost none of his passion for the business and was at that time watching developments in the trade-union movement with growing anxiety. Carr's were doing well, but if a general strike were called, as Theodore suspected early in 1926 that it would be, no one knew what might happen. Theodore had done his best to keep his workers happy, but he knew most of them had been members of trade unions for a long time now and that if loyalty to union membership was called for, he would find it pointless appealing to their loyalty to Carr's instead. In the event, Carr's were lucky. When the General Strike came on 5 May 1926, the only workers affected were the printers, the cardboard-box makers and the transport men. The chief problem for Carr's was obtaining deliveries, but they managed to keep going, just, and the only workers who had to be laid off were a few joiners. There was no disorder in Carlisle as a whole, either, though a Volunteer Service Committee of local middle-class dignitaries was set up in the old prison. The deputy chairman was Ronald Carr, Theodore's cousin, but it turned out that he had little to do. The chaos and collapse of trade that Theodore had envisaged did not happen in Carlisle.

But he had other worries of a personal nature, which had nothing to do with the industrial unrest. His eyesight was bothering him and he was diagnosed as suffering from diabetes. He was put on a strict diet, which he found tedious but not nearly as annoying as not being able to drive, because his sight had deteriorated so rapidly. It was agony for him, with his love of cars, to have a chauffeur, and he became increasingly bad-tempered. His wife pointed out that now he was over sixty he must expect to slow down and must take care of himself, but Theodore rejected this depressing idea. Whatever the consequences, he had no desire to slow down, as Bertram had done. But in fact it was Bertram who suffered the consequences of being a Carr, with a family history, in the male line, of heart trouble. On 30 May 1927 he died suddenly of heart failure, two weeks before his second wedding anniversary. The shock for Theodore was profound. Bertram was the one brother he had been close to; in the business sense he and Bertram *were*, in effect, the Carrs. He was the only person to whom Theodore could really talk and in whom he could confide, and though Bertram had retired, he had always been available to discuss problems and ideas.

The funeral was a big affair, the cortège driving all the way from High Dyke to Carlisle cemetery. As well as virtually the entire Carr family, hundreds of Carr's employees were present. The biscuit works was closed down so that those who wanted to pay their respects could do so, and most of them did. Bertram had been popular. He was easier in manner than Theodore and, though rarely on the factory floor himself, knew many of the workers from the various works' social functions, where he mixed much more freely than his brother. More than any other death at that time, Bertram's marked the end of another era at Carr's. After it, Theodore began to worry about who would take over from him. The fact of his own mortality seemed to strike him harder than it had done after his son's death during the war.

Theoretically there was no need for anxiety. The position had changed since Stanley's death and there were those in the next generation who, by 1927, were well on the way to being able to take over when the time came, not that Theodore actually anticipated giving way yet, whatever his state of health. Ronald Carr, Theodore's cousin, was aged only thirty-five. Ronald had had a difficult early childhood, which left its mark on him. His father, James, who died when his son was seven, had drawn an absolutely rigid line between what was right and what was wrong and, unlike his own father, the ever-gentle J.D., was terrifying to his young son in his fanatically religious zeal. Ronald was made to accompany his father on his regular drives round the villages near Carlisle in a four-wheeled iron-tyred wagonette, distributing religious tracts, which were scattered so plentifully that it seemed to him they must be setting some kind of peculiar paperchase. These outings made him feel not only embarrassed but frightened. Some of the villages were known to be in Roman Catholic areas and, as an imaginative child, he had visions of himself and his father being captured and subjected to unmentionable tortures as heretics. Home life was no more reassuring. The Cavendish Mount house always seemed full of similar evangelical enthusiasts who had come to help spread the word, and the environment was one of constant prayer and the reading of texts. It left Ronald feeling isolated and lonely, but he proved to be tough enough to survive this indoctrination without being thoroughly oppressed by it.

When his father died while Ronald was still young, the rest of the Carr family felt sorry for him and rallied round, involving him in their various leisure pursuits. Theodore took him, with his own children, to learn how to sail, and of course for drives in his car. It made him an exciting figure to the boy, who sensed that this much older cousin was the same kind of strong personality as his own father had been. The difference, to his relief, was that Theodore did not preach religion all the time. His obsession was the family biscuit works. Like all young Carrs, Ronald had already been taken to visit the factory but, apart from enjoying the tasting of biscuits, he had felt no immediate passion for it. His uncle Henry's sons, Laurence and Frank, played their part in his upbringing too. Laurence was not yet married, so he had no family in which to include Ronald, but he took him climbing in the Lake District, and Frank, also still a bachelor, taught him to fish. But Ronald was more wary of Frank, the last of his family to be a lay preacher. (He preached regularly at Cumwhitton Parish Hall, where James had also preached.) It was much more fun for the boy to go with Harold, Theodore's youngest brother, and learn to shoot. Because of all these relatives, Ronald had at least something to look forward to on holiday from school and all these connections could not help but give him a sense of family.

He knew, of course, that all male Carrs were expected to go into the family business, but while he was growing up he wanted to get away not only from Carr's but from Carlisle. His education at Repton public school had fitted him for something more challenging and he went on to Pembroke College, Cambridge, with no idea of what he wanted to do afterwards, but convinced that he had escaped what he saw as the treadmill of biscuit manufacturing. In spite of loving his mother, he planned to go home to Carlisle as little as possible. But the war changed everything for Ronald, as it did for so many young men. Unlike Theodore's son Stanley, he not only survived the war but came out of it with some glory. He was mentioned twice in despatches in 1915, going on to win the MC on the Somme. On the same day that Stanley was killed, Ronald had led an attack to secure Schwaben and, though wounded, continued to lead his men. The notes on this advance show that 'in the second trench Captain Carr tackled three of the enemy single-handed and accounted for two of these before he was knocked out by a second wound'. His award of the MC was published in the *London Gazette* of 14 November 1916. He was a major at twenty-two, and gave every appearance of having relished his military career.

Impressive stories circulated in the factory of exactly how many Germans Mr Ronald had personally bay-oneted and there were furtive but admiring looks at the scar on his face. Some of the women, like Maggie Robson, the head forewoman in the 1920s, had known him since he was four years old, when he was brought round the factory by his father. By now Ronald was a family man. He had made a wartime marriage to Vida Maxwell, and had two children, Margaret and Douglas Nicholson (known as Nick). After the war, Ronald did not return to Cambridge to complete his education. The war and marriage had changed his priorities. Instead, he went straight into the biscuit works and, to his surprise, quickly became as passionate about the business as his cousin was. Theodore recognised Ronald's ability and was certainly pleased by his evident dedication, though he had found it hard to avoid a touch of natural bitter-ness that his young cousin had survived the war when his own son had not. At the peace celebration dinner given by Carr's, Theodore had gone so far as to confess this openly to the assembled throng and a hush had fallen over them for a moment. It was touching enough to halt the cheers and laughter for a while, to hear him say how painful it was to see Ronald among them and not Stanley, but embarrassing for Ronald. But, of course, Theodore did have another son, Ivan, whom he still hoped to groom to take over from him.

Their relationship was good. Even before the death of his brother Stanley, Ivan had shared with his father a love of boats and sailing, and they were at their closest when indulging this passion. As a small boy, Ivan's greatest treat had been going with Theodore, just the two of them, to Silloth, driving wickedly fast, and, when they got there, sailing on the ebb tide down the Solway Firth to come alongside one of the great sailing ships bringing wheat to Carr's mill. Just as Theodore first realised what Carr's stood for when he was given labels to cut out during his attack of measles, so Ivan, aged seven, realised the full import of the family name as he sat with his father in the cabin of a ship that had come from Australia. The captain was a Spaniard, and as he and Theodore talked, drinking whisky and toasting Carr's, Ivan listened and pieced together what his father actually did and what the family firm was all about. It seemed so romantic to think of ships sailing right across the world to provide Carr's mill with the wheat it needed, and it made the business of producing biscuits suddenly thrilling, instead of mundane.

But, like Ronald, Ivan had no intention at first of going into the biscuit works. Stanley's death altered things of course. Ivan was now his father's only son and expectations were high. He was only ten when his brother was killed, but it was obvious, even to a child, that all the hopes invested in Stanley would now weigh down on him. Meanwhile, he was still being educated, first at prep school and then at Oundle, and he hated both. Unlike Dorothy, called home to look after her mother when Stanley was killed, Ivan would much have preferred to be at home. He was bullied, he loathed all the games they were forced to play, and spent most of his schooldays lurking in the music room. There was a good deal of the rebel in his character, though this never took the form of rebellion against his own father. He longed for Theodore's visits to him at school, loving the excursions in the new Sunbeam car, and the highlight of

his schooldays was when Theodore took him to Belfast
to pick up a motor-cruiser he had bought in 1920, while
he was an MP. The two of them sailed it back to the
Solway in heavy seas and Ivan was full of admiration
for the boldness, even rashness, that his father showed
as a mariner.

Deciding to go into the family business after all was
something Ivan did more by default than anything else,
but once he had made the decision he was surprised, as
Ronald had been, at how much he enjoyed learning
what it was all about. There was more variety in the
work than he had imagined and much more involvement
with all kinds of people, to which he responded. In fact,
he proved himself better with people than his father,
who had often been brusque and impatient. Ivan was
not a typical Carr, in that, though tall, he was not big
and heavy, and he was rather more obviously sensitive
than most of them cared to be. His father sent him as
part of his training to Workington, Whitehaven and
Maryport, those western ports in Cumberland, which
had fallen on very hard times, and he was shocked by the
visible destitution he witnessed there. Theodore, who
sometimes worried that Ivan had been overindulged and
sheltered from the realities of the world, was pleased by
this reaction. Ivan was at last appreciating the value of
money, as Theodore felt that all Carrs should. He did
not want his son to imagine that being a Carr gave him
an automatic right to easy money. On the contrary,
when Ivan asked his father for money to buy a boat,
Theodore would lend him the £250 only on condition
that a proper agreement was drawn up with a solicitor
and that it was repaid according to the terms he stated.

So Ronald and Ivan were the two front-runners to
take over the business, though Allen, Bertram's son,
who was twenty-four when his father died and had
taken a degree in commerce at Birmingham University,

was a possible contender. He joined the business just after the General Strike, starting in the offices. Frank had no sons (he had one adopted daughter) and Laurence's only son, Ian, was not born until 1928. That left Harold, now forty-seven and in Home Sales, but he had never been as dedicated as Theodore and was not really interested in taking over control. He was conscientious enough, under his brother's direction, but Harold was more thrilled by flying over the Solway than by manufacturing triumphs. He had two sons, Stephen and Geoffrey, who both came into the business, but there was no doubt that beside Ronald they were relatively insignificant when the succession was considered. Not that it was openly considered. Theodore brooded about it, but then put it to the back of his mind and concentrated on the present.

He was keener than ever, at the end of the 1920s, to find ways to bind his workers closer to Carr's, preferably at low, or no, cost. Miss Wynne came up with an excellent idea in 1928. She suggested that they start a works' magazine, to which both employees and management would contribute and which could report news of interest to all concerning Carr's. Theodore immediately endorsed this, and what was called *The Topper Off* (a 'topper off' being the person who carried out the final inspection of the biscuits, before they were packed) was duly launched. Its avowed purpose was that of 'connecting everyone with the Firm to be interested in the welfare of the company'. In short, to cultivate team spirit within Carr's. And there was certainly an emphasis on teams – football, hockey, cricket – all of which sent in their match reports. Then there were the retirement lists of those who had worked for Carr's for many years, which did indeed act as good advertisements for team spirit. There would be a photograph of someone retiring who had devoted forty years or more to the firm, together with a brief piece (in which they were sure to say how happy they had been working for such a wonderful firm as Carr's), and a description of the leaving presents they had been given. Forty years or more qualified you for a gold watch, anything less for a couple of oak chairs or a canteen of cutlery.

But there were more interesting contributions, which did gradually create some sense of corporate identity. Miss Wynne began a women's page, making a plea that it should consist of more than recipes and beauty tips – 'we should like this page to reflect as many sides of a woman's life as possible'. (She printed accounts of women workers in a rubber-goods factory in China, which someone she knew had sent her, as an example.) The directors of Carr's were expected to do their bit too, and there were regular pages about trips made abroad (Carrying Carr's Products Round the Tropics), together with personal accounts of what the directors got up to in their leisure time. Harold Carr contributed stories of his experiences as an amateur flyer. The works' annual outings (still on the go, but not for the whole work force now that it was so large, and no longer paid for by Carr's) received good coverage. Miss Wynne was determined that the choice of destination should be more exciting than the inevitable Lake District or Blackpool, and organised a trip abroad, to Bruges, with some art history thrown in. The culture went down well and a new tradition was begun, though this kind of semi-educational trip was never as popular as the outings to good old Blackpool. Any prizes won by Carr's biscuits at the exhibitions of the day were naturally highlighted, and there were several of these in the 1920s, in Paris, Amsterdam and Berlin.

The message sent to Carr's workers by the magazine was that they were privileged to be part of a firm, still a family firm, that cared for their welfare so sincerely and which, in hard times, was still doing so well. Or, as *The Topper Off* reported, 'By land, sea and air the name of Carr is ever associated with those who lead.' They were lucky, and they should not forget it.

This was, on the whole, still thought true at the time, just as true as it had been when J.D. began, even though by then there were other factories offering similar wages and working conditions which, in the Founder's day, there had not been. Carr's in the 1840s was unique in Carlisle, whereas Carr's in the 1920s was not. But it was the most popular factory for girls to work in, and a great deal of that popularity arose from precisely that sense of cohesion the Carrs had made a point of creating. Just under 3,000 workers were now employed, thirty-five times the original work force, and most of them were women who had chosen to come into the factory at the age of fourteen. In Carlisle, if you were a working-class girl, for whom factory work was the only option, then Carr's was reckoned the best choice.

Getting taken on was not easy. In 1916, Viola Young's mother took her to the Juvenile Employment Office in Fisher Street, where she asked if Carr's had a vacancy. They did, but Viola, like all the other candidates for Carr's, had to have a medical, which she greatly dreaded because she did not like the prospect of removing her clothes. But the medical was basic enough, merely testing that her heart and lungs were sound, that she had no lice and that she was free of skin diseases. Once the medical was passed, she simply presented herself, with the other girls, at the impressive main gate, where the gateman checked her in and took her on to the factory floor. There she was shown what to do in five minutes flat and told to get on with it, while she was watched to see how she coped.

The usual way to start a young girl off was to put her on to what were called 'tuppenny packets'. This consisted of picking the correct number of biscuits off the conveyor-belt and wrapping them up. It sounded easy but it was surprisingly fiddly to do properly and took some getting used to. Meanwhile, each new girl would be trying to adapt to the heat and noise and the general shock of being in a factory which, to Ernestine Little, seemed like an animal swallowing her up. It took the average girl about two weeks to get the knack of doing the twopenny packets quickly, though it took Ernestine longer, but once she had learned it she was put on piece-work (which had been introduced by the mid-1920s). She found this a terrible strain – 'I never lifted my head all day and it was so hot.'

If the week's quota was not achieved, there was no pay beyond the basic 5s 6d (for a fourteen-year-old). Everything depended on speed and efficiency and those who were slow or clumsy did not last. They were supervised closely all the time and found the discipline as harsh as it had been at school. Permission was needed to go to the lavatory, and though talking was allowed, so long as it did not interfere with production, 'silly' behaviour was not (giggling, nudging each other, and making faces were all 'silly'). The room in which the twopenny-packet girls worked was up six flights of stone stairs and for at least a month they never left it during working hours to go to any other department. If they did, if for some reason they were sent, Ernestine Little described it as 'like crossing the River Jordan'. They went to the dining-room for their dinner break, but otherwise the rest of the huge factory was unknown to them, although they were given a talk about its history later on.

Once a girl was assigned to a particular department after her inauguration with twopenny packets, it was unlikely that she would be moved. A woman could work at Carr's for years and never see inside another room. At sixteen, they earned 10s 6d a week, but because of the tyranny of piece-work, the slow ones might end up getting even less – and a woman was paid only for what she produced. Out of that wage she had to provide herself with a white wrap-over overall, which did up at the back, and a hat. The days of Carr's providing protective clothing were over. In the mid-1920s these overalls cost 1s 11d to buy, but many of the girls made their own (material was six pence a yard, and one and a half yards was enough). If a girl could not afford either to buy or make the essential overall, then Carr's issued her with one and kept back three pence a week from her wage until it was paid off. She laundered it herself, and it had to be kept scrupulously clean. The girls had to work for eighteen months before they were entitled to a week's holiday with pay, but this was thought fair: as Viola Young said, nobody wanted to see someone who had just waltzed into the works claiming that precious paid holiday without having earned it.

Since the girls could be stuck for years in whatever department they were assigned to, it was crucial how the assigning was done. This depended both on physique and skill. A big, strong girl like Mary Johnson (who came to Carr's after working in another factory and liked it much better) would find herself carrying heavy trays from the ovens to the packers, while a dextrous girl would be given a bowl and certain ingredients and put to mixing (these were the days before automatic mixers for all types of biscuits). This job was thought of as enviable, assuming, as it did, a certain expertise and giving the satisfaction of seeing the result of one's work. It was pleasant, too, at that level, handling the sugar, flour and fats and felt like real work, quite creative in its own way. But the most desired location was the chocolate room. Everyone liked being sent there – the work was easier and the product more attractive –

though having to own two overalls was a drawback. (Drops of chocolate stained so badly and were hard to remove, so it was necessary to have a second overall in reserve.) The only really unpopular job was in the Matzo room. Betty Brown, who worked on the Matzos in the 1920s, did not like it because the meal used in the biscuits flew about and got into everyone's hair in spite of their caps. She was always a little in awe of the supervising rabbis, who sat watching them, sipping special tea from glasses, although she pronounced them 'very nice people'.

Promotion in Carr's could be, and often was, rapid. The Carrs believed in advancing promising, keen workers with all speed. But the problem with the women was that they were not nearly as eager to be promoted as might have been expected, given that it meant more money. An ordinary worker not on piecework made twenty-five shillings a week in the early 1920s, whereas a forewoman, or chargehand as she was sometimes called, could make twice that for the same number of hours. The problem was not only that the women seemed reluctant to accept the responsibility, but that they did not want to separate themselves from the camaraderie of being part of the gang. It was a feeling of togetherness, which Carr's had fostered, and it was precious, too precious for many to risk losing. Once a woman accepted promotion she had to see that everyone was in their right place at the right time, keep an eye on the conveyor-belts, making sure there were no gaps, examine the biscuits coming off the belts for quality, and train new people. But added to these duties were two others, far more onerous. Forewomen had to report breakdowns on the belts and negotiate with the male mechanics to have these fixed, which they hated to do, since the men always made them feel inferior. And they had to deal with the management if there was any grievance in their departments. If the next Workers' Welfare Association meeting was a long way off, or if a problem was thought not to be a union matter, it was up to the forewoman to go to the various bosses and complain. This made them feel unpopular both with workers (who never thought they did enough) and with management (who thought they complained too much).

As a family the Carrs prided themselves, of course, on the relationship between management and workers and it was true there was, theoretically, easy access to the offices from the factory floor. Forewomen knew they could go at any time and request to see the works manager, or even a director, and they would not be refused or thought out of order. But it was still a difficult thing for them to do, a matter of overcoming a sense (however unintentional) of intimidation. This was partly to do with clothes, partly with the organisation of the offices. The forewoman wore an overall, the manager, or director, a suit; the boss sat at a desk a long way from the door (or what felt to the forewoman a long way), and he sat while she stood. It was better to confront one of the management actually on the factory floor and shriek at them above the noise, but naturally those shrieked at preferred their offices. In the 1920s Mr Ronald was the most approachable. As Theodore had once done, and J.D. before him, he walked round the factory every day and could always be stopped in his tracks and appealed to. Maurice Hutchinson, Ernest's son, was another boss who was comparatively easy to talk to: he would listen and was prepared to concede a point, which some others never would on principle. And Miss Wynne, though not exactly management, was fair and just and would sometimes act as go-between.

But even in this family firm the hierarchy was rigid, the divide between employers and employees great, and the system of benevolent despotism, begun with

J.D., was still in place. The more intelligent and politically aware of the workers very often could not understand their own loyalty to Carr's. Mary Bolton, who became a chargehand, certainly could not. She wondered why she felt it. What was this feeling based on? There was no denying that all the work force felt they somehow belonged when they worked in Carr's; they really did feel part of a family and they liked this feeling. Yet surely it was all an illusion, as the trade-union stewards constantly reminded them. What did the Carrs actually do for them? Allow them to work for low wages in what, by then, were conditions no better than those in other factories. Was this treating them like a family, giving them the benefits of a family relationship? Hardly. But there was the social life – the clubs, the outings, the celebratory dinners, the magazine – and the women cited these advantages to each other whenever the subject came up of going somewhere else for more money. What they had at Carr's *was* valued, there was no doubt about that. And so was knowing the family and everything about it; seeing Ronald's children come round the factory, just as he had done, gave a sense of continuity that was very family-like. The bosses were not faceless people, the firm not run from some unknown headquarters.

Yet it was in danger of changing, this atmosphere, as the 1930s began. Theodore knew it as well as anyone, but then he had always been acutely aware of the mood of the times. The loyalty that family firms felt they had worked so hard to earn was in jeopardy, even if it had not yet been eroded. Working in a factory, even one with such a good reputation as Carr's, was no longer the only alternative for a girl leaving school with no qualifications, who did not want to go into domestic service. There were now other options, ones that had not existed in J.D.'s time. Few women had been shop

assistants in Carlisle until the mid-nineteenth century –
though, of course, many of them had their own market
stalls and ran their own small shops in the villages
around the city – and there had not in any case been
many large shops for them to work in. But as the
century progressed, houses in the city centre had been
demolished and in their place appeared large, purpose-
built shops, which became known as emporiums and
later as department stores. The first to merit this description in Carlisle was Robinson's, completed in 1902, and
thought of as a wonder to behold, with its plate-glass
windows and impressive frontage. It employed eighty
women shop assistants, who thought themselves infinitely superior to any factory worker (though their
wages were not so different). Girls wanted to work there
or in one of the other big stores that opened in the next
thirty years, so Carr's had new competition for its female
labour. Instead of being a first-choice job it became very
much a last one. And for the brighter girls, who had
taken the newly available shorthand and typing courses,
Carr's offices were only one of many opportunities open
to them.

It was also true that the girls who did come to Carr's
now were different – not so docile, not so easily regimented, and much more aware of their rights. Girls as
young as fifteen joined a union. There was a little room
in a building opposite the factory where subs could be
paid and there was a regular little procession to it on pay
day. Theodore knew the days when he had addressed the
work force in front of a hopeful union official, and had
persuaded them to stand firm (publicly at least) against
joining, were long since over. So the thing to do now
was to recognise the inevitable – virtually all the workers
were unionised – and work to make sure there would
be no call for strike action within Carr's itself. The
continuing prosperity of the firm helped: everyone liked

being part of success, even if its fruits were not exactly trickling down to them. In 1927, Carr & Co. Ltd became a public company, but all the ordinary shares were still held by members of the Carr family and the directors, and these were lucrative shares, reflecting how well Carr's were still doing. The average annual profit of the biscuit company was four times its pre-war average.

Only Theodore saw behind this boom and was worried. He read the unemployment figures and saw that they were rising. He thought the minority government recently elected, in 1929, unstable, and he registered the unreliability of public tastes, which led to demand fluctuating wildly in a way it had never done before, a tendency aggravated by advertising, which was becoming more and more aggressive. J.D., who had always realised the power of advertising and, of course, been quick to exploit it, had not had to operate in a biscuit world becoming so overcrowded. Carr's, like all the biscuit firms, had to show constant ingenuity in trying to think up imaginative ways of attracting new customers and keeping them. The days of being content with merely placing advertisements in newspapers and periodicals were by now well over, and even poster hoardings, used since the beginning of the century, were no longer enough on their own. Free gifts of biscuits had been a persuasive form of advertising since the 1860s. Now something new was needed to amuse and catch the eye, but which could also be valued for its own sake and kept.

In 1929 Carr's came up with the idea of giving away a booklet which told the story of their biscuits as a pastiche of *Alice in Wonderland*. This fifteen-page booklet had coloured illustrations and was witty and fun. Entitled *Alice in Biscuit Land*, it had all the biscuits describing themselves in rhyme to the King and Queen of Hearts, who then awarded medals and honours according to their estimation of each type of biscuit:

Full Cream Rich Tea stepped out from the ranks, bowed to the King and Queen, and commenced in a high treble voice to recite the following verse:

Rich Tea is my name,
You'll have heard of my fame,
But it reaches its apex with Carr's.
Not too plain nor too sweet
You'll find me a treat,
Which not even Nannie debars.

The booklet was distributed by the travellers to retailers and proved an immediate success.

Apart from competitive advertising, there was another sort of competition. There was the effect, in the 1920s, of the huge growth in smoking (many people grew to prefer a cigarette instead of a biscuit with their tea or coffee) and of the health measures taken post-war to encourage the eating of fruit (an apple instead of a biscuit). All these factors gave Theodore cause for concern. Keeping Carr's abreast of the times was a difficult business and he felt the weight of it, even while in public he trumpeted the firm's success, and never more so than in 1929 at the British Industries Fair, where Carr's had several miles of stands at the White City Stadium. Their display was spectacular and drew admiring crowds, all eager to sample the two best-known biscuits, the good old Table Water and the Club Cheese. Production was now up to 20,000 ten-pound tins a week, and Carr's were riding high. Shortly afterwards Theodore entertained royalty in Carlisle, giving a lunch for Princess Helena Victoria, Queen Victoria's fifth child, who came to reopen the new YMCA, which he had been involved in reconstructing.

But Theodore was not a well man. That year, 1929, he had to give up sailing as well as driving, because he could no longer see well enough to steer safely. This was a terrible blow which left him dependent on others for his relaxation. He was told he needed a cataract operation, perhaps on each eye, and facing up to the necessary hospitalisation was something he kept putting off. When finally, on the edge of blindness, he was obliged to submit, he went into a nursing home in Edinburgh, but the resulting operations were not entirely successful. One eye was restored well enough for him to be able to see with the help of a very strong lens, but the other did not respond. He came home with severely restricted sight, though he could at least steer his motor-cruiser again and that cheered him. He took a long convalescence, sailing round the entire coast and islands of Scotland, but, though he relished the sense of freedom it gave him, he felt far from his old energetic self. His wife expected him to retire, but he would not consider it and no one could make him. Work was life to Theodore and he was not going to relinquish it at the age of a mere sixty-three. He would not even take long holidays – once he felt he had recovered, that was enough of idleness. He could easily afford good holidays but had no interest in them. It had been a battle for Edith to get him to go to the South of France to meet their daughter Dorothy when she was on her way home after a visit to her sister, who had married and now lived in India.

The lack of recuperative holidays in the sun might not have mattered, had Theodore been sensible and rested properly, but he hated to rest. It bored him and did more damage than good, though unlike some businessmen he did have leisure interests in which he could have indulged. He was musical – the workers at Carr's had given him a piano when he married – and liked singing and he was also a football fan. But compared with running Carr's, these things were puny and gave him little satisfaction. His masterfulness and sheer drive had to be channelled and found an outlet only in being managing director of both of the Carr companies. So he worked as hard as ever, tiring himself but determined to keep going at least until the end of the next decade, which he saw as potentially dangerous for a family firm like Carr's. After a celebration for the firm's centenary in 1931, for which he had ambitious plans, and once the next few years had been safely negotiated, then he might consider stepping down and making way for Ronald and Ivan.

But in mid-January 1931, on a business trip to London, Theodore became ill. He had taken the Carlisle –London train scores of times and the journey had become so routine that it could hardly be claimed to be a strain. His wife and daughter Dorothy saw him off, thinking only that he looked a little pale and old, but he had aged a great deal since his cataract operations and they had never really adjusted to this difference. He arrived in London, spent the night in a hotel and went to a meeting next morning to do with the milling side of Carr's. During the meeting he felt ill, but struggled on until a pain in his chest and down his arm brought him to a standstill. A doctor, Sir Thomas Horder, was summoned and had no trouble diagnosing the obvious – a severe heart attack. Theodore was admitted to a nursing home and his wife informed. Edith was, from the very first, alarmed and wanted to leave immediately for London, but she was assured that her husband was in good hands and that he himself was adamant he did not want her to travel in such cold weather. It would only cause him further anxiety, which would be bad for him. So she allowed herself to be persuaded to wait; and when, after a week, he seemed to be recovering fully and a date was being discussed for his return home, she thought the danger over. But then, on 30 January, Theodore took a sudden turn for the worse and his wife was told to come at once. She, Ivan and Dorothy set off immediately, but by the time they reached the nursing home Theodore had died, early on 31 January.

It was a tremendous shock to everyone in his family and to the people of Carlisle. In spite of his diabetes and the cataract operations, Theodore had seemed so strong and resilient that no one was prepared. Flags flew at half-mast at the Town Hall, and the funeral, on 3 February, was a very public occasion. The church, St James, was packed and the Bishop of Carlisle delivered an address. He said he did not believe in orations at funerals – 'silence is usually best' – but that Theodore Carr had played such a great part in the life of Carlisle that he felt in this case a few words were appropriate. It was, said the Bishop, due to Theodore Carr's wisdom, courage and initiative that Carlisle had escaped great unemployment. He had not been a Party man, but had been ready 'to take immediate steps to meet pressing . . . duties and claims'. In fact, one of his characteristics had been to refuse any work he thought he might not be able to finish, so once he had taken on a job, one always knew it would be brought to a successful completion. Above all, said the Bishop, Theodore Carr was a kind man, a quality not noticeable in most hard-headed manufacturers.

There was an enormous crowd at the cemetery, where Theodore was buried on the high ground near the war memorial. Eighty-eight employees from the flour mills were there (a special train brought them from Silloth) and almost the entire work force from the biscuit works. There was a long list of family mourners, among whom was Mary, his stepmother, and Mildred (described as 'sister', not half-sister). All the male Carrs were present, uncomfortably aware that there was no one obvious successor to Theodore. Frank could manage the flour mills, Harold the biscuit works, but could either Ronald or Ivan, the two heirs apparent, eventually take on both and become, like Theodore, the presiding and unifying force? It seemed unlikely. So what would happen? Would Carr's continue as two companies, now really as separate and distinct as they technically had been since 1908? Only Theodore's position as Managing Director of both had kept them linked. And now that his powerful presence had been removed, would Carr's stay independent, still largely controlled by the family, or would it lose its identity and be merged with a bigger firm, where 'family' would have no meaning? Would J.D.'s sacred trust be broken?

The gloom on the faces of the Carrs at Theodore's funeral was not entirely due to grief at his death.

Epilogue

———————— • ————————

WHEN THEODORE CARR died in 1931, one hundred years exactly since his grandfather Jonathan Dodgson Carr had begun his bread and biscuit business in Carlisle and so successfully established the family fortunes, there were only three Carrs among the seven directors of the two companies, all grandsons of the Founder. At Carr's Flour Mills there was only Frank Carr, who was the obvious choice to succeed Theodore there as chairman. At Carr & Co. Ltd, the biscuit works, there were Harold and Ronald Carr and the succession was not nearly so obvious. Harold was the senior. He had come into the family business in 1902, at the age of twenty-two, and had therefore been working for it for almost thirty years when Theodore died. But Ronald, aged thirty-seven, though he had only been working for Carr & Co. Ltd since the end of the First World War, a mere thirteen years to Harold's thirty, had already shown leadership qualities that Harold lacked.

Seniority won, as it was bound to in a family firm where justice was more important than who was the better man. Harold became chairman of the biscuit works, but neither he nor Frank, chairman of the flour mills, provided the link at boardroom level that Theodore had done. The two companies were both still owned by the Carr family, but the way was open for them to become more and more separate, less and less mutually dependent. They also each developed a different company policy. At the biscuit works, Harold's main drive was towards marketing. He was not an engineer, as his brother Theodore had been, and had little knowledge of the methods of production. What most concerned him was the distribution of the finished product. Theodore had always kept a close eye on efficient production and was constantly modernising equipment and experimenting, but now less attention was paid to this. At the flour mills, Frank became convinced that managing the company's finances was as important as managing the actual mills and he was worried about the loans that had been made, under Theodore, from the flour company to the biscuit works. He thought that Carr's Flour Mills' reserves, if there were any, would be better off wisely invested elsewhere.

In the next decade of extremely difficult trading conditions, when Britain suffered the worst trade depression of her history, the biscuit works had a harder time than the flour mills, but both survived as family companies, even though profits declined. During the Second World War, both the Silloth mills and the Carlisle biscuit works benefited from their remote positions: they both escaped bombing. But in the post-war period, when Ronald Carr had taken over at the biscuit works (he become chairman in 1937 when Harold died) and Ivan Carr at the flour mills (when Frank died in 1942), the competition from other, more powerful biscuit companies began to bite and to force a decision that no Carr liked to contemplate: either to merge with, or be taken over by, another company. At the end of the 1950s an offer was made by Lyons, which was refused. But in 1964, Cavenhams made a cash offer for the entire ordinary share capital which it was felt wise to accept. James Goldsmith gave his assurance that the Carlisle biscuit works would be kept in full operation. Almost a decade later, in 1972, United Biscuits bought Carr & Co. Ltd from the Cavenham group. Carr's biscuit works were finished as a family company.

But they were not quite finished as a flour-milling company. Ivan Carr, Theodore's son, kept Carr's Flour Mills family-controlled (though it changed its name to Carr's Milling Industries in 1950) until the mid-1960s. After that, though family shareholdings were still considerable, the Carrs could no longer claim the company as theirs. Today, the family holdings are well below 10 per cent, though the myth continues locally that Carr's is still family-owned. Ian Carr, great-grandson of J. D. Carr, remained chairman until September 1997, completing thirty-three years' service. There is now no family connection except for those few remaining shareholders. Ian was the last of the Carrs.

*

This brief summary tells nothing of the underlying struggle that went on after Theodore Carr's death to remain true to the inheritance Jonathan Dodgson had left, but at the same time to adapt to mid-twentieth-century conditions. The practical problems that confront all small family firms were faced with varying degrees of success by the Carrs, but what was far more difficult for them was to face up to a whole new business philosophy.

Ivan Carr had ideas about the conduct of business which were every bit as inflexibly high-minded as his great-grandfather's had been and which clashed first with Ronald's and then with Ian's ideas. Addressing a gathering of Young Millers in 1956, he prefaced his talk with a quotation from Plato, 'The noblest of all investigations is the study of what man should be and what he should pursue.' He then went on to define business as 'an experiment in co-operation', before outlining how he considered this co-operation should be achieved in a factory. This, in short, was to recommend 'the attitude of a benevolent father', exactly the same recipe for success that J.D. had used 125 years before in startlingly different times, when such advice was not reckoned patronising and socially unacceptable.

But Ivan had even more to say along these nineteenth-century lines: 'I believe that government by an inherited head is the least bad,' he asserted, because 'the head by birthright is secure on his throne', which made him 'superior to any professional manager'. What was important was how this superiority was used – 'it is up to us to give until the pips squeak for the well-being of our businesses. For the well-being of the whole shooting-match – Staff, Workers, Boys, Girls, Colleagues, Customers, Shareholders, Suppliers, and perhaps most important of all, Posterity.' 'The professional manager', Ivan continued, 'could never match such unselfish dedication because in his efforts to do well for his company he allows the making of good profits – perhaps our most important single duty – to become his ONLY duty.' That, for a Carr, would never do.

An introduction to a booklet about Carr's Flour Mills, issued during Ivan's time, waxed lyrical on the same subject of responsibility going beyond mere profit. It described how, ever since its foundation, the mills had always had 'a Carr guiding it down the years'. Throughout its history 'a Carr stood guard; shielding, watching, improving, extending; loyally served by generations of honest skilful men, whose memories are built into the very fabric of the business; but he who took supreme responsibility, who must answer for it all, who must one day pass the torch to another of his kin, was always a Carr'. But there were some Carrs who thought this kind of thing both pompous and a bit ridiculous. One of them was Ronald. He was as passionately involved in the running of the biscuit works as Ivan was in the flour mills, but his philosophy was different, far more down-to-earth and much more concerned with the need to make profits. 'The differences between Ronald and me are wide,' Ivan acknowledged in a letter to another cousin, ' . . . and largely ideological at root.' He saw Ronald as ruthless in the pursuit of profit, whereas he thought of himself as putting other things first. Ronald had only to hint that the shareholders were restive for Ivan to be furious. He refused to be influenced by shareholders' complaints.

But it was to the young Ian Carr that Ivan was even more forthright later on. Ian was Laurence's son, born in 1928 when his father was fifty-seven. He had started off in the biscuit works, under Ronald, but then transferred to the flour mills in 1962. Writing to Ian soon after he had joined Carr's Flour Mills Ltd, Ivan emphasised that his aim in life was not to increase shareholders' profits, but 'to keep our Silloth mill in full employment . . . there would be human suffering and distress if our mill did not continue to run full-time'. He confessed himself deeply unhappy that in order to keep profits high and meet competition 'growth has been forced upon us and I don't like it . . . while in the past I used to be in intimate touch with the rank and file, nowadays I am alas further away with less time and opportunity to spend with everybody in the company. To my shame and sorrow I don't even know the names of the girls working in the hut'. He was proud that the company had survived – 'in the last ten years fifty-six mills have folded up . . . in the last year, twenty-five have sold out' – but he was aware of 'the hateful need to live under the shadow of a whacking overdraft'.

Ian responded that it was old-fashioned and out of date *not* to have an overdraft, but Ivan would not accept this – 'you tell me we must spend more, not less, and you say that if we do accumulate a liquid reserve it might be distributed to shareholders.' He was appalled at the thought of this, telling Ian, 'our policy has been one of cautious, reluctant, conservative spending; coupled with adventurous unorthodox trading and management'. That was how Ivan wanted it to stay. He could not bear what he saw as his young cousin's 'obsession with profit-making'. Carr's existed to *serve the customer*, and if that customer wanted only two bags of flour, then he should be given them, however unprofitable the transaction. 'I do not care a fig for Unilevers . . . or for the way they behave. We are *unique*. We are *out of the ordinary*. We do not copy anyone else, least of all the big companies. It is for you to cherish and safeguard our reputation for uniqueness, not to throw it away and turn us into a company just the same as thousands of others, each with its dreary, commonplace parrot cry . . . "We are in business to make profit."'

*

In 1996 no fewer than 75 per cent of all British companies were family-owned. Taken altogether, this means that about half the entire work force of the country is employed by such companies, so what goes on within the management of them matters enormously. But of these family-owned companies, only 13 per cent have survived to the third generation, largely because of the issue of succession. The Carrs were lucky for so long: there was always someone capable and willing to succeed (even if some were more capable than others). They kept the business, divided into its two companies, family-owned and partially managed for 133 years, and when Carr's & Co. Ltd had to sell out, it was not because the succession failed – there were still Carrs working there who could have taken over – but because the economic climate made the survival of a small firm impossible. At the flour mills, the succession did fail: no Carr was available to take over from Ian.

So far as its workers are concerned, Carr's is still thought of (wrongly, of course) as a family business. The traditions of over a century and a half do not die in a takeover. When United Biscuits were selecting factories to close down, they kept Carlisle's biscuit works open because of its excellent labour relations: there was rarely any trouble at Carr's and that made it valuable. But everyone is aware that the benefits that come from being a family-owned business have gone, for workers as well as for bosses. That 'family feeling', which kept employees loyal to Carr's, may have been partly a cleverly created illusion, but it was there and it was valued. Being part of a conglomerate is not the same at all. Whether it matters to production is doubtful, but it matters to how people feel. The ideals of Jonathan Dodgson Carr, which for so long permeated the place, have entirely gone. Nobody feels cared for, watched over, worried about – even if, when they did, that concern was a benevolent despotism that kept workers always subservient.

The death of a family business is a very strange death. There is no corpse to grieve over. It is all a matter of spirit, and in Carlisle that spirit is strong. All that was good about Carr's is recalled, all that was less good barely remembered. No matter how much better paid, how much shorter their hours and how much more secure their employment, today's factory workers in the old Carr's factory lack what those who worked there up to 1964 speak of still – the sense of belonging to a unit they could grasp and understand. It is this that makes the history of Carr's more than just the story of one family's manufacturing career: it is also part of a pattern repeated in the last hundred years all over the country, a tale of private enterprise, starting so humbly, turning into business success, catapulting its owners into another class and towards positions of power and influence in one city. The power waned with control of the firm, but the memory of what Carrs had once been, and what in other cities other family firms had been, did not. Even today, the same thing can happen again, over and over again: one man, or woman, one entrepreneur, one family, building into something huge and carrying within it, as it grows, the seeds of its transformation – the takeover by some gigantic corporation. Always people seem to look back fondly and proudly to the first beginnings, finding in them both fascination – so much from so little – and inspiration.

Sources and
Acknowledgements

———————— • ————————

I T WILL be obvious that the main sources for this book are family papers, owned by various descendants of Jonathan Dodgson Carr, and papers concerning the history of the two firms, Carr & Co. Ltd and Carr's Flour Mills Ltd. The business records were gathered together in the first place by Dr Clare Burgess, a former Managing Director of Carr's Milling Industries Ltd (previously Carr's Flour Mills Ltd), in order to produce a book intended to celebrate the 150th anniversary of the original firm. Dr Burgess died before this was completed and the work was taken over by Sir John Burgess, assisted by Susan Dench. But Sir John also died, and by this time the anniversary had been missed, so the book was never published. I have used these records as a source for everything relating to the business history and have been able to refer to the Directors' Minute Books and other documents upon which Dr Burgess based his manuscript. This text, together with all the research material, is in the possession of Ian Carr and I am grateful to him for allowing me access to it.

Ian Carr also let me see personal family records (and many photographs). Two other Carr family members have given me invaluable help. Mary Leggett, descended from Jonathan Dodgson Carr through his son George, has sent me, from Canada, letters and memoirs that appear to have been rare in the family – sensitive, full of domestic detail and beautifully written. I am more grateful than I can say to have had them, as well as an early photo of J.D. and his family. But it is to Courtenay Latimer, descended from J. D. Carr through his son Thomas William, that I owe the greatest debt. Not only has he dug out every scrap of personal material he possesses, but he has in effect acted as an unpaid research assistant and found additional information for me on a whole host of subjects, from Theodore Carr's schooling to the war records of Stanley and Ronald Carr. His interest and enthusiasm have never failed to encourage me. Other Carrs have also helped with memories, in particular Isobel Carr (to whom I am grateful for permission to read her late husband's memoir, which Dr Burgess had used) and Margaret and Douglas Nicholson Carr. James N. Carr arranged for me to tour the McVities factory, and I am grateful to Peter Whiteley, a former manager, who took us round.

In spite of help from all these people there were many gaps in the family's history, so I turned to Carlisle's local archives and in particular to copies of local newspapers which are kept there. Cumbria Record Office (in the Castle) holds the *Carlisle Journal* (founded in 1798), which from 1831 has hardly an issue without mention of one Carr or another; and the Carlisle *Patriot* (founded in 1815) on microfilm is in Carlisle Library in The Lanes, as are copies (on microfilm) of the Cumberland *Pacquet* (founded in 1774). The *Cumberland News* (founded in 1910 and formerly the *Patriot*) is also kept in the Castle. There are many other local sources there to which I had been directed by Susan Dench, concerning all the associations and charity organisations in which J. D. Carr in particular was so heavily involved.

But the biggest problem turned out to be finding out

about Carr's employees. Here I was rescued by the discovery of a vast collection of tapes in Tullie House, oral histories of elderly people in Carlisle, many of whom had worked at Carr's from the late nineteenth century onwards. My thanks to Susan Dalloe, Senior Keeper of Human History, for arranging access to these tapes. I have relied on them extensively, and on a complete collection of *The Topper Off*, Carr's house magazine, also lodged in Tullie House. This did not begin production until 1928, but in its first issues there are reminiscences of some of the retiring workers which stretch back to the 1840s. My thanks to David Clarke, Senior Curator and Collections Manager, for access to these volumes. Another oral history was not on tape but was given to me in person by the late Athol MacGregor. He was in the next room to my father in a Carlisle nursing home. His memory, at the age of ninety-four, was formidably sharp and he was able not only to take me through his own time at Carr's (he started work there in 1916) but also his father's and grandfather's, which took me back very nearly to the founding of the factory.

Nobody can do any work on the history of Carlisle without becoming indebted to Denis Perriam, who has not only immense knowledge but always seems to find time to impart it. He has helped me this time particularly on houses and buildings. My thanks, also, to the staff of Carlisle Library, particularly Stephen White, the Local Studies Librarian, for locating photographs and maps.

It is mostly self-evident where I have used the different sources, but where it is not I have indicated the sources in the brief chapter notes that follow. This is especially true where secondary sources are concerned. Instead of a bibliography, I have listed books as they were used.

CHAPTER I: A QUAKER CHILDHOOD IN KENDAL

General Quaker background: *The Journal of George Fox* (pub. Friends Utd. Press, 1908); *John Bright and the Quakers*, J. Travis Mills; *Portrait in Grey*, John Punshon (Quaker Home Service, 1984): all in Friends House, Euston Road, London, the Library of the Religious Society of Friends, where there are many records to consult.

Kendal: *Annals of Kendal*, Cornelius Nicholson (1831); *Kirbie-Kendall*, J. F. Curwen (1900); Cumbria Record Office, Kendal, for Quaker minutes: Kendal Monthly Meeting Minutes 1827–58 (ref. WDFC/FI/19) and Kendal Women's Monthly Meeting Minutes 1823–37 (ref. WDFC/FI/27): Cumbria Record Office, Kendal.

Quaker meeting-houses: *Quaker Meeting-houses in the Lake District*, David M. Butler (Friends Historical Society, 1978).

Contents of the Carrs' house: advertisement for the sale of the house, found for me by Richard Hall (assistant archivist).

Quaker education: *Quakers and Education*, W. A. C. Stewart.

CHAPTER 2: 'CHEAP BREAD'

Thomas Brockbank: from memoir by his daughter Mary.

Carlisle in 1831: N. Parson and W. White: *History, Directory & Gazetteer of Counties of Cumberland & Westmorland* (1829).

Caldewgate: autobiography of William Farish, *The Struggles of a Handloom Weaver* (Caliban Books edition, 1996); Transactions of Cumberland & Westmorland Archaeological & Antiquarian Society, vol. LXXXIV, June Barnes.

Quaker minutes: Carlisle Preparative Meetings 1824–47; Carlisle Monthly Meeting for Ministers and Elders 1831–45 (ref. D/FCF2/109), Cumbria Record Office, Carlisle.

CHAPTER 3: A GIANT OF A MAN

Biscuit manufacturing: *Quaker Enterprise in Biscuits*, T. A. B. Corley (Hutchinson, 1972).

Royal Warrant: A *Short History of the Royal Warrant*, Betty Whittington (The Royal Warrant Holders Association, 1961).

Yearly meetings: *Pen Pictures of London Yearly Meetings*, J. Penney: records in Friends House, London.

CHAPTER 4: THE RICH DESSERTS

Housing, health in Carlisle: 'Report to General Board of Health in the City of Carlisle', R. Rawlinson (1850).

Carlisle in the 1840s: Mannix and Whelan: *History, Directory & Gazetteer of Counties of Carlisle & Westmorland* (1847). Silloth railway: 'The Silloth Branch', Part I and II, Alan Earnshaw (published in the magazine *Backtrack*).

CHAPTER 5: THE SONS AND THE SCHISM

John Irving's diary: extracts in *The Topper Off*.

Reading-room and Temperance Hall: Carlisle West End Society Minute Book (ref. DSO 77/1+3 CROC). Cumbria Record Office, Carlisle.

Disowning of Henry and James Carr: Monthly Meeting Minute Book 1862–77 (ref. D/FCF/2/110 CROC), which contains the original letters written by the Carrs to the Society.

CHAPTER 6: DEATHS AND DUTIES

Elizabeth (Lizzie) Carr: from memoir by Dorothy Carr. Wilfrid's and Dodgson's deaths: from memoir by Mary Brockbank.

CHAPTER 7: '. . . FROM DARKNESS INTO LIGHT'

Carlisle in the 1880s: *Carlisle*, D. R. Perriam (Bookcase, Cumbria County Library, and Tullie House, 1992); *Carlisle*, Sydney Towill (pub. Phillimore & Co., 1991); *175 Years of Carlisle*: Archive Publications (1990).

Theodore's education: *Memories of the Old Hall School 1845–1995* (commemorative booklet).

Theodore's car: *Pageant of Motoring* (Carlisle Great Fair publication, 1975) added to family descriptions; also account in *The Autocar* (16 October 1897).

Ernest Carr: Directors' Minutes Book of Carr & Co. Ltd contains letters to and from him.

John Sanderson: report in the Carlisle *Patriot* supplied by Helen Strickland, his great-great-granddaughter.

CHAPTER 8: MACHINES, MILLS AND MISSIONARIES
Carr's vans, Carlisle traffic: *Pageant of Motoring* (see above); *Tramways of the City of Carlisle*, George S. Hearse (1962).

CHAPTER 9: STRIKES AND WAR
Bertram's South American trip: described in a series of articles he wrote for the *Cumberland News* (1915) called 'Under the Southern Cross'.

CHAPTER 10: THE FINEST HOUR
Bertram as Mayor: Proceedings of the Council and Committees 1917–18 (Carlisle library/The Castle).
Woodrow Wilson: *A President's Love Affair with the Lake District*, Andrew Wilson (Lakeland Press Agency, 1996).

CHAPTER 11: CHANGING TIMES
Stanley's war record: The Manchester Museum of the King's Regiment; Tameside Local Studies Library.
Ronald's war record: Regimental Museum of the King's Own Royal Border Regiment, 'The Border Regiment in the Great War'.
Ivan Carr: *Gusts and Zephyrs*, F. Ivan Carr (private publication).

ILLUSTRATION CREDITS
I am extremely grateful to the following not only for permission to reproduce photographs and other illustrations but for their invaluable help in tracking them down and supplying prints:
Front endpaper 'Glovers Row, Carlisle 1835', watercolour by W. H. Nutter (1819–1872): Tullie House Museum & Art Gallery, Carlisle. *Back endpaper* Market Place and Crown and Mitre Hotel, Carlisle: Heritage Services, Carlisle Library.
Plate section 1 Heritage Services, Carlisle Library, for plates 5, 14. Tullie House Museum & Art Gallery, Carlisle, for plate 4 ('Carlisle Market Cross from English Street, 1835', watercolour by W. H. Nutter). Members of the Carr family for plates 1, 2, 3, 6, 7, 8, 9, 10, 11, 12, 13, 15. *Plate section 2* Heritage Services Carlisle Library, for plates 4, 5. Members of the Carr family for plates 1, 2, 3, 6, 7, 8, 9.

Index